Keys to American History

★★★

Understanding Our Most Important Historic Documents

Richard Panchyk

CHICAGO
REVIEW
PRESS

Library of Congress Cataloging-in-Publication Data

Panchyk, Richard.
  The keys to American history : understanding our most important historic documents / Richard Panchyk.
      p. cm.
  Includes bibliographical references and index.
  ISBN 978-1-55652-716-6—ISBN 978-1-55652-804-0 (paper)
  1. United States—History—Sources. I. Title.

  E173.P25 2009
  973—dc22
                            2008010662

Cover design: Monica Baziuk
Cover photographs: Courtesy of the Library of Congress
Interior design: Sarah Olson
Photo credits: Images on the following pages are used courtesy of the Library of Congress: 2, 5, 9, 13, 16, 18, 25, 35, 42, 56, 71, 72 (portrait), 78, 81, 91, 101, 120–121, 129, 132, 138, 158, 162, 168, 169, 176, 185, 189, 194, 197, 206, 213, 216, 217. Images on the following pages are used courtesy of the National Archives: 19, 22, 26, 28, 32, 38, 50, 51, 52, 59, 63, 68, 69, 72 (document), 74, 86, 94, 95, 98, 107, 109, 113, 116, 123, 125, 126, 135, 142, 145, 149, 151, 154, 157, 166, 172, 178, 180, 183, 186, 190, 200, 203, 207, 211, 214. Images on the following pages are from the author's collection: 66, 106, 112, 119, 124, 222, 226.

© 2008 by Richard Panchyk
All rights reserved
Published by Chicago Review Press, Incorporated
814 North Franklin Street
Chicago, Illinois 60610
ISBN 978-1-55652-716-6 (cloth)
ISBN 978-1-55652-804-0 (paper)
Printed in China
5 4 3 2 1

Contents

Introduction

Our country's written history is a momentous tale that stretches back four hundred years to the arrival of the first European settlers. Our struggles and triumphs have been epic, and these tales can be found in most American history books, having been interpreted for easy digestion by their authors.

I wanted to take a different approach with this book, and give the reader food for thought. Because many of the key moments in American history are associated with documents of some kind, I feel it is difficult to understand our history without reading these primary sources. These are the actual words written and spoken by the leaders of our country; for example, the Declaration of Independence and Constitution are perhaps our greatest primary sources. To this day, these documents demonstrate the determination and freethinking that drove the founding fathers.

Of course, the Declaration and Constitution are but two of countless thousands of documents, laws, proclamations, and speeches that have been offered over the years. Each one has the power to shed light on a particular aspect of our history and bring it to vivid life.

In reality it would be impossible and impractical to place so many documents into a book. A few dozen of these moments hold the "keys to American history"; these are some of the more pivotal documents that should be read in order to understand the bigger picture of our nation's history. Though I have provided a brief introduction to each moment, the reader should understand that each document I cover is worthy of its own book.

It was no easy task to select the most important moments in our nation's history. Most of these moments are associated with a document of some sort; some are associated with an important speech. There are documents of various types such as laws, acts, proclamations, and constitutional amendments. All of the documents selected for this book had an impact on life in the United States; some changed things for the better, and others changed things for the worse. Some of these historic documents had an immediate effect while in other cases the effect was more gradual. Included here is a subjective sampling to provide the reader with a chronological overview of moments in our history.

These words are a window into the minds and lives of the past. A historic document is a time machine that transports the reader into another world. Some documents are written in very obscure language while others are crystal in their clarity.

The words in the speeches and documents here at times ignited rebellion and at other times achieved unity. Some words soothed Americans while others caused anger and frustration. Sometimes the same words caused different reactions to white or black people, Northerners or Southerners, Democrats or Republicans. As mentioned, there are both written and oral documents in this book. You might think that speeches are intended to be heard more than read, but in the days before radio, television, and the Internet, only a select few people actually heard any particular speech; the vast majority of people read it the next day in a newspaper.

Some of these documents were crucial to the future of the democracy, while others were important to the expansion of settlement across the nation. Some documents are long and some are brief. Each one is an adventure in history, a rich tapestry of hopes, dreams, compromises, and demands that make us who we are—Americans.

Because history is subjective, I recognized that while reading an original document with a brief introduction might provide a snapshot in time, it could not provide the rich context of our nation as it stood at the time. It could not provide the thoughts and feelings of Americans of different political and social backgrounds.

To make reading this book a much richer experience, I include a feature called "What They Were Saying," which provides interesting quotes from a variety of nineteenth and twentieth century speeches, newspapers, and history books. These quotes about many of the key moments and documents in our history are both fascinating and important because their viewpoint is so close in time to the event itself. Most of these supplemental quotes are from within ten to twenty years of the event. Today our perspective on those events may be quite different from that of someone of that generation. Things that we scarcely give a second thought to today may have been very important one hundred years ago, and things that were controversial one hundred years ago may be accepted as routine today. These quotes have the power to reveal the intensity with which the now-forgotten triumphs and sorrows of the past were felt at the time. I have intentionally included fewer quotes for the more recent events.

It is my hope that the reader will find this book a practical reference, a window into our country's fascinating history, and an inspiration to do further reading on American history.

Author's Note

In many cases, the original documents covered by this book are very lengthy. To keep the book at a manageable size and highlight the more important passages, I have omitted some of the less significant or more repetitive sections of these documents. In some cases, it is clear by the discontinuity of section numbers of a particular Act what has been left out. In other cases, ellipses are used to show where part of a document has been edited out. Some important documents, including the Declaration of Independence and the Constitution, are included in their entirety, as are some of the more brief works.

Questions to Consider

Many ordinary history texts are presented as predigested material for readers to swallow whole. As mentioned earlier, this book strives to give readers food for thought. It is helpful to ponder some questions as you read through this book. For example, what meaning or importance did the event in question have at the time? How was it perceived to impact the country and, looking back, what were its actual effects? Does it still have an impact today? For the various quotes and accounts from newspapers and history books, what was the perspective of the person writing the piece? Did the person have a bias or were they neutral? Were their fears justified? Were their hopes realized? Try to determine what is fact and what is opinion. How would you comment on the more recent events in our history?

Foundations

★★

The official history of our nation begins with the Declaration of Independence, but our roots here go back nearly 170 years earlier to the first European settlement at Jamestown. Many of the foundations of American government and political philosophy were laid during those years. As the colonies grew in population and prospered commercially, their collective conscience began to flower while England began to exercise more control and authority over the colonies via taxation. Through unity in opposition to their English mother country, they began to develop thoughts of a single entity, a republic formed from the individual colonies. Though the concept seems natural in retrospect, it was by no means a given at the time. Discarding the monarchy and introducing democracy was a great and weighty step. The Articles of Confederation, the first attempt at a national governing document, were a starting point but were not strong enough to propel the nation forward. The Constitution, which followed in 1787, was a powerful and comprehensive document that would help steer the nation through both good and trying times.

1606 First Charter of Virginia

By 1606 it had already been more than one hundred years since Europeans first explored the New World. Since then a succession of explorers of many nationalities had come to the Americas in search of riches and an easy passage to the Pacific. They also excited interest in Europe about the possibility of settling in the New World. In fact, by the dawn of the seventeenth century, spices and gold were no longer a priority; rather, laying claim to the vast lands of the Americas was of critical importance. It was in England's interest to get settlers to the East Coast of North America quickly in order to legitimize the country's claim on land in the New World; a claim by itself was relatively abstract, but settlements were another thing entirely. The Spanish were already founding settlements to the south. Other countries were positioning themselves to enter the fray as well. The Dutch would soon occupy what is now New York, and the Swedish would claim land (in present-day Delaware) during the early part of the seventeenth century. But in the end, the English were able to control the entire Eastern Seaboard.

The original land patent from King James to the London Company and the Plymouth Company made possible the first English settlement in what would become the United States. Interestingly, recognition of the existing native population can be found within the patent in a reference to hopes that the colonists could bring the savages to "human Civility" and a "settled and quiet Government."

Pocahontas is presented to King James I in England.

JAMES, by the Grace of God, King of England, Scotland, France and Ireland, Defender of the Faith, &c. WHEREAS our loving and well-disposed Subjects . . . have been humble Suitors unto us, that We would vouchsafe unto them our Licence, to make Habitation, Plantation, and to deduce a colony of sundry of our People into that part of America commonly called VIRGINIA, and other Parts and Territories in America . . .

And to that End, and for the more speedy Accomplishment of their said intended Plantation and Habitation there, are desirous to divide themselves into two several Colonies and Companies; the one consisting of certain Knights, Gentlemen, Merchants, and other Adventurers, of our City of London and elsewhere, which are, and from time to time shall be, joined unto them, which do desire to begin their Plantation and Habitation in some fit and convenient Place, between four and thirty and one and forty Degrees of the said Latitude, alongst the Coasts of Virginia, and the Coasts of America aforesaid: And the other consisting of sundry Knights, Gentlemen, Merchants, and other Adventurers, of our Cities of Bristol and Exeter, and of our Town of Plimouth, and of other Places, which do join themselves unto that Colony, which do desire to begin their Plantation and Habitation in some fit and convenient Place, between eight and thirty Degrees and five and forty Degrees of the said Latitude, all alongst the said Coasts of Virginia and America, as that Coast lyeth:

We, greatly commending, and graciously accepting of, their Desires for the Furtherance of so noble a Work, which may, by the Providence of Almighty God, hereafter tend to the Glory of his Divine Majesty, in propagating of Christian Religion to such People, as yet live in Darkness and miserable Ignorance of the true Knowledge and Worship of God, and may in time bring the Infidels and Savages, living in those parts, to human Civility, and to a settled and quiet Government: DO, by these our Letters Patents, graciously accept of, and agree to, their humble and well-intended Desires;

AND do therefore, for Us, our Heirs, and Successors, GRANT and agree, that the said Sir Thomas Gates, Sir George Somers, Richard Hackluit, and Edward-Maria Wingfield, Adventurers of and for our City of London, and all such others, as are, or shall be, joined unto them of that Colony, shall be called the first Colony; And they shall and may begin their said first Plantation and Habitation, at any Place upon the said-Coast of Virginia or America, where they shall think fit and convenient, between the said four and thirty and one and forty Degrees of the said Latitude; And that they shall have all the Lands, Woods, Soil, Grounds, Havens, Ports, Rivers, Mines, Minerals, Marshes, Waters, Fishings, Commodities, and Hereditaments, whatsoever, from the said first Seat of their Plantation and Habitation by the Space of fifty Miles of English Statute Measure, all along the said Coast of Virginia and America, towards the West and Southwest, as the Coast lyeth, with all the Islands within one hundred Miles directly over against the same Sea Coast; And also all the Lands . . . from the said Place of their first Plantation and Habitation for the space of fifty like English Miles, all alongst the said Coasts of Virginia and America, towards the East and Northeast, or towards the North, as the Coast lyeth, together with all the Islands within one hundred Miles, directly over against the said Sea Coast, And also all the Lands . . . from the same fifty Miles every way on the Sea Coast, directly into the main Land by the Space of one hundred like English Miles; . . .

AND we do also ordain, establish, and agree, for Us, our Heirs, and Successors, that each of the said

Colonies shall have a Council, which shall govern and order all Matters-and Causes, which shall arise, grow, or happen, to or within the same several Colonies, according to such Laws, Ordinances, and Instructions, as shall be, in that behalf, given and signed with Our Hand or Sign Manual, and pass under the Privy Seal of our Realm of England; Each of which Councils shall consist of thirteen Persons, to be ordained, made, and removed, from time to time, according as shall be directed and comprised in the same instructions; . . .

And that also there shall be a Council, established here in England, which shall, in like manner, consist of thirteen Persons, to be for that Purpose, appointed by Us, our Heirs and Successors, which shall be called our Council of Virginia; And shall, from time to time, have the superior Managing and Direction, only of and for all Matters that shall or may concern the Government, as well of the said several Colonies . . .

Also we do, for Us, our Heirs, and Successors, DECLARE, by these Presents, that all and every the Persons being our Subjects, which shall dwell and inhabit within every or any of the said several Colonies and Plantations, and every of their children, which shall happen to be born within any of the Limits and Precincts of the said several Colonies and Plantations, shall HAVE and enjoy all Liberties, Franchises, and Immunities, within any of our other Dominions, to all Intents and Purposes, as if they had been abiding and born, within this our Realm of England, or any other of our said Dominions.

Pilgrims Sign the Mayflower Compact 1620

The passengers of the Mayflower were under no illusions about their lives in the New World. They did not come here to escape from the yokes of government; they came for freedom to practice their religion without being persecuted. One of their first orders of business upon landing (at what would become Massachusetts but was then called "the northern parts of Virginia") was to create an understanding among themselves about the nature of their existence in America. The "Body Politick" they formed upon arrival represented the seeds of what would eventually grow into the great tree of American democracy. Though they found their own way and eventually split from the mother country, our founding fathers all had roots in England. Documents such as the Mayflower Compact are reminders that our democracy owes a great deal to the English system of government, beginning in 1215 with the Magna Carta.

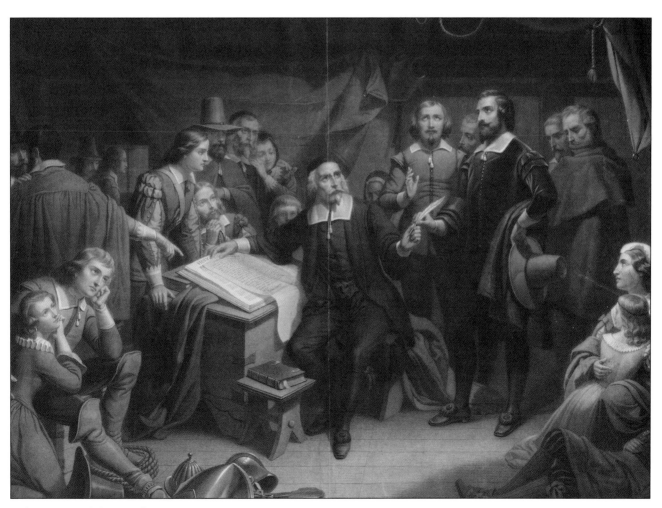

The signing of the Mayflower Compact, 1620.

In the name of God, Amen. We, whose names are underwritten, the Loyal Subjects of our dread Sovereign Lord King James, by the Grace of God, of Great Britain, France, and Ireland, King, Defender of the Faith, &c. Having undertaken for the Glory of God, and Advancement of the Christian Faith, and the Honour of our King and Country, a Voyage to plant the first Colony in the northern Parts of Virginia; Do by these Presents, solemnly and mutually, in the Presence of God and one another, covenant and combine ourselves together into a civil Body Politick, for our better Ordering and Preservation, and Furtherance of the Ends aforesaid: And by Virtue hereof do enact, constitute, and frame, such just and equal Laws, Ordinances, Acts, Constitutions, and Officers, from time to time, as shall be thought most meet and convenient for the general Good of the Colony; unto which we promise all due Submission and Obedience.

In witness whereof we have hereunto subscribed our names at Cape-Cod the eleventh of November, in the Reign of our Sovereign Lord King James, of England, France, and Ireland, the eighteenth, and of Scotland the fifty-fourth, Anno Domini; 1620.

What They Were Saying

from a letter to the Pilgrims upon their departure for America, written by their pastor, 1620:

Note: Some of the spelling, punctuation, and capitalization has been changed for ease of reading.

Lastly, whereas you are to become a body politic, using amongst yourselves civil government, and are not furnished with persons of special eminency above the rest, to be chosen by you into office of government; let your wisdom and godliness appear not only in choosing such persons as do entirely love, and will promote the common good; but also in yielding unto them all due honor and obedience in their lawful administrations, not beholding in them the ordinariness of their persons, but God's ordinance for your good; not being like the foolish multitude, who more honor the gay coat, than either the virtuous mind of the man, or the glorious ordinance of God. But you know better things, and that the image of the Lord's power and authority, which the magistrate beareth, is honorable, in how mean persons soever; and this duty you may the more willingly, and ought the more conscionably to perform, because you are (at least for the present) to have them for your ordinary governors, which yourselves shall make choice of for that work.

Connecticut Constitution 1639

Three decades after the first European settlers arrived in the New World, citizens from Windsor, Wethersfield, and Hartford, three central Connecticut towns along the Connecticut River, met and devised a set of governing rules called the Fundamental Orders. That document was the first constitution of any colony in America and a very decent one at that. Though not as sophisticated as modern-day state constitutions, the Connecticut Constitution was robust enough that it stood the test of time for nearly two hundred years and served as a model and inspiration for other colonies.

Note: Some of the spelling, punctuation, and capitalization has been changed for ease of reading.

Forasmuch as it hath pleased the Allmighty God by the wise disposition of his divine providence so to order and dispose of things that we the Inhabitants and Residents of Windsor, Hartford, and Wethersfield are now cohabiting and dwelling in and upon the River of Connectecotte and the lands thereunto adjoining; and well knowing where a people are gathered together the word of God requires that to maintain the peace and union of such a people there should be an orderly and decent Government established according to God, to order and dispose of the affairs of the people at all seasons as occasion shall require; do therefore associate and conjoin ourselves to be as one Public State or Commonwealth; and do for ourselves and our Successors and such as shall be adjoined to us at any time hereafter, enter into Combination and Confederation together, to maintain and preserve the liberty and purity of the Gospel of our Lord Jesus which we now profess, as also the discipline of the Churches, which according to the truth of the said Gospel is now practiced amongst us; as also in our Civil affairs to be guided and governed according to such Laws, Rules, Orders, and Decrees as shall be made, ordered, and decreed as followeth:—

1. It is Ordered, sentenced, and decreed, that there shall be yearly two General Assemblies or Courts, the one the second Thursday in April, the other the second Thursday in September following; the first shall be called the Court of Election, wherein shall be yearly chosen from time to time so many Magistrates and other public Officers as shall be found requisite: Whereof one to be chosen Governor for the year ensuing and until another be chosen, and no other Magistrate to be chosen for more than one year: provided always there be six chosen besides the Governor, which being chosen and sworn according to an Oath recorded for that purpose, shall have power to administer justice according to the Laws here established, and for want thereof, according to the rule of the Word of God. . . .

2. It is Ordered, sentenced, and decreed, that the election of the aforesaid Magistrates shall be on this manner: every person present and qualified for choice shall bring in (to the persons deputed to receive them) one single paper with the name of him written in it whom he desires to have Governor, and he that hath the greatest number of papers shall be Governor for that year. And the rest of the Magistrates or public officers to be chosen in this manner: the Secretary for the time being shall first read the names of all that are to be put to choice and then shall severally nominate them distinctly, and every one that would have the person nominated to be chosen shall bring in one single paper written upon, and he that would not have him chosen shall bring in a blank; and every one that hath more written papers than blanks shall be a Magistrate for that year; which papers shall be received and told by one or more that shall be then chosen by the court and sworn to be faithful therein; but in case there should not be six chosen as aforesaid, besides the Governor, out of those which are nominated, then he or they which have the most written papers shall be a

Magistrate or Magistrates for the ensuing year, to make up the aforesaid number.

3. It is Ordered, sentenced, and decreed, that the Secretary shall not nominate any person, nor shall any person be chosen newly into the Magistracy which was not propounded in some General Court before, to be nominated the next Election; and to that end it shall be lawful for each of the Towns aforesaid by their deputies to nominate any two whom they conceive fit to be put to election; and the Court may add so many more as they judge requisite.

4. It is Ordered, sentenced, and decreed, that no person be chosen Governor above once in two years, and that the Governor be always a member of some approved congregation, and formerly of the Magistracy within this Jurisdiction; and all the Magistrates, Freemen of this Commonwealth . . .

5. It is Ordered, sentenced, and decreed, that to the aforesaid Court of Election the several Towns shall send their deputies, and when the Elections are ended they may proceed in any public service as at other Courts. Also the other General Court in September shall be for making of laws, and any other public occasion, which concerns the good of the Commonwealth.

6. It is Ordered, sentenced, and decreed, that the Governor shall, either by himself or by the Secretary, send out summons to the Constables of every Town for the calling of these two standing Courts one month at least before their several times: And also if the Governor and the greatest part of the Magistrates see cause upon any special occasion to call a General Court, they may give order to the Secretary so to do within fourteen days' warning. . . .

7. It is Ordered, sentenced, and decreed, that after there are warrants given out for any of the said General Courts, the Constable or Constables of each Town, shall forthwith give notice distinctly to the inhabitants of the same, in some public assembly or by going or sending from house to house, that at a place and time by him or them limited and set, they meet and assemble themselves together to elect and choose certain deputies to be at the General Court. . . .

8. It is Ordered, sentenced, and decreed, that Windsor, Hartford, and Wethersfield shall have power, each Town, to send four of their Freemen as their deputies to every General Court; and Whatsoever other Town shall be hereafter added to this Jurisdiction, they shall send so many deputies as the Court shall judge meet, a reasonable proportion to the number of Freemen that are in the said Towns being to be attended therein; which deputies shall have the power of the whole Town to give their votes and allowance to all such laws and orders as may be for the public good, and unto which the said Towns are to be bound.

9. It is Ordered and decreed, that the deputies thus chosen shall have power and liberty to appoint a time and a place of meeting together before any General Court, to advise and consult of all such things as may concern the good of the public, as also to examine their own Elections.

American colonists in the mid-1760s were unhappy with new laws enacted by the English government. One law, the Quartering Act of March 1765, mandated that Americans offer lodgings to British officers. Another unpleasant law was the Stamp Act, also enacted in March 1765. The colonists were angry. They did not accept that these taxes were necessary for "defraying the expences of defending, protecting, and securing" the colonies. Many colonists believed the Stamp Act to be excessive—it included taxes on everything from newspapers to playing cards to university degrees. Almost every conceivable product made of paper was taxed, and fines were laid out for those who failed to follow the provisions of the act. Most importantly, it amounted to taxation without representation—the colonists did not have any say in the government that controlled them, so they felt they should not have to pay taxes.

In October 1765 a special congress was convened in New York City, consisting of twenty-eight representatives from nine colonies. Their fruitful fifteen-day meeting resulted in the creation of a document of remonstrances against Great Britain, a precursor to the Declaration of Independence

eleven years later. It was also a new experience for the colonies—working together as one united body in opposition to their oppressor. The outcry helped lead to the repeal of the Stamp Act in 1766, signaling the beginning of the end for England's reign over the colonies. Rather than exerting more control over the American territory, England began to lose its grip on the New World.

A period newspaper proclaims the repeal of the Stamp Act.

from the Stamp Act

. . . be it enacted . . . there shall be raised, levied, collected, and paid unto his Majesty, his heirs, and successors, throughout the colonies and plantations in America which now are, or hereafter may be, under the dominion of his Majesty, his heirs and successors . . .

For every skin or piece of vellum or parchment, or sheet or piece of paper, on which shall be ingrossed, written, or printed, any petition, bill, answer, claim, plea, replication, rejoinder, demurrer, or other pleading in any court of chancery or equity within the said colonies and plantations, a stamp duty of one shilling and six pence. . . .

For every skin or piece of vellum or parchment, or sheet or piece of paper, on which shall be ingrossed, written or printed, any grant, appointment, or admission of or to any publick beneficial office or employment, for the space of one year, or any lesser time, of or above the value of twenty pounds per annum sterling money, in salary, fees, and perquisites, within the said colonies and plantations, (except commissions and appointments of officers of the army, navy, ordnance, or militia, of judges, and of justices of the peace) a stamp duty of ten shillings. . . .

For every skin or piece of vellum or parchment, of sheet of piece of paper, on which shall be ingrossed, written, or printed any licence for retailing wine, to be granted to any person who shall not take out a licence for retailing of spirituous liquors, within the said colonies and plantations, a stamp duty of four pounds.

For every skin or piece of vellum or parchment, of sheet of piece of paper, on which shall be ingrossed, written, or printed, any probate of a will, letters of administration, or of guardianship for any estate above the value of twenty pounds sterling money . . . a stamp duty of five shillings. . . .

And for and upon every pack of playing cards, and all dice, which shall be sold or used within the said colonies and plantations, the several stamp duties following (that is to say)

For every pack of such cards, the sum of one shilling.

And for every pair of such dice, the sum of ten shillings. . . .

For every advertisement to be contained in any gazette, news paper, or other paper, or any pamphlet which shall be so printed, a duty of two shillings.

For every almanack or calendar, for any one particular year, or for any time less than a year, which shall be written or printed on one side only of any one sheet, skin, or piece of paper parchment, or vellum, within the said colonies and plantations, a stamp duty of two pence. . . .

X. Provided always, That this act shall not extend to charge any proclamation, forms of prayer and thanksgiving, or any printed votes of any house of assembly in any of the said colonies and plantations.

from the Stamp Act Congress Declaration of Rights

The members of this congress, sincerely devoted, with the warmest sentiments of affection and duty to His Majesty's person and government, inviolably attached to the present happy establishment of the Protestant succession, and with minds deeply impressed by a sense of the present and impending misfortunes of the British colonies on this continent; having considered as maturely as time would permit, the circumstances of said colonies, esteem it our indispensable duty to make the following declarations, of our humble opinions, respecting the most essential rights and liberties of the colonists, and of the grievances under which they labor, by reason of several late acts of Parliament.

1st. That His Majesty's subjects in these colonies owe the same allegiance to the crown of Great Britain that is owing from his subjects born within the realm, and all due subordination to that august body, the Parliament of Great Britain.

2d. That His Majesty's liege subjects in these colonies are entitled to all the inherent rights and privileges of his natural born subjects within the kingdom of Great Britain.

3d. That it is inseparably essential to the freedom of a people, and the undoubted rights of Englishmen, that no taxes should be imposed on them, but with their own consent, given personally, or by their representatives.

4th. That the people of these colonies are not, and from their local circumstances cannot be, represented in the House of Commons in Great Britain.

5th. That the only representatives of the people of these colonies are persons chosen therein, by themselves; and that no taxes ever have been or can be constitutionally imposed on them but by their respective legislatures.

6th. That all supplies to the crown being free gifts of the people, it is unreasonable and inconsistent with the principles and spirit of the British constitution for the people of Great Britain to grant to His Majesty the property of the colonists.

7th. That trial by jury is the inherent and invaluable right of every British subject in these colonies.

8th. That the late act of Parliament entitled, "An act for granting and applying certain stamp duties, and other duties in the British colonies and plantations in America, etc.," by imposing taxes on the inhabitants of these colonies, and the said act, and several other acts, by extending the jurisdiction of the courts of admiralty beyond its ancient limits, have a manifest tendency to subvert the rights and liberties of the colonists.

9th. That the duties imposed by several late acts of Parliament, from the peculiar circumstances of these colonies, will be extremely burthensome and grievous, and, from the scarcity of specie, the payment of them absolutely impracticable.

10th. That as the profits of the trade of these colonies ultimately center in Great Britain, to pay for the manufactures which they are obliged to take from thence, they eventually contribute very largely to all supplies granted there to the crown.

11th. That the restrictions imposed by several late acts of Parliament on the trade of these colonies will render them unable to purchase the manufactures of Great Britain.

12th. That the increase, prosperity, and happiness of these colonies depend on the full and free enjoyment of their rights and liberties, and an intercourse, with Great Britain, mutually affectionate and advantageous.

13th. That it is the right of the British subjects in these colonies to petition the king or either house of Parliament.

Lastly, That it is the indispensable duty of these colonies to the best of sovereigns, to the mother-country, and to themselves, to endeavor, by a loyal and dutiful address to His Majesty, and humble application to both houses of Parliament, to procure the repeal of the act for granting and applying certain stamp duties, of all clauses of any other acts of Parliament whereby the jurisdiction of the admiralty is extended as aforesaid, and of the other late acts for the restriction of the American commerce.

What They Were Saying

Lord Camden, of the House of Peers (British Parliament), 1765:

My position is this. I repeat it, I will maintain it to my last hour; taxation and representation are inseparable. This position is founded on the laws of nature. It is more, it is itself an eternal law of nature. For whatever is a man's own, it is absolutely his own. No man has a right to take it from him without his consent. Whoever attempts to do it, attempts an injury; whoever does it, commits a robbery.

William Pitt, of the House of Commons (British Parliament), 1765:

You have no right to tax America. I rejoice that America has resisted. Three millions of our fellow subjects so lost to every sense of virtue, as tamely to give up their liberties, would be fit instruments to make slaves of the rest . . . Upon the whole, I will beg leave to tell the house what is really my opinion. It is, that the stamp-act be repealed absolutely, totally, and immediately. That the reason for the repeal be assigned, because it is founded on an erroneous principle. At the same time, let the sovereign authority of this country over the colonies, be asserted in as strong; terms as can be devised, and be made to extend to every point of legislation whatsoever. That we may bind their trade, confine their manufactures and exercise every power whatsoever, except that of taking their money out of their pockets without their consent!

from the New York group Sons of Liberty, 1766:

Resolved: That we will go to the last extremity and venture our lives and fortunes effectively to prevent the said Stamp-Act from ever taking place in this city and province. Resolved: That any person who shall deliver out or receive any instrument of writing upon stamped paper . . . agreeable to the said act shall incur the highest resentment of this society, and be branded with ever-lasting infamy. Resolved: That the persons who carry on business as formerly on unstamped paper . . . shall be protected to the utmost power of this society . . . Resolved: That we will to the utmost of our power maintain the peace and good order of this city so far as it can be done consistently with the preservation of our rights and privileges

Tea Act 1773

During the eighteenth century, tea was a more valuable commodity than it is today. Tea plants only grew in warm climates in distant lands and had to be transported by ship across thousands of miles to get to America. Though earlier taxes from the 1760s had been repealed, England retained a small tax on tea and granted a monopoly for selling tea to America to the East India Company. Even though their tax was lower than what British citizens paid for their tea, the colonists rebelled. They refused to buy the tea that was to be taxed and were angry over being taxed without representation. They were also upset about being forced to buy through the East India Company. Tea-carrying East India Company ships approaching New York and Philadelphia were not allowed to dock. In Boston, however, the governor prevented the people from sending the newly arrived ships away. Samuel Adams and other patriots argued for the rejection of the tea ships, but the governor held firm. After days of tension, a few dozen men dressed as Native

Americans boarded the ships and dumped 342 crates (45 tons) of precious tea into the Boston Harbor, in what became known as the Boston Tea Party. In response, an angry Parliament devised a bill that shut down the port of Boston for business until the city repaid what had been lost in tea (one of the so-called Intolerable Acts passed by a furious English government). A year later, in September 1774, the first Continental Congress met to show support for Massachusetts and to proclaim their right of self-government.

A British print from 1774 shows Bostonians "paying the excise-man" as tea is being dumped in the background.

THE BOSTONIANS PAYING THE EXCISE-MAN OR TARRING & FEATHERING

from the Tea Act

An act to allow a drawback of the duties of customs on the exportation of tea to any of his Majesty's colonies or plantations in America; to increase the deposit on bohea tea to be sold at the India Company's sales; and to impower the commissioners of the treasury to grant licences to the East India Company to export tea duty-free.

WHEREAS by an act, made in the twelfth year of his present Majesty's reign . . . it is amongst other things, enacted, That for and during the space of five years, to be computed from and after the fifth day of July, one thousand seven hundred and seventy-two, there shall be drawn back and allowed for all teas which shall be sold after the said fifth day of July, one thousand seven hundred and seventy-two, at the publick sale of the united company of merchants of England trading to the East Indies, or which after that time shall be imported, by licence, in pursuance of the said therein and hereinafter mentioned act, made in the eighteenth year of the reign of his late majesty King George the Second, and which shall be exported from this kingdom, as merchandise, to Ireland, or any of the British colonies or plantations in America, three-fifth parts of the several duties of customs which were paid upon the importation of such teas; which drawback or allowance, with respect to such teas as shall be exported to Ireland, shall be made to the exporter, in such manner, and under such rules, regulations, securities, penalties, and forfeitures, as any drawback or allowance was then payable, out of the duty of customs upon the exportation of foreign goods to Ireland; and with respect to such teas as shall be exported to the British colonies and plantations in America, the said drawback or allowance shall be made in such manner, and under such rules, regulations, penalties, and forfeitures, as any drawback or allowance payable out of the duty of customs upon foreign goods exported to foreign parts, was could, or might be made, before the passing of the said act of the twelfth year of his present Majesty's reign, (except in such cases as are otherwise therein provided for:) and whereas it may tend to the benefit and advantage of the trade of the said united company of merchants of England trading to the East Indies, if the allowance of the drawback of the duties of customs upon all teas sold at the publick sales of the said united company, after the tenth day of May, one thousand seven hundred and seventy-three, and which shall be exported from this kingdom, as merchandise, to any of the British colonies or plantations in America, were to extend to the whole of the said duties of customs payable upon the importation of such teas; may it therefore please your Majesty that it may be enacted; and be it enacted by the King's most excellent majesty, by and with the advice and consent of the lords spiritual and temporal, and commons, in this present parliament assembled, and by the authority of the same, That there shall be drawn back and allowed for all teas, which, from and after the tenth day of May, one thousand seven hundred and seventy-three, shall be sold at the publick sales of the said united company, or which shall be imported by licence, in pursuance of the said act made in the eighteenth year of the reign of his late majesty King George the Second, and which shall, at any time hereafter, be exported from this kingdom, as merchandise, to any of the British colonies or plantations in America, the whole of the duties of customs payable upon the importation of such teas; which drawback or allowance shall be made to the exporter in such manner, and under such rules, regulations, and securities, and subject to the like penalties and forfeitures, as the former drawback or allowance granted by the said recited act of the twelfth year of his present Majesty's reign, upon tea exported to the said British colonies and plantations in America was, might, or could be made, and was subject to by the said recited act, or any other act of parliament now in force, in as full and ample manner, to all intents and purposes, as if the several clauses relative thereto were again repeated and re-enacted in this present act.

II. And whereas by one other act made in the eighteenth year of the reign of his late majesty King George the Second . . . it is, amongst other things, enacted, That every person who shall, at any publick sale of tea made by the united company of merchants of England trading to the East Indies, be declared to be the best bidder for any lot or lots of tea, shall, within three days after being so declared the best bidder or bidders for the same, deposit with the said united company, or such clerk or officer as the said company shall appoint to receive the same, forty shillings for every tub and for every chest of tea.

# What They Were Saying

Samuel Adams (patriot, future Declaration of Independence signer), circa 1769:

We will not submit to any tax, nor become slaves. We will take up arms, and spend our last drop of blood before the King and Parliament shall impose on us, and settle crown officers in this country to dragoon us. The country was first settled by our ancestors, therefore we are free, and want no king. The times were never better in Rome than when they had no king and were a free state; and as this is a great empire, we shall have it in our power to give laws to England.

from a letter by John Dickinson, a patriot whose nickname was "the Penman of the Revolution," 1773:

I am very sorry for the Piece of Intelligence you were pleased to communicate to me in your last, five Ships, loaded with tea, on their Way to America, and this with a View not only to enforce the Revenue Act, but to establish a Monopoly for the East-India Company, who have espoused the Cause of the Ministry; and hope to repair their broken Fortunes by the Ruin of American freedom and Liberty! No Wonder the Minds of the People are exasperated, as you say, to a degree of Madness. . . .

The Monopoly of Tea, is, I dare say, but a small Part of the Plan they have formed to strip us of our Property. But thank GOD, we are . . . British Subjects, who are born to Liberty, who know its Worth, and who prize it high. We are engaged in a mighty Struggle. The Cause is of the utmost Importance, and the Determination of it will fix our Condition as Slaves or Freemen. It is not the paltry Sum of Three-Pence which is now demanded, but the Principle upon which it is demanded, that we are contending against. Before we pay any Thing, let us see whether we have any Thing we can call our own to pay . . .

Our Houses, Stores and Wharves are at our own Disposal. Resolve, therefore, nobly resolve and publish to the World your Resolutions, that no Man will receive the Tea, no Man will let his Stores, nor suffer the Vessel, that brings it, to moor at his Wharf, and that if any Person assists in unlading, landing or storing it, he shall ever after be deemed an Enemy to his Country, and never be employed by his Fellow Citizens. I am sure, from what I have formerly known of our porters, there is not a Man among them, that will lend a Hand; and I question, whether among the whole Class of Labourers that ply about the Wharves, there will be found One, who would not rather go without his Dinner than, for double Wages, touch the accursed Trash. Believe me, my Friend, there is a Spirit of Liberty and a love of their Country among every Class of Men among us, which Experience will evince, and which shew them worthy the Character of free-born Americans.

1776 Thomas Paine's *Common Sense*

Common Sense, by Thomas Paine, was a stirring pamphlet about the monarchy of England and the future of the colonies. Born in 1737, political philosopher and activist Thomas Paine was a newcomer to the colonies. He had arrived in 1774 after having met Benjamin Franklin in London. The British-born Paine was soon to become a fervent supporter of American independence. Paine's *Common Sense* (originally published anonymously) was a fiery piece in which emotional pleas were put forth alongside political facts. *Common Sense* was the perfect name for Paine's work, as it embraced everything that colonists wished to say. After he wrote *Common Sense* and another pamphlet supporting American independence, he received a sum of three thousand dollars from the government in 1785 in thanks for his support of the struggle for independence. He returned to Europe in 1787 and published a defense of the French Revolution in 1791. Called *The Rights of Man*, it was a fervent rebuttal to a work by Edmund Burke that opposed the French Revolution and criticized the British government. Paine was forced to leave Britain in 1792 and spent many years in France, hoping for a British revolution. He finally returned to the United States in 1802, where he died in 1809.

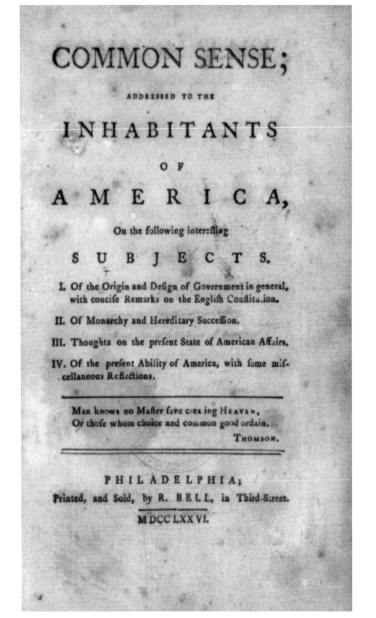

COMMON SENSE;

ADDRESSED TO THE

INHABITANTS

OF

AMERICA,

On the following interesting

SUBJECTS.

I. Of the Origin and Design of Government in general, with concise Remarks on the English Constitution.

II. Of Monarchy and Hereditary Succession.

III. Thoughts on the present State of American Affairs.

IV. Of the present Ability of America, with some miscellaneous Reflections.

Man knows no Master save creating HEAVEN,
Or those whom choice and common good ordain.
THOMSON.

PHILADELPHIA;
Printed, and Sold, by R. BELL, in Third-Street.
MDCCLXXVI.

Perhaps the sentiments contained in the following pages, are not YET sufficiently fashionable to procure them general favour; a long habit of not thinking a thing WRONG, gives it a superficial appearance of being RIGHT, and raises at first a formidable outcry in defense of custom. But the tumult soon subsides. Time makes more converts than reason. As a long and violent abuse of power, is generally the Means of calling the right of it in question (and in Matters too which might never have been thought of, had not the Sufferers been aggravated into the inquiry) and as the King of England hath undertaken in his OWN RIGHT, to support the Parliament in what he calls THEIRS, and as the good people of this country are grievously oppressed by the combination, they have an undoubted privilege to inquire into the pretensions of both, and equally to reject the usurpation of either. In the following sheets, the author hath studiously avoided every thing which is personal among ourselves. Compliments as well as censure to individuals make no part thereof. The wise, and the worthy, need not the triumph of a pamphlet; and those whose sentiments are injudicious, or unfriendly, will cease of themselves unless too much pains are bestowed upon their conversion. The cause of America is in a great measure the cause of all mankind. Many circumstances hath, and will arise, which are not local, but universal, and through which the principles of all Lovers of Mankind are affected, and in the Event of which, their Affections are interested. The laying a Country desolate with Fire and Sword, declaring War against the natural rights of all Mankind, and extirpating the Defenders thereof from the Face of the Earth, is the Concern of every Man to whom Nature hath given the Power of feeling; of which Class, regardless of Party Censure, is the AUTHOR . . .

There is something exceedingly ridiculous in the composition of Monarchy; it first excludes a man from the means of information, yet empowers him to act in cases where the highest judgment is required. The state of a king shuts him from the World, yet the business of a king requires him to know it thoroughly; wherefore the different parts, by unnaturally opposing and destroying each other, prove the whole character to be absurd and useless. . . .

I HAVE never met with a man, either in England or America, who hath not confessed his opinion, that a separation between the countries would take place one time or other: And there is no instance in which we have shown less judgment, than in endeavoring to describe, what we call, the ripeness or fitness of the continent for independence.

As all men allow the measure, and vary only in their opinion of the time, let us, in order to remove mistakes, take a general survey of things, and endeavor if possible to find out the VERY time. But I need not go far, the inquiry ceases at once, for the TIME HATH FOUND US. The general concurrence, the glorious union of all things, proves the fact.

What They Were Saying

from *Memoirs of the Reign of George III*, 1796:

This extraordinary production [a piece written by the British Edmund Burke] gave rise to numberless replies, of which by far the most memorable was that written by Thomas Paine, the author of the famous pamphlet styled COMMON SENSE, which by its almost magical effect: on the minds of the people of America, at a most important crisis, paved the way for the declaration of independency. His present work, RIGHTS OF MAN, was written with no less power of intellect and force of language; and made a correspondent, perhaps an indelible, impression upon the public mind. Not content with pointing out and exposing with the most sarcastic severity the absurdities and misrepresentations of Mr. Burke—not content with painting in just and striking colors the abuses and corruptions of the existing government, he with daring and unhallowed hand attacked the principles of the [British] constitution itself—describing it in terms the most indecent as radically vicious and tyrannical; and reprobating the introduction of aristocracy or monarchy, under whatever modifications, into any form of government, as a flagrant usurpation and invasion of the unalienable rights of man.

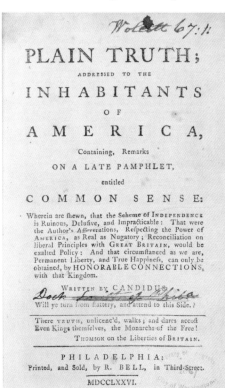

from *The Life of Thomas Paine*, 1809:

Speaking a language which the colonists had felt but not thought, its popularity, terrible in its consequences to the parent country, was unexampled in the history of the press. At first, involving the colonists, it was thought, in the crime of rebellion, and pointing to a road leading inevitably to ruin, it was read with indignation and alarm, but when the reader, (and everybody read it) recovering from the first shock, reperused it, its arguments, nourishing his feelings and appealing to his pride, reanimated his hopes and satisfied his understanding, that COMMON SENSE, backed by the resources and force of the colonies, poor and feeble as they were, could alone rescue them from the unqualified oppression with which they were threatened. The unknown author, in the moments of enthusiasm which succeeded, was hailed as an angel sent from heaven to save from all the horrours of slavery, by his timely, powerful, and unerring councils, a faithful, but abused, a brave, but misrepresented people.

A pamphlet opposing independence issued in response to Common Sense, 1776.

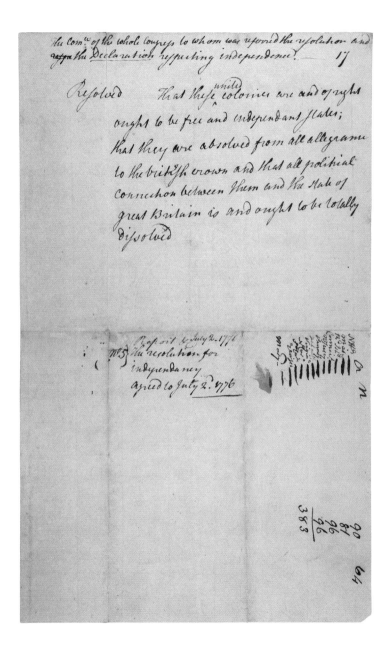

Hostilities had already broken out between England and the colonies by 1776, but the conflict remained nothing more than an attempt by the mother country to suppress insurrection. An official call for the colonies' independence from England would change that and elevate the colonists' struggle to a different level, both in the eyes of the Americans and in the eyes of England and the rest of the world. Richard Henry Lee (1732–1794) of Virginia drafted a brief and to the point resolution that put into words what many colonists were already thinking. This resolution, though debated for some time by the Congress, was seconded by John Adams and finally adopted in July 1776. It led directly to the creation by Thomas Jefferson of the Declaration of Independence (of which Lee was a signer).

Resolved, That these United Colonies are, and of right ought to be, free and independent States, that they are absolved from all allegiance to the British Crown, and that all political connection between them and the State of Great Britain is, and ought to be, totally dissolved.

That it is expedient forthwith to take the most effectual measures for forming foreign Alliances.

That a plan of confederation be prepared and transmitted to the respective Colonies for their consideration and approbation.

 What They Were Saying

from a speech by Richard Henry Lee urging the adoption of his resolution, 1776:

Why . . . do we longer delay? Why still deliberate? Let this happy day give birth to an American republic. Let her arise, not to devastate and to conquer, but to re-establish the reign of peace and of law. The eyes of Europe are fixed upon us; she demands of us a living example of freedom, that may exhibit a contrast, in the felicity of the citizen, to the ever increasing tyranny which desolates her polluted shores. She invites us to prepare an asylum, where the unhappy may find solace, and the persecuted repose. She entreats us to cultivate a propitious soil, where that generous plant which first sprung and grew in England, but is now withered by the poisonous blasts of Scottish tyranny, may revive and flourish, sheltering under its salubrious and interminable shade, all the unfortunate of the human race. If we are not this day wanting in our duty, the names of the American legislators of 1776, will be placed by posterity, at the side of Theseus, Lycurgus and Romulus, of the three Williams of Nassau, and of all those whose memory has been, and ever will be, dear to virtuous men and good citizens.

from *Biography of the Signers to the Declaration of Independence*, 1828:

Mr. Lee was chosen to move the resolution in Congress; he knew that the implacable hatred of tyrants would pursue him for revenge, and that the uncertain issue of war, might place him in their power; but foreign states could form no alliance with rebels, and England was not resting on her own mighty resources: necessity urged, and Mr. Lee had ever listened to the voice of his country; he depended, for his safety, on the extent of her territories, her capabilities of defence, and the alliances which the declaration of independence would procure, or he despised the consequences, and was deaf to the suggestions of fear. This motion [Lee's Resolution], which was followed by a protracted debate of several days, was introduced by one of the most luminous and eloquent speeches, ever delivered by its illustrious mover.

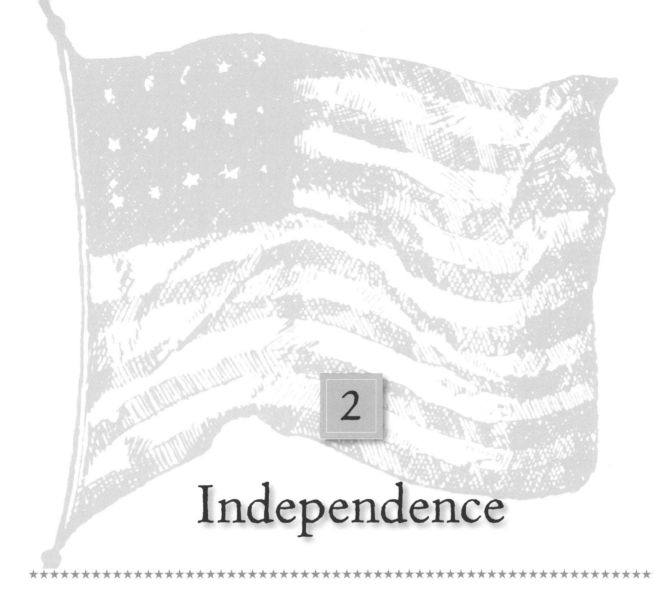

2

Independence

★★

In 1774 King George III of England said of the situation in America, "The die is cast, the colonies must either triumph or submit." The colonies did not submit. It took some years and considerable bloodshed, but the colonies triumphed. With the assistance of their newly minted French allies, whose hatred of the English was a motivating force in their alliance with America, the colonies vanquished their mother country. The king of England at first refused to give up the colonies even after his armies had surrendered, but eventually came to his senses. Benjamin Franklin helped draft a peace treaty, and the United States was at last free of English rule. A provisional governing document called the Articles of Confederation was created, but by 1787 it was evident that it did not give the federal government enough authority. A convention was called to draft a new document. The resulting Constitution and subsequent Bill of Rights would become the cornerstones of the American way of life and stand the test of time.

1776 Declaration of Independence

Perhaps no other document in American history carries the status of the Declaration of Independence. This document, drafted by Thomas Jefferson in June 1776 in just over two weeks, would be legendary by virtue of its being our assertion of freedom from England. But the Declaration's real genius lies in its combination of flowing eloquence and simple expression. It is the ultimate recognition that it would be impossible to recover from the damages inflicted upon the colonists by their mother country. The document begins humbly enough, citing "a decent respect to the opinions of mankind" that requires a clear and detailed explanation of their grievances. The long list of complaints against England is an exclamation point upon the "Life, Liberty and the pursuit of Happiness" mentioned in the introduction. The closing of the document explains how England had been "deaf to the voice of justice" despite attempts by the colonies to have their concerns heard. The Declaration and subsequent fight for freedom inspired the French Revolution and led countless other nations to fight for democracy. The Declaration was heard loud and clear at the time, and it still echoes loudly today.

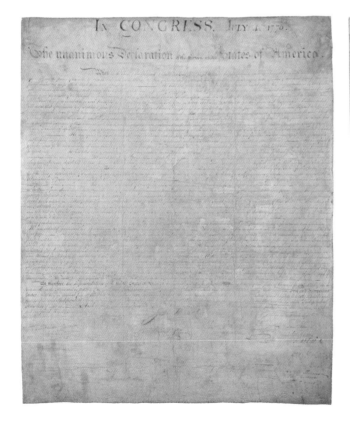

When in the Course of human events, it becomes necessary for one people to dissolve the political bands which have connected them with another, and to assume among the powers of the earth, the separate and equal station to which the Laws of Nature and of Nature's God entitle them, a decent respect to the opinions of mankind requires that they should declare the causes which impel them to the separation.

We hold these truths to be self-evident, that all men are created equal, that they are endowed by their Creator with certain unalienable Rights, that among these are Life, Liberty and the pursuit of Happiness. That to secure these rights, Governments are instituted among Men, deriving their just powers from the consent of the governed,— That whenever any Form of Government becomes destructive of these ends, it is the Right of the People to alter or to abolish it, and to institute new Government, laying its foundation on such principles and organizing its powers in such form, as to them shall seem most likely to effect their Safety and Happiness. Prudence, indeed, will dictate that Governments long established should not be changed for light and transient causes; and accordingly all experience hath shewn that mankind are more disposed to suffer, while evils are sufferable, than to right themselves by abolishing the forms to which they are accustomed. But when a long train of abuses and usurpations, pursuing invariably the same Object evinces a design to reduce them under absolute Despotism, it is their right, it is their duty, to throw off such Government, and to provide new Guards for their future security.— Such has been the patient sufferance of these Colonies; and such is now the necessity which constrains them to alter their former Systems of Government. The history of the present King of Great Britain is a history of repeated injuries and usurpations, all having in direct object the establishment of an absolute Tyranny over these States. To prove this, let Facts be submitted to a candid world.

He has refused his Assent to Laws, the most wholesome and necessary for the public good.

He has forbidden his Governors to pass Laws of immediate and pressing importance, unless suspended in their operation till his Assent should be obtained; and when so suspended, he has utterly neglected to attend to them.

He has refused to pass other Laws for the accommodation of large districts of people, unless those people would relinquish the right of Representation in the Legislature, a right inestimable to them and formidable to tyrants only.

He has called together legislative bodies at places unusual, uncomfortable, and distant from the depository of their public Records, for the sole purpose of fatiguing them into compliance with his measures.

He has dissolved Representative Houses repeatedly, for opposing with manly firmness his invasions on the rights of the people.

He has refused for a long time, after such dissolutions, to cause others to be elected, whereby the Legislative powers, incapable of Annihilation, have returned to the People at large for their exercise; the State remaining in the mean time exposed to all the dangers of invasion from without, and convulsions within.

He has endeavoured to prevent the population of these States; for that purpose obstructing the Laws for Naturalization of Foreigners; refusing to pass others to encourage their migrations hither, and raising the conditions of new Appropriations of Lands.

He has obstructed the Administration of Justice by refusing his Assent to Laws for establishing Judiciary powers.

He has made Judges dependent on his Will alone, for the tenure of their offices, and the amount and payment of their salaries.

He has erected a multitude of New Offices, and sent hither swarms of Officers to harass our people and eat out their substance.

He has kept among us, in times of peace, Standing Armies without the Consent of our legislatures.

He has affected to render the Military independent of and superior to the Civil power.

He has combined with others to subject us to a jurisdiction foreign to our constitution, and unacknowledged by our laws; giving his Assent to their Acts of pretended Legislation:

For Quartering large bodies of armed troops among us:

For protecting them, by a mock Trial, from punishment for any Murders which they should commit on the Inhabitants of these States:

For cutting off our Trade with all parts of the world:

For imposing Taxes on us without our Consent:

For depriving us in many cases, of the benefits of Trial by Jury:

For transporting us beyond Seas to be tried for pretended offences:

For abolishing the free System of English Laws in a neighbouring Province, establishing therein an Arbitrary government, and enlarging its Boundaries so as to render it at once an example and fit instrument for introducing the same absolute rule into these Colonies:

For taking away our Charters, abolishing our most valuable Laws, and altering fundamentally the Forms of our Governments:

For suspending our own Legislatures, and declaring themselves invested with power to legislate for us in all cases whatsoever.

He has abdicated Government here, by declaring us out of his Protection and waging War against us.

He has plundered our seas, ravaged our Coasts, burnt our towns, and destroyed the lives of our people.

He is at this time transporting large Armies of foreign Mercenaries to compleat the works of death, desolation, and tyranny, already begun with circumstances of Cruelty & perfidy scarcely paralleled in the most barbarous ages, and totally unworthy the Head of a civilized nation.

He has constrained our fellow Citizens taken Captive on the high Seas to bear Arms against their Country, to become the executioners of their friends and Brethren, or to fall themselves by their Hands.

He has excited domestic insurrections amongst us, and has endeavoured to bring on the inhabitants of our frontiers, the merciless Indian Savages, whose known rule of warfare, is an undistinguished destruction of all ages, sexes and conditions.

In every stage of these Oppressions We have Petitioned for Redress in the most humble terms: Our repeated Petitions have been answered only by repeated injury. A Prince, whose character is thus marked by every act which may define a Tyrant, is unfit to be the ruler of a free people.

Nor have We been wanting in attentions to our British brethren. We have warned them from time to time of attempts by their legislature to extend an unwarrantable jurisdiction over us. We have reminded them of the circumstances of our emigration and settlement here. We have appealed to their native justice and magnanimity, and we have conjured them by the ties of our common kindred to disavow these usurpations, which, would inevitably interrupt our connections and correspondence. They too have been deaf to the voice of justice and of consanguinity. We must, therefore, acquiesce in the necessity, which denounces our Separation, and hold them, as we hold the rest of mankind, Enemies in War, in Peace Friends.

We, therefore, the Representatives of the united States of America, in General Congress, Assembled, appealing to the Supreme Judge of the world for the rectitude of our intentions, do, in the Name, and by Authority of the good People of these Colonies, solemnly publish and declare, That these united Colonies are, and of Right ought to be Free and Independent States, that they are Absolved from all Allegiance to the British Crown, and that all political connection between them and the State of Great Britain, is and ought to be totally dissolved; and that as Free and Independent States, they have full Power to levy War, conclude Peace, contract Alliances, establish Commerce, and to do all other Acts and Things which Independent States may of right do. And for the support of this Declaration, with a firm reliance on the protection of divine Providence, we mutually pledge to each other our Lives, our Fortunes, and our sacred Honor.

What They Were Saying

from a letter by John Adams, July 5, 1776:

Yesterday was decided the greatest question which was ever decided among men. A resolution was passed unanimously, "that these United States are, and of right ought to be, free and independent states." The day is passed. The 4th of July '76, will be a memorable epoch in the history of America. I am apt to believe it will be celebrated by succeeding generations, as the great anniversary festival. It ought to be commemorated as the day of deliverance by solemn acts of devotion to Almighty God.

from King George III, 1779:

No man in my dominions desires solid peace more than I do. But no inclination to get out of the present difficulties, which certainly keep my mind very far from a state of ease, can incline me to enter into the destruction of the empire . . . The present contest with America I cannot help seeing as the most serious in which this country was ever engaged. It contains such a train of consequences, as must be examined to feel its real weight . . . step by step the demands of America have risen. Independence is their object, which every man not willing to sacrifice every object to a momentary and inglorious peace must concur with me in thinking this country can never submit to. Should America succeed in that, the West Indies must follow not in independence, but dependence on America. Ireland would soon follow, and this island reduce itself to a poor island indeed.

from a speech by Jeremiah Reeve delivered at Canterbury, Connecticut, July 4, 1802:

Most certainly, a day like this—a day on which the patriots of '76 drew up those resolutions in which millions of our fellow creatures are deeply interested, and perhaps will continue so, even through succeeding generations. I say, a day like this, will always be celebrated in some way or another, by every one whose breast glows with the least spark of patriotism or sensibility . . . What son of freedom is there, who, upon the least reflection does not feel his heart dilate with gratitude to the great disposer of all things, who has in this age of the world, placed him in a country like this? . . . Where the people are ruled by mild and salutary laws; and where each member of society, (whether ruler or subject) is equally governed and protected by the laws.

Members of the Declaration Committee in 1776, including Jefferson, seated left, and Franklin, second from right.

1778 Treaty of Alliance with France

Relations between France and England were tense during the eighteenth century. As they were under British control, the American colonists had to contend with the French during several eighteenth-century conflicts, including the long French and Indian Wars that pitted the English, colonists, and their Native American allies against the French and their own Native American allies. Once the colonists declared their independence from the English in 1776, it seemed logical for the French (with a little persuasion from Benjamin Franklin) to side with them, or more precisely, against the English. The French assistance during the war, including French ships, thousands of French troops, and much-needed monetary aid, was decisive; it countered the German mercenaries who were helping the British. In fact, the French king got more than he bargained for by helping America. So taken were many French with the cause for freedom that they were soon inspired to conduct a revolt of their own beginning in 1789. The French Revolution was born, leading to the beheading of King Louis XVI and Queen Marie Antoinette. The outcome in France was not nearly as positive as it had been in America; chaos reigned for some time, and Napoleon Bonaparte declared himself emperor in 1804.

Note: Original spelling is used in the introductory clause, but is corrected in the remainder of the document excerpts.

The most Christian King and the United States of North America . . . having this Day concluded a Treaty of amity and Commerce, for the reciprocal advantage of their Subjects and Citizens have thought it necessary to take into consideration the means of strengthening those engagements and of rondring them useful to the safety and tranquility of the two parties, particularly in case Great Britain in Resentment of that connection and of the good correspondence which is the object of the said Treaty, should break the Peace with france, either by direct hostilities, or by hindring her commerce and navigation, in a manner contrary to the Rights of Nations, and the Peace subsisting between the two Crowns; and his Majesty and the said united States having resolved in that Case to join their Councils and efforts against the Enterprises of their common Enemy, the respective Plenipotentiaries, impower'd to concert the Clauses & conditions proper to fulfil the said Intentions, have, after the most mature Deliberation, concluded and determined on the following Articles.

Article 1—If War should break out between France and Great Britain during the continuance of the present War between the United States and England, his Majesty and the said United States, shall make it a common cause, and aid each other mutually with their good Offices, their Counsels, and their forces, according to the exigence of Conjunctures as becomes good & faithful allies. . . .

Article 3—The two contracting parties shall each on its own Part, and in the manner it may judge most proper, make all the efforts in its Power, against their common Enemy, in order to attain the end proposed. . . .

Article 5—If the United States should think fit to attempt the reduction of the British power remaining in the northern parts of America, or the Islands of Bermudas, those countries or islands in case of success, shall be confederated with or dependent upon the said United States. . . .

Article 8—Neither of the two Parties shall conclude either truce or peace with Great Britain, without the formal consent of the other first obtained; and they mutually engage not to lay down their arms, until the independence of the United States shall have been formally or tacitly assured by the Treaty or Treaties that shall terminate the War. . . .

 What They Were Saying

from a letter by Thomas Paine, 1781:

Perhaps no two events ever united so intimately and forcibly to combat and expel prejudice, as the revolution of America and the alliance with France . . . Perhaps there never was an alliance on a broader basis, than that between America and France, and the progress of it is worth attending to. The countries had been enemies, not properly of themselves, but through the medium of England. They, originally, had no quarrel with each other, nor any cause for one, but what arose from the interest of England, and her arming America against France. . . . An alliance not formed for the mere purpose of a day, but on just and generous grounds, and with equal and mutual advantages; and the easy, affectionate manner in which the parties have since communicated, has made it an alliance not of courts only, but of countries.

1781 Articles of Confederation

In this short-lived governing document, one can see many of the seeds of the Constitution. As early as June 1776, Congress authorized the creation of the Articles of Confederation. The resulting document was accepted by Congress in 1777 and officially adopted in 1781 after the British surrender. It was certainly a start, but it was only the colonists' first attempt at creating a governing document. Under the Articles, the new country was more a "league of friendship" than a strongly united nation. The office of president as we know it today was not provided for. In Article IX there was a provision for a Committee of States, over which one person would be selected to preside, a president. No provisions were made for allowing the federal government to request money from the states to pay for its operation, and the federal government did not have the authority to regulate commerce. Interestingly, an invitation was extended to Canada to join the United States. After a few years, the founding fathers realized that this document was not going to be sufficient for the new republic, and work began on a new governing document in 1787. The Articles of Confederation were used until the newly written Constitution was ratified in 1789.

TO ALL WHOM these Presents shall come, we the undersigned Delegates of the States affixed to our Names send greeting . . .

Article I
The Stile of this Confederacy shall be "The United States of America."

Article II
Each state retains its sovereignty, freedom, and independence, and every power, jurisdiction, and right, which is not by this Confederation expressly delegated to the United States, in Congress assembled.

Article III
The said States hereby severally enter into a firm league of friendship with each other, for their common defense, the security of their liberties, and their mutual and general welfare, binding themselves to assist each other, against all force offered to, or attacks made upon them, or any of them, on account of religion, sovereignty, trade, or any other pretense whatever.

Article IV
The better to secure and perpetuate mutual friendship and intercourse among the people of the different States in this Union, the free inhabitants of each of these States, paupers, vagabonds, and fugitives from justice excepted, shall be entitled to all privileges and immunities of free citizens in the several States; and the people of each State shall have free ingress and regress to and from any other State, and shall enjoy therein all the privileges of trade and commerce, subject to the same duties, impositions, and restrictions as the inhabitants thereof respectively . . .

Article V
. . . Freedom of speech and debate in Congress shall not be impeached or questioned in any court or place out of Congress, and the members of Congress shall be protected in their persons from arrests or imprisonments, during the time of their going to and from, and attendance on Congress, except for treason, felony, or breach of the peace.

Article VI
. . . No State shall engage in any war without the consent of the United States in Congress assembled, unless such State be actually invaded by enemies, or shall have received certain advice of a resolution being formed by some nation of Indians to invade such State, and the danger is so imminent as not to admit of a delay till the United States in Congress assembled can be consulted . . .

Article IX
The United States in Congress assembled, shall have the sole and exclusive right and power of determining on peace and war . . . of sending and receiving ambassadors—entering into treaties and alliances, provided that no treaty of commerce shall be made whereby the legislative power of the respective States shall be restrained from imposing such imposts and duties on foreigners, as their own people are subjected to, or from prohibiting the exportation or importation of any species of goods or commodities whatsoever . . .

The United States in Congress assembled shall also be the last resort on appeal in all disputes and differences now subsisting or that hereafter may arise between two or more States concerning boundary, jurisdiction or any other cause whatever; which authority shall always be exercised in the manner following . . .

The United States in Congress assembled shall also have the sole and exclusive right and power of regulating the alloy and value of coin struck by their own authority, or by that of the respective States—fixing the standard of weights and measures throughout the United States—regulating the trade and managing all affairs with the Indians, not members of any of the States, provided that the legislative right of any State within its own limits be not infringed or violated . . .

The United States in Congress assembled shall have authority to appoint a committee, to sit in the recess of Congress, to be denominated "A Committee of the States," and to consist of one delegate from each State; and to appoint such other committees and civil officers as may be necessary for managing the general affairs of the United States under their direction—to appoint one of their number to preside, provided that no person be allowed to serve in the office of president more than one year in any term of three years; to ascertain the necessary sums of money to be raised for the service of the United States, and to appropriate and apply the same for defraying the public expenses—to borrow money, or emit bills on the credit of the United States, transmitting every half year to the respective States an account of the sums of money so borrowed or emitted—to build and equip a navy—to agree upon the number of land forces, and to make requisitions from each State for its quota, in proportion to the number of white inhabitants in such State; which requisition shall be binding, and thereupon the legislature of each State shall appoint the regimental officers, raise the men and clothe, arm and equip them in a soldier-like manner, at the expense of the United States; and the officers and men so clothed, armed and equipped shall march to the place appointed, and within the time agreed on by the United States in Congress assembled . . .

Article XI
Canada acceding to this confederation, and adjoining in the measures of the United States, shall be admitted into, and entitled to all the advantages of this Union; but no other colony shall be admitted into the same, unless such admission be agreed to by nine States.

 What They Were Saying

from remarks by James Wilson, one of the drafters of the Constitution, 1787:

On the glorious conclusion of our conflict with Britain, what high expectations were formed concerning us by others! What high expectations did we form concerning ourselves! Have those expectations been realized? No. What has been the cause? Did our citizens lose their perseverance and magnanimity? No. Did they become insensible of resentment and indignation at any highhanded attempt that might have been made to injure or enslave them? No. What then has been the cause? The truth is, we dreaded danger only on one side: This we manfully repelled. But on another side, danger, not less formidable, but more insidious, stole in upon us; and our unsuspicious tempers were not sufficiently attentive, either to its approach or to its operations. Those, whom foreign strength could not overpower, have well nigh become the victims of internal anarchy.

If we become a little more particular, we shall find that the foregoing representation is by no means exaggerated. When we had baffled all the menaces of foreign power, we neglected to establish among ourselves a government, that would ensure domestic vigour and stability. What was the consequence? The commencement of peace was the commencement of every disgrace and distress that could befall a people in a peaceful state. Devoid of national power, we could not prohibit the extravagance of our importations, nor could we derive a revenue from their excess.

from the _Monthly Review_ in London, 1793:

The chief faults in these articles had their fource in that jealousy of power, which generally prevails among a people who have shaken off what they conceived to be an oppressive yoke, and have successfully asserted their liberties. Having long been accustomed to see authority and oppression united, they find it difficult to distinguish two ideas which they have acquired a habit of associating. They confess the necessity of laws to restrain licentiousness, as well as to regulate the proceedings of government: but they are apt to look with aversion on those who are appointed to execute them, as men who wish to elevate themselves above the level of their fellow-citizens, and to acquire a power independent of them. They forget that, in a republic, the magistrate, of whom they are thus suspicious, holds his power only for a short period; that when this is expired, he must retire to the station of a private citizen; and, if he has laid any burthen on the community, must afterward bear his portion of it.

from _A Treatise Concerning Political Enquiry and the Liberty of the Press_, 1800:

Possessed of an unity of interest, and conscious of the necessity of associating their means of defence, the American Colonies become united by a compact of Confederation

. . . Upon the restoration of peace we became taught by experience to discover the feebleness and inefficiency of our former Articles of Confederation, and were finally led to the adoption of our present general Constitution.

1783 Treaty of Paris

The war did not end instantly after General Cornwallis surrendered to the Americans at Yorktown, Virginia, in 1781. British troops remained in America and bloody skirmishes continued to take place. Once the stubborn King George III finally yielded and realized that the American colonies were lost for good, a more final and definitive peace was possible. John Adams, John Jay, and Benjamin Franklin were the key American peace negotiators. Franklin worked with David Hartley, a member of Parliament appointed by the British government, to develop the treaty. In November 1782 articles of peace were signed; the actual treaty was not ready for another year. It was signed in Paris in September 1783, and the remaining British troops finally left the United States on November 25, 1783, Evacuation Day. At last the United States received official recognition from Great Britain as an independent nation. The tone of the document was quite conciliatory, mentioning a return to the "good correspondence and friendship" of the past.

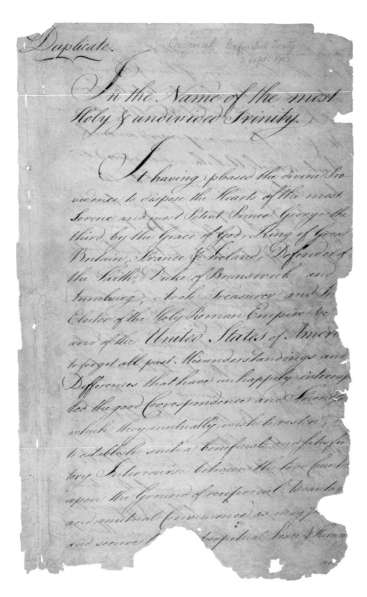

It having pleased the Divine Providence to dispose the hearts of the most serene and most potent Prince George the Third . . . and of the United States of America, to forget all past misunderstandings and differences that have unhappily interrupted the good correspondence and friendship which they mutually wish to restore, and to establish such a beneficial and satisfactory intercourse between the two countries upon the ground of reciprocal advantages and mutual convenience as may promote and secure to both perpetual peace and harmony; and having for this desirable end already laid the foundation of peace and reconciliation by the Provisional Articles signed at Paris on the 30th of November 1782, by the commissioners empowered on each part, which articles were agreed to be inserted in and constitute the Treaty of Peace proposed to be concluded between the Crown of Great Britain and the said United States, but which treaty was not to be concluded until terms of peace should be agreed upon between Great Britain and France and his Britannic Majesty should be ready to conclude such treaty accordingly . . .

Article 1

His Brittanic Majesty acknowledges the said United States, viz., New Hampshire, Massachusetts Bay, Rhode Island and Providence Plantations, Connecticut, New York, New Jersey, Pennsylvania, Delaware, Maryland, Virginia, North Carolina, South Carolina and Georgia, to be free, sovereign, and independent States; that he treats with them as such; and for himself, his heirs, and successors, relinquishes all claims to the Government, propriety, and territorial rights of the same and every part thereof.

Article 2

And that all disputes which might arise in future on the subject of the boundaries of the said United States may be prevented, it is hereby agreed and declared, that the following are and shall be their boundaries . . .

Article 5

It is agreed that the Congress shall earnestly recommend it to the legislatures of the respective States to provide for the restitution of all estates, rights, and properties, which have been confiscated belonging to real British subjects; and also of the estates, rights, and properties of persons resident in districts in the possession on his Majesty's arms and who have not borne arms against the said United States. . . .

Article 6

That there shall be no future confiscations made nor any prosecutions commenced against any person or persons for, or by reason of, the part which he or they may have taken in the present war; and that no person shall, on that account, suffer any future loss or damage, either in his person, liberty or property . . .

Article 7

There shall be a firm and perpetual peace between His Brittanic Majesty and the said States, and between the subjects of the one and the citizens of the other, wherefore all hostilities both by sea and land shall from henceforth cease. All prisoners on both sides shall be set at liberty, and his Brittanic Majesty shall with all convenient speed . . . withdraw all his armies, garrisons, and fleets from the said United States, and from every post, place, and harbor within the same; leaving in all fortifications, the American artilery that may be therein . . .

# What They Were Saying

from a letter from David Hartley to Benjamin Franklin, September 1783:

It is with the sincerest pleasure that I congratulate you on the happy event which took place yesterday, viz. the signature of the definitive treaty between our two countries. I consider it as the auspicious presage of returning confidence, and of the future intercourse of all good offices between us. I doubt not that our two countries will entertain the same sentiments, and that they will behold with satisfaction the period which terminates the memory of their late unhappy dissensions, and which leads to the renewal of all the ancient ties of amity and peace. I can assure you that his Britannic majesty, and his confidential servants, entertain the strongest desire of a cordial good understanding with the United States of America. . . . Let us then join our hearts and hands together in one common cause, for the reunion of all our ancient affections and common interests.

from a letter from Benjamin Franklin to David Hartley, September 1783:

Your friendly congratulations on the signature of the definitive treaty, meet with cordial returns on our part; and we sincerely rejoice with you in that event by which the ruler of nations has been graciously pleased to give peace to our two countries. We are no less ready to join our endeavors than our wishes with yours, to concert such measures for regulating the future intercourse between Great Britain and the United States, as by being consistent with the honor and interest of both, may tend to increase and perpetuate mutual confidence and goodwill . . . The unrestrained course already given by the States to the British commerce with them, and the unconditional liberation of prisoners, at a time when more caution would not have been singular, are marks of liberality and confidence, which we flatter ourselves will be equalled by the magnanimity of his majesty and the people of Great Britain.

General Washington's Farewell to His Soldiers 1783

After the Treaty of Paris had been signed in November 1783, General George Washington was finally able to disband his army. First, on December 4, he said a private farewell to his officers at a tavern in New York City. On December 23, he gave his army an eloquent farewell. He did not simply exclaim slogans of inevitable victory. He was completely honest in admitting the "feeble condition" the army found itself in during the war. From there he moved on to the future and the bounty of American riches to which the returning soldier had to look forward. His message was filled with optimism and imbued with the spirit of a newly born nation in search of its destiny. The Revolution has a very special and unique place among all American conflicts; its legendary status would only grow through the nineteenth century (the founding of the Daughters of the American Revolution took place in 1890, for example) in tandem with that of its leader. Little did Washington or his country realize that his retirement would be short-lived, and he would soon return to the spotlight as the nation's first president.

General Washington addressing his army.

The disadvantageous circumstances on our part, under which the war was undertaken, can never be forgotten. The singular interpositions of Providence in our feeble condition were such, as could scarcely escape the attention of the most unobserving; while the unparalleled perseverance of the armies of the United States, through almost every possible suffering and discouragement for the space of eight long years, was little short of a standing miracle. It is not the meaning nor within the compass of this address, to detail the hardships peculiarly incident to our service, or to describe the distresses, which in several instances have resulted from the extremes of hunger and nakedness, combined with the rigors of an inclement season; nor is it necessary to dwell on the dark side of our past affairs.

Every American officer and soldier must now console himself for any unpleasant circumstances, which may have occurred, by a recollection of the uncommon scenes in which he has been called to act no inglorious part, and the astonishing events of which he has been a witness; events which have seldom, if ever before, taken place on the stage of human action; nor can they probably ever happen again. For who has before seen a disciplined army formed at once from such raw materials? Who, that was not a witness, could imagine, that the most violent local prejudices would cease so soon; and that men, who came from the different parts of the continent, strongly disposed by the habits of education to despise and quarrel with each other, would instantly become but one patriotic band of brothers? Or who, that was not on the spot, can trace the steps by which such a wonderful revolution has been effected, and such a glorious period put to all our warlike toils?

It is universally acknowledged, that the enlarged prospects of happiness, opened by the confirmation of our independence and sovereignty, almost exceeds the power of description. And shall not the brave men, who have contributed so essentially to these inestimable acquisitions, retiring victorious from the field of war to the field of agriculture, participate in all the blessings, which have been obtained?

In such a republic, who will exclude them from the rights of citizens, and the fruits of their labors? In such a country, so happily circumstanced, the pursuits of commerce and the cultivation of the soil will unfold to industry the certain road to competence. To those hardy soldiers, who are actuated by the spirit of adventure, the fisheries will afford ample and profitable employment; and the extensive and fertile regions of the West will yield a most happy asylum to those, who, fond of domestic enjoyment, are seeking for personal independence. Nor is it possible to conceive, that any one of the United States will prefer a national bankruptcy, and a dissolution of the Union, to a compliance with the requisitions of Congress, and the payment of its just debts; so that the officers and soldiers may expect considerable assistance, in recommencing their civil occupations, from the sums due to them from the public, which must and will most inevitably be paid.

In order to effect this desirable purpose, and to remove the prejudices, which may have taken posession of the minds of any of the good people of the States, it is earnestly recommended to all the troops, that, with strong attachments to the Union, they should carry with them into civil society the most conciliating dispositions, and that they should prove themselves not less virtuous and useful as citizens, than they have been persevering and victorious as soldiers . . .

The Commander-in-chief conceives little is now wanting, to enable the soldier, to change the military character into that of the citizen, but that steady and decent tenor of behavior, which has generally distinguished, not only the army under his immediate command, but the different detachments and separate armies, through the course of the war. From their good sense and prudence he anticipates the happiest consequences; and, while he congratulates them on the glorious occasion, which renders their services in the field no longer necessary, he wishes to express the strong obligations he feels himself under for the assistance he has received from every class and in every instance.

He presents his thanks in the most serious and affectionate manner to the general officers, as well for their counsel on many interesting occasions, as for their ardor in promoting the success of the plans he had adopted; to the commandants of regiments and corps, and to the other officers, for their great zeal and attention in carrying his orders promptly into execution; to the staff, for their alacrity and exactness in performing the duties of their several departments; and to the noncommissioned officers and private soldiers, for their extraordinary patience and suffering, as well as their invincible fortitude in action. To the various branches of the army, the General takes this last and solemn opportunity of professing his inviolable attachment and friendship. He wishes more than bare professions were in his power; that he were really able to be useful to them all in future life. He flatters himself, however, they will do him the justice to believe, that whatever could with propriety be attempted by him has been done. And being now to conclude these his last public orders, to take his ultimate leave in a short time of the military character, and to bid a final adieu to the armies he has so long had the honor to command, he can only again offer in their behalf his recommendations to their grateful country, and his prayers to the God of armies. May ample justice be done them here, and may the choicest of Heaven's favors, both here and hereafter, attend those, who, under the Divine auspices, have secured innumerable blessings for others. With these wishes and this benediction, the Commander-in-chief is about to retire from service. The curtain of separation will soon be drawn, and the military scene to him will be closed for ever.

 What They Were Saying

from a resolution passed by Virginia Legislature, 1783:

Resolved, That the executive be requested to take measures for procuring a statue of General Washington, to be of the finest marble and best workmanship, with the following inscription on its pedestal: "The general assembly of the Commonwealth of Virginia have caused this statue to be erected as a monument of affection and gratitude to George Washington, who, uniting to the endowments of the hero, the virtues of the patriot, and exerting both in establishing the liberties of his country, has rendered his name dear to his fellow citizens, and given the world an immortal example of true glory."

George Washington, 1783:

I am just beginning to experience the ease and freedom from public cares, which, however desirable, takes some time to realize; for strange as it may seem, it is nevertheless true, that it was not until lately I could get the better of my usual custom of ruminating, as soon as I awoke in the morning, on the business of the ensuing day; and of my surprise at finding, after revolving many things in my mind, that I was no longer a public man, or had any thing to do with public transactions. I feel now however, as I conceive a wearied traveller must do, who, after treading many a painful step with a heavy burden on his shoulders, is eased of the latter, having reached the haven to which all the former were directed; and from his house-top is looking back, and tracing with an eager eye, the meanders by which he escaped the quick-sands and mires which lay in his way, and into which none but the all powerful Guide and Dispenser of human events could have prevented his falling.

1787 Northwest Ordinance

During the mid-1780s the land west of the Appalachian Mountains was considered to be the western frontier of the United States. Congress passed a law in 1785 that provided for the division and sale of frontier land at affordable rates. This was beneficial both to adventurous souls and to veterans of the Revolution looking for a place to settle. The Northwest Ordinance of 1787 set up the rules for expansion of the United States to Ohio and beyond. It laid out a system of government for the territory and delineated that between three and five states should be formed out of that area. The federal government would appoint a governor and judges, and the citizens would elect representatives. According to the Northwest Ordinance, slavery was not to be allowed in the Northwest Territory, while religious tolerance and education ("religion, morality, and knowledge") were to be promoted. The states formed out of the area were Ohio (admitted 1803), Indiana (admitted 1816), Illinois (admitted 1818), Michigan (admitted 1837), and Wisconsin (admitted 1848). In some cases, the development of infrastructure was all that prevented the states from becoming more populous and entering the union sooner.

An ORDINANCE for the GOVERNMENT of the TERRITORY of the UNITED STATES, North-West of the RIVER OHIO.

Be it ordained by the United States in Congress assembled, That the said territory, for the purpose of temporary government, be one district . . .

Be it ordained by the authority aforesaid, That there shall be appointed from time to time by Congress, a governor, whose commission shall continue in force for the term of three years, unless sooner revoked by Congress; he shall reside in the district, and have a freehold estate therein in 1,000 acres of land, while in the exercise of his office.

There shall be appointed from time to time by Congress, a secretary, whose commission shall continue in force for four years unless sooner revoked; he shall reside in the district, and have a freehold estate therein in 500 acres of land, while in the exercise of his office. It shall be his duty to keep and preserve the acts and laws passed by the legislature, and the public records of the district, and the proceedings of the governor in his executive department, and transmit authentic copies of such acts and proceedings, every six months, to the Secretary of Congress: There shall also be appointed a court to consist of three judges, any two of whom to form a court, who shall have a common law jurisdiction, and reside in the district, and have each therein a freehold estate in 500 acres of land while in the exercise of their offices; and their commissions shall continue in force during good behavior.

The governor and judges, or a majority of them, shall adopt and publish in the district such laws of the original States, criminal and civil, as may be necessary and best suited to the circumstances of the district, and report them to Congress from time to time: which laws shall be in force in the district until the organization of the General Assembly therein, unless disapproved of by Congress; but afterwards the Legislature shall have authority to alter them as they shall think fit.

The governor, for the time being, shall be commander in chief of the militia, appoint and commission all officers in the same below the rank of general officers; all general officers shall be appointed and commissioned by Congress. . . .

So soon as there shall be five thousand free male inhabitants of full age in the district, upon giving proof thereof to the governor, they shall receive authority, with time and place, to elect representatives from their counties or townships to represent them in the general assembly:

Provided, That, for every five hundred free male inhabitants, there shall be one representative, and so on progressively with the number of free male inhabitants shall the right of representation increase, until the number of representatives shall amount to twenty-five; after which, the number and proportion of representatives shall be regulated by the legislature:

Provided, That no person be eligible or qualified to act as a representative unless he shall have been a citizen of one of the United States three years, and be a resident in the district, or unless he shall have resided in the district three years; and, in either case, shall likewise hold in his own right, in fee simple, two hundred acres of land within the same;

Provided, also, That a freehold in fifty acres of land in the district, having been a citizen of one of the states, and being resident in the district, or the like freehold and two years residence in the district, shall be necessary to qualify a man as an elector of a representative.

The representatives thus elected, shall serve for the term of two years; and, in case of the death of a representative, or removal from office, the governor shall issue a writ to the county or township for which he was a member, to elect another in his stead, to serve for the residue of the term. . . .

And, for extending the fundamental principles of civil and religious liberty, which form the basis whereon these republics, their laws and constitutions are erected; to fix and establish those principles as the basis of all laws, constitutions, and governments, which forever hereafter shall be formed in the said territory: to provide also for the establishment of States, and permanent government therein, and for their admission to a share in the federal councils on an equal footing with the original States, at as early periods as may be consistent with the general interest:

It is hereby ordained and declared by the authority aforesaid, That the following articles shall be considered as articles of compact between the original States and the people and States in the said territory and forever remain unalterable, unless by common consent, to wit:

Article 1. No person, demeaning himself in a peaceable and orderly manner, shall ever be molested on account of his mode of worship or religious sentiments, in the said territory.

Article 2. The inhabitants of the said territory shall always be entitled to the benefits of the writ of habeas corpus, and of the trial by jury; of a proportionate representation of the people in the legislature; and of judicial proceedings according to the course of the common law. All persons shall be bailable, unless for capital offenses, where the proof shall be evident or the presumption great. All fines shall be moderate; and no cruel or unusual punishments shall be inflicted. No man shall be deprived of his liberty or property, but by the judgment of his peers or the law of the land . . .

Article 3. Religion, morality, and knowledge, being necessary to good government and the happiness of mankind, schools and the means of education shall forever be encouraged. The utmost good faith shall always be observed towards the Indians; their lands and property shall never be taken from them without their consent; and, in their property, rights, and liberty, they shall never be invaded or disturbed, unless in just and lawful wars authorized by Congress; but laws founded in justice and humanity, shall from time to time be made for preventing wrongs being done to them, and for preserving peace and friendship with them. . . .

Article 5. There shall be formed in the said territory, not less than three nor more than five States. . . . And, whenever any of the said States shall have sixty thousand free inhabitants therein, such State shall be admitted, by its delegates, into the Congress of the United States, on an equal footing with the original States in all respects whatever, and shall be at liberty to form a permanent constitution and State government: Provided, the constitution and government so to be formed, shall be republican, and in conformity to the principles contained in these articles; and, so far as it can be consistent with the general interest of the confederacy, such admission shall be allowed at an earlier period, and when there may be a less number of free inhabitants in the State than sixty thousand.

Article 6. There shall be neither slavery nor involuntary servitude in the said territory, otherwise than in the punishment of crimes whereof the party shall have been duly convicted: Provided, always, That any person escaping into the same, from whom labor or service is lawfully claimed in any one of the original States, such fugitive may be lawfully reclaimed and conveyed to the person claiming his or her labor or service as aforesaid.

 What They Were Saying

Representative Gabriel Richard during a congressional debate, 1825:

Make this road [a Detroit to Chicago road] now, when you have the full sovereignty over the Territory of Michigan, before it becomes an independent State, and you may easily anticipate how beneficial this road will be to your finances. There are more than seventeen millions of acres of, generally, good and fertile land, in Michigan proper, (without speaking of the ninety-four millions of acres in the Northwest Territory.) Without a road to go to those lands, they have no value. We are credibly informed, that, on our inland seas, I mean Lakes Erie, St. Clair, Huron, and Michigan, no less than one hundred and fifty vessels are plying up and down, on board of which whole families do come, sometimes, with their wagons, horses, sheep, and milk-cows; land in Detroit, ready to go in search of good land, to settle on it, and having their money ready to give to the Receiver of the Land Office. No road to go into that immense wilderness! What disappointment! During about twelve months, last elapsed, more than one hundred thousand dollars have been actually paid into the hands of the Receivers of Public Moneys, in the Territory of Michigan, for land purchased. How much more would have been paid, if the proposed road had been made! We can learn from the Commissioner of the General Land Office, that about ten surveyors have been employed in surveying public lands in the interior of Michigan Territory, between Detroit and Chicago, during last winter. These lands will soon be advertised to be sold. If there is no road to come to them, who will purchase them? But let this road be made; let it be determined by this House that it shall be made; then you will have purchasers enough: they will come as a torrent from the Eastern states. It cannot be questioned that the land along the intended road will sell for two or three hundred per cent, more than it would if there were no such road; and so, in nearly the same proportion, the adjacent lands will be increased in price. If you ask me what will this road cost? I beg leave to answer, it will cost nothing to the Government. I might say it will cost less than nothing. The half of the land along the road only, will, after the road is made, or determined to be made, sell for a great deal more than the whole would, without the road. What an immense profit for your Treasury you can derive from the sale of this immense wilderness, which remains entirely unprofitable, if you have no road to come at it! This road is, therefore, to be beneficial to your finances, and your military operations, and to all parts of the Union . . .

1789 Constitution of the United States

Fifty-five men, known as deputies, ranging in age from twenty-six to eighty-one, and representing the various states, came together at the Constitutional Convention in May 1787 in Philadelphia. Over a period of 116 days, the framers of the Constitution discussed, collaborated, wrote, and revised. Compromises had to be made between those who favored a strong central government and those who desired that the states retain more power. Smaller states were satisfied with the final result because, while representation in one body of Congress (the House) was based on population, each state would be represented equally in the other body (the Senate).

The Constitution of the United States is a work of genius precisely because it maintains the fine balance between specific and vague. On the one hand, it lays out the concrete details of the organization of the government and the rules regarding the election of the president and members of Congress. On the other hand, there are many places within the document where the words are open to interpretation. For example, "High crimes and Misdemeanors" constitute reasons for a president to be impeached. Some may argue that the Constitution is not a living document but a rigid guidebook. However, in looking at the decisions of the Supreme Court over the past two hundred years, it becomes clear that different justices have interpreted the same phrases in the Constitution in different ways.

The ultimate flexibility of the Constitution is the provision for amendments to be made, so long as three-fourths of the states approve them. The fundamentals of the original document still stand, but the amendments to the Constitution have refined and adjusted the original document as times have changed. Our Constitution is so flexible that a new amendment can be passed to repeal an earlier amendment. This is exactly what happened with the Twenty-first Amendment in 1933, which repealed the Eighteenth Amendment (prohibiting the sale of alcohol in 1919). What types of laws are important enough to become amendments? This is one debate that has been conducted for more than two hundred years.

Benjamin Franklin speaking at the Constitutional Convention in 1787.

We the People of the United States, in Order to form a more perfect Union, establish Justice, insure domestic Tranquility, provide for the common defence, promote the general Welfare, and secure the Blessings of Liberty to ourselves and our Posterity, do ordain and establish this Constitution for the United States of America.

Article I, Section 1

All legislative Powers herein granted shall be vested in a Congress of the United States, which shall consist of a Senate and House of Representatives.

Article I, Section 2

The House of Representatives shall be composed of Members chosen every second Year by the People of the several States, and the Electors in each State shall have the Qualifications requisite for Electors of the most numerous Branch of the State Legislature.

No Person shall be a Representative who shall not have attained to the Age of twenty five Years, and been seven Years a Citizen of the United States, and who shall not, when elected, be an Inhabitant of that State in which he shall be chosen.

Representatives and direct Taxes shall be apportioned among the several States which may be included within this Union, according to their respective Numbers, which shall be determined by adding to the whole Number of free Persons, including those bound to Service for a Term of Years, and excluding Indians not taxed, three fifths of all other Persons. The actual Enumeration shall be made within three Years after the first Meeting of the Congress of the United States, and within every subsequent Term of ten Years, in such Manner as they shall by Law direct. The Number of Representatives shall not exceed one for every thirty Thousand, but each State shall have at Least one Representative; and until such enumeration shall be made, the State of New Hampshire shall be entitled to chuse three, Massachusetts eight, Rhode-Island and Providence Plantations one, Connecticut five, New-York six, New Jersey four, Pennsylvania eight, Delaware one, Maryland six, Virginia ten, North Carolina five, South Carolina five, and Georgia three.

When vacancies happen in the Representation from any State, the Executive Authority thereof shall issue Writs of Election to fill such Vacancies.

The House of Representatives shall chuse their Speaker and other Officers; and shall have the sole Power of Impeachment.

Article I, Section 3

The Senate of the United States shall be composed of two Senators from each State, chosen by the Legislature thereof for six Years; and each Senator shall have one Vote.

Immediately after they shall be assembled in Consequence of the first Election, they shall be divided as equally as may be into three Classes. The Seats of the Senators of the first Class shall be vacated at the Expiration of the second Year, of the second Class at the Expiration of the fourth Year, and of the third Class at the Expiration of the sixth Year, so that one third may be chosen every second Year; and if Vacancies happen by Resignation, or otherwise, during the Recess of the Legislature of any State, the Executive thereof may make temporary Appointments until the next Meeting of the Legislature, which shall then fill such Vacancies.

No Person shall be a Senator who shall not have attained to the Age of thirty Years, and been nine Years a Citizen of the United States, and who shall not, when elected, be an Inhabitant of that State for which he shall be chosen.

The Vice President of the United States shall be President of the Senate, but shall have no Vote, unless they be equally divided.

The Senate shall chuse their other Officers, and also a President pro tempore, in the Absence of the Vice

President, or when he shall exercise the Office of President of the United States.

The Senate shall have the sole Power to try all Impeachments. When sitting for that Purpose, they shall be on Oath or Affirmation. When the President of the United States is tried, the Chief Justice shall preside: And no Person shall be convicted without the Concurrence of two thirds of the Members present.

Judgment in Cases of Impeachment shall not extend further than to removal from Office, and disqualification to hold and enjoy any Office of honor, Trust or Profit under the United States: but the Party convicted shall nevertheless be liable and subject to Indictment, Trial, Judgment and Punishment, according to Law.

Article I, Section 4

The Times, Places and Manner of holding Elections for Senators and Representatives, shall be prescribed in each State by the Legislature thereof; but the Congress may at any time by Law make or alter such Regulations, except as to the Places of chusing Senators.

The Congress shall assemble at least once in every Year, and such Meeting shall be on the first Monday in December, unless they shall by Law appoint a different Day.

Article I, Section 5

Each House shall be the Judge of the Elections, Returns and Qualifications of its own Members, and a Majority of each shall constitute a Quorum to do Business; but a smaller Number may adjourn from day to day, and may be authorized to compel the Attendance of absent Members, in such Manner, and under such Penalties as each House may provide.

Each House may determine the Rules of its Proceedings, punish its Members for disorderly Behaviour, and, with the Concurrence of two thirds, expel a Member.

Each House shall keep a Journal of its Proceedings, and from time to time publish the same, excepting such Parts as may in their Judgment require Secrecy; and the Yeas and Nays of the Members of either House on any question shall, at the Desire of one fifth of those Present, be entered on the Journal.

Neither House, during the Session of Congress, shall, without the Consent of the other, adjourn for more than three days, nor to any other Place than that in which the two Houses shall be sitting.

Article I, Section 6

The Senators and Representatives shall receive a Compensation for their Services, to be ascertained by Law, and paid out of the Treasury of the United States. They shall in all Cases, except Treason, Felony and Breach of the Peace, be privileged from Arrest during their Attendance at the Session of their respective Houses, and in going to and returning from the same; and for any Speech or Debate in either House, they shall not be questioned in any other Place.

No Senator or Representative shall, during the Time for which he was elected, be appointed to any civil Office under the Authority of the United States, which shall have been created, or the Emoluments whereof shall have been encreased during such time; and no Person holding any Office under the United States, shall be a Member of either House during his Continuance in Office.

Article I, Section 7

All Bills for raising Revenue shall originate in the House of Representatives; but the Senate may propose or concur with Amendments as on other Bills.

Every Bill which shall have passed the House of Representatives and the Senate, shall, before it become a Law, be presented to the President of the United States: If he approve he shall sign it, but if not he shall return it, with his Objections to that House in which it shall have originated, who shall enter the Objections at large on their Journal, and proceed to reconsider it. If after such Reconsideration two thirds of that House shall agree to pass the Bill, it shall be sent, together with the Objections, to the other House, by which it shall likewise be reconsidered, and if approved by two thirds of that House, it shall become a Law. But in all such Cases the Votes of both Houses shall be determined by yeas and Nays, and the Names of the Persons voting for and against the Bill shall be entered on the Journal of each House respectively. If any Bill shall not be returned by the President within ten Days (Sundays excepted) after it shall have been presented to him, the Same shall be a Law, in like Manner as if he had signed it, unless the Congress by their Adjournment prevent its Return, in which Case it shall not be a Law.

Every Order, Resolution, or Vote to which the Concurrence of the Senate and House of Representatives may be necessary (except on a question of Adjournment) shall be presented to the President of the United

States; and before the Same shall take Effect, shall be approved by him, or being disapproved by him, shall be repassed by two thirds of the Senate and House of Representatives, according to the Rules and Limitations prescribed in the Case of a Bill.

Article I, Section 8
The Congress shall have Power To lay and collect Taxes, Duties, Imposts and Excises, to pay the Debts and provide for the common Defence and general Welfare of the United States; but all Duties, Imposts and Excises shall be uniform throughout the United States;

To borrow Money on the credit of the United States;

To regulate Commerce with foreign Nations, and among the several States, and with the Indian Tribes;

To establish an uniform Rule of Naturalization, and uniform Laws on the subject of Bankruptcies throughout the United States;

To coin Money, regulate the Value thereof, and of foreign Coin, and fix the Standard of Weights and Measures;

To provide for the Punishment of counterfeiting the Securities and current Coin of the United States;

To establish Post Offices and post Roads;

To promote the Progress of Science and useful Arts, by securing for limited Times to Authors and Inventors the exclusive Right to their respective Writings and Discoveries;

To constitute Tribunals inferior to the supreme Court;

To define and punish Piracies and Felonies committed on the high Seas, and Offences against the Law of Nations;

To declare War, grant Letters of Marque and Reprisal, and make Rules concerning Captures on Land and Water;

To raise and support Armies, but no Appropriation of Money to that Use shall be for a longer Term than two Years;

To provide and maintain a Navy;

To make Rules for the Government and Regulation of the land and naval Forces;

To provide for calling forth the Militia to execute the Laws of the Union, suppress Insurrections and repel Invasions;

To provide for organizing, arming, and disciplining, the Militia, and for governing such Part of them as may be employed in the Service of the United States,

reserving to the States respectively, the Appointment of the Officers, and the Authority of training the Militia according to the discipline prescribed by Congress;

To exercise exclusive Legislation in all Cases whatsoever, over such District (not exceeding ten Miles square) as may, by Cession of particular States, and the Acceptance of Congress, become the Seat of the Government of the United States, and to exercise like Authority over all Places purchased by the Consent of the Legislature of the State in which the Same shall be, for the Erection of Forts, Magazines, Arsenals, dock-Yards, and other needful Buildings;—And

To make all Laws which shall be necessary and proper for carrying into Execution the foregoing Powers, and all other Powers vested by this Constitution in the Government of the United States, or in any Department or Officer thereof.

Article I, Section 9
The Migration or Importation of such Persons as any of the States now existing shall think proper to admit, shall not be prohibited by the Congress prior to the Year one thousand eight hundred and eight, but a Tax or duty may be imposed on such Importation, not exceeding ten dollars for each Person.

The Privilege of the Writ of Habeas Corpus shall not be suspended, unless when in Cases of Rebellion or Invasion the public Safety may require it.

No Bill of Attainder or ex post facto Law shall be passed.

No Capitation, or other direct, Tax shall be laid, unless in Proportion to the Census or enumeration herein before directed to be taken.

No Tax or Duty shall be laid on Articles exported from any State.

No Preference shall be given by any Regulation of Commerce or Revenue to the Ports of one State over those of another; nor shall Vessels bound to, or from, one State, be obliged to enter, clear, or pay Duties in another.

No Money shall be drawn from the Treasury, but in Consequence of Appropriations made by Law; and a regular Statement and Account of the Receipts and Expenditures of all public Money shall be published from time to time.

No Title of Nobility shall be granted by the United States: And no Person holding any Office of Profit or Trust under them, shall, without the Consent of the

Congress, accept of any present, Emolument, Office, or Title, of any kind whatever, from any King, Prince, or foreign State.

Article I, Section 10
No State shall enter into any Treaty, Alliance, or Confederation; grant Letters of Marque and Reprisal; coin Money; emit Bills of Credit; make any Thing but gold and silver Coin a Tender in Payment of Debts; pass any Bill of Attainder, ex post facto Law, or Law impairing the Obligation of Contracts, or grant any Title of Nobility.

No State shall, without the Consent of the Congress, lay any Imposts or Duties on Imports or Exports, except what may be absolutely necessary for executing its inspection Laws: and the net Produce of all Duties and Imposts, laid by any State on Imports or Exports, shall be for the Use of the Treasury of the United States; and all such Laws shall be subject to the Revision and Controul of the Congress.

No State shall, without the Consent of Congress, lay any Duty of Tonnage, keep Troops, or Ships of War in time of Peace, enter into any Agreement or Compact with another State, or with a foreign Power, or engage in War, unless actually invaded, or in such imminent Danger as will not admit of delay.

Article II, Section 1
The executive Power shall be vested in a President of the United States of America. He shall hold his Office during the Term of four Years, and, together with the Vice President, chosen for the same Term, be elected, as follows:

Each State shall appoint, in such Manner as the Legislature thereof may direct, a Number of Electors, equal to the whole Number of Senators and Representatives to which the State may be entitled in the Congress: but no Senator or Representative, or Person holding an Office of Trust or Profit under the United States, shall be appointed an Elector.

The Electors shall meet in their respective States, and vote by Ballot for two Persons, of whom one at least shall not be an Inhabitant of the same State with themselves. And they shall make a List of all the Persons voted for, and of the Number of Votes for each; which List they shall sign and certify, and transmit sealed to the Seat of the Government of the United States, directed to the President of the Senate. The President of the Senate shall, in the Presence of the Senate and House of Representatives, open all the Certificates, and the Votes shall then be counted. The Person having the greatest Number of Votes shall be the President, if such Number be a Majority of the whole Number of Electors appointed; and if there be more than one who have such Majority, and have an equal Number of Votes, then the House of Representatives shall immediately chuse by Ballot one of them for President; and if no Person have a Majority, then from the five highest on the List the said House shall in like Manner chuse the President. But in chusing the President, the Votes shall be taken by States, the Representation from each State having one Vote; A quorum for this purpose shall consist of a Member or Members from two thirds of the States, and a Majority of all the States shall be necessary to a Choice. In every Case, after the Choice of the President, the Person having the greatest Number of Votes of the Electors shall be the Vice President. But if there should remain two or more who have equal Votes, the Senate shall chuse from them by Ballot the Vice President.

The Congress may determine the Time of chusing the Electors, and the Day on which they shall give their Votes; which Day shall be the same throughout the United States.

No Person except a natural born Citizen, or a Citizen of the United States, at the time of the Adoption of this Constitution, shall be eligible to the Office of President; neither shall any Person be eligible to that Office who shall not have attained to the Age of thirty five Years, and been fourteen Years a Resident within the United States.

In Case of the Removal of the President from Office, or of his Death, Resignation, or Inability to discharge the Powers and Duties of the said Office, the Same shall devolve on the Vice President, and the Congress may by Law provide for the Case of Removal, Death, Resignation or Inability, both of the President and Vice President, declaring what Officer shall then act as President, and such Officer shall act accordingly, until the Disability be removed, or a President shall be elected.

The President shall, at stated Times, receive for his Services, a Compensation, which shall neither be increased nor diminished during the Period for which he shall have been elected, and he shall not receive within that Period any other Emolument from the United States, or any of them.

Before he enter on the Execution of his Office, he shall take the following Oath or Affirmation:—"I do solemnly swear (or affirm) that I will faithfully execute the Office of President of the United States, and will to the best of my Ability, preserve, protect and defend the Constitution of the United States."

Article II, Section 2

The President shall be Commander in Chief of the Army and Navy of the United States, and of the Militia of the several States, when called into the actual Service of the United States; he may require the Opinion, in writing, of the principal Officer in each of the executive Departments, upon any Subject relating to the Duties of their respective Offices, and he shall have Power to grant Reprieves and Pardons for Offences against the United States, except in Cases of Impeachment.

He shall have Power, by and with the Advice and Consent of the Senate, to make Treaties, provided two thirds of the Senators present concur; and he shall nominate, and by and with the Advice and Consent of the Senate, shall appoint Ambassadors, other public Ministers and Consuls, Judges of the supreme Court, and all other Officers of the United States, whose Appointments are not herein otherwise provided for, and which shall be established by Law: but the Congress may by Law vest the Appointment of such inferior Officers, as they think proper, in the President alone, in the Courts of Law, or in the Heads of Departments.

The President shall have Power to fill up all Vacancies that may happen during the Recess of the Senate, by granting Commissions which shall expire at the End of their next Session.

Article II, Section 3

He shall from time to time give to the Congress Information of the State of the Union, and recommend to their Consideration such Measures as he shall judge necessary and expedient; he may, on extraordinary Occasions, convene both Houses, or either of them, and in Case of Disagreement between them, with Respect to the Time of Adjournment, he may adjourn them to such Time as he shall think proper; he shall receive Ambassadors and other public Ministers; he shall take Care that the Laws be faithfully executed, and shall Commission all the Officers of the United States.

Article II, Section 4

The President, Vice President and all civil Officers of the United States, shall be removed from Office on Impeachment for, and Conviction of, Treason, Bribery, or other high Crimes and Misdemeanors.

Article III, Section 1

The judicial Power of the United States shall be vested in one supreme Court, and in such inferior Courts as the Congress may from time to time ordain and establish. The Judges, both of the supreme and inferior Courts, shall hold their Offices during good Behaviour, and shall, at stated Times, receive for their Services a Compensation, which shall not be diminished during their Continuance in Office.

Article III, Section 2

The judicial Power shall extend to all Cases, in Law and Equity, arising under this Constitution, the Laws of the United States, and Treaties made, or which shall be made, under their Authority;—to all Cases affecting Ambassadors, other public Ministers and Consuls;—to all Cases of admiralty and maritime Jurisdiction;—to Controversies to which the United States shall be a Party;—to Controversies between two or more States;—between a State and Citizens of another State;—between Citizens of different States;—between Citizens of the same State claiming Lands under Grants of different States, and between a State, or the Citizens thereof, and foreign States, Citizens or Subjects.

In all Cases affecting Ambassadors, other public Ministers and Consuls, and those in which a State shall be Party, the supreme Court shall have original Jurisdiction. In all the other Cases before mentioned, the supreme Court shall have appellate Jurisdiction, both as to Law and Fact, with such Exceptions, and under such Regulations as the Congress shall make.

The Trial of all Crimes, except in Cases of Impeachment, shall be by Jury; and such Trial shall be held in the State where the said Crimes shall have been committed; but when not committed within any State, the Trial shall be at such Place or Places as the Congress may by Law have directed.

Article III, Section 3

Treason against the United States, shall consist only in levying War against them, or in adhering to their Enemies, giving them Aid and Comfort. No Person shall be convicted of Treason unless on the Testimony of two Witnesses to the same overt Act, or on Confession in open Court.

The Congress shall have Power to declare the Punishment of Treason, but no Attainder of Treason shall work Corruption of Blood, or Forfeiture except during the Life of the Person attainted.

Article IV, Section 1

Full Faith and Credit shall be given in each State to the public Acts, Records, and judicial Proceedings of every other State. And the Congress may by general Laws prescribe the Manner in which such Acts, Records and Proceedings shall be proved, and the Effect thereof.

Article IV, Section 2

The Citizens of each State shall be entitled to all Privileges and Immunities of Citizens in the several States.

A Person charged in any State with Treason, Felony, or other Crime, who shall flee from Justice, and be found in another State, shall on Demand of the executive Authority of the State from which he fled, be delivered up, to be removed to the State having Jurisdiction of the Crime.

No Person held to Service or Labour in one State, under the Laws thereof, escaping into another, shall, in Consequence of any Law or Regulation therein, be discharged from such Service or Labour, but shall be delivered up on Claim of the Party to whom such Service or Labour may be due.

Article IV, Section 3

New States may be admitted by the Congress into this Union; but no new State shall be formed or erected within the Jurisdiction of any other State; nor any State be formed by the Junction of two or more States, or Parts of States, without the Consent of the Legislatures of the States concerned as well as of the Congress.

The Congress shall have Power to dispose of and make all needful Rules and Regulations respecting the Territory or other Property belonging to the United States; and nothing in this Constitution shall be so construed as to Prejudice any Claims of the United States, or of any particular State.

Article IV, Section 4

The United States shall guarantee to every State in this Union a Republican Form of Government, and shall protect each of them against Invasion; and on Application of the Legislature, or of the Executive (when the Legislature cannot be convened), against domestic Violence.

Article V

The Congress, whenever two thirds of both Houses shall deem it necessary, shall propose Amendments to this Constitution, or, on the Application of the Legislatures of two thirds of the several States, shall call a Convention for proposing Amendments, which, in either Case, shall be valid to all Intents and Purposes, as Part of this Constitution, when ratified by the Legislatures of three fourths of the several States, or by Conventions in three fourths thereof, as the one or the other Mode of Ratification may be proposed by the Congress; Provided that no Amendment which may be made prior to the Year One thousand eight hundred and eight shall in any Manner affect the first and fourth Clauses in the Ninth Section of the first Article; and that no State, without its Consent, shall be deprived of its equal Suffrage in the Senate.

Article VI

All Debts contracted and Engagements entered into, before the Adoption of this Constitution, shall be as valid against the United States under this Constitution, as under the Confederation.

This Constitution, and the Laws of the United States which shall be made in Pursuance thereof; and all Treaties made, or which shall be made, under the Authority of the United States, shall be the supreme Law of the Land; and the Judges in every State shall be bound thereby, any Thing in the Constitution or Laws of any State to the Contrary notwithstanding.

The Senators and Representatives before mentioned, and the Members of the several State Legislatures, and all executive and judicial Officers, both of the United States and of the several States, shall be bound by Oath or Affirmation, to support this Constitution; but no religious Test shall ever be required as a Qualification to any Office or public Trust under the United States.

Article VII

The Ratification of the Conventions of nine States, shall be sufficient for the Establishment of this Constitution between the States so ratifying the Same.

The Word, "the," being interlined between the seventh and eighth Lines of the first Page, the Word "Thirty" being partly written on an Erazure in the fifteenth Line of the first Page, The Words "is tried" being interlined between the thirty second and thirty third Lines of the first Page and the Word "the" being interlined between the forty third and forty fourth Lines of the second Page.

Attest William Jackson Secretary

Done in Convention by the Unanimous Consent of the States present the Seventeenth Day of September in the Year of our Lord one thousand seven hundred and Eighty seven and of the Independence of the United States of America the Twelfth In witness whereof We have hereunto subscribed our Names . . .

What They Were Saying

from *Federalist Paper #1* by Alexander Hamilton, 1787:

After an unequivocal experience of the inefficacy of the subsisting federal government, you are called upon to deliberate on a new Constitution for the United States of America. The subject speaks its own importance; comprehending in its consequences nothing less than the existence of the Union, the safety and welfare of the parts of which it is composed, the fate of an empire in many respects the most interesting in the world. It has been frequently remarked that it seems to have been reserved to the people of this country, by their conduct and example, to decide the important question, whether societies of men are really capable or not of establishing good government from reflection and choice, or whether they are forever destined to depend for their political constitutions on accident and force. If there be any truth in the remark, the crisis at which we are arrived may with propriety be regarded as the era in which that decision is to be made; and a wrong election of the part we shall act may, in this view, deserve to be considered as the general misfortune of mankind.

from *A Compend of History*, 1828:

One of the most serious evils, to which the constitution of our government is liable . . . is the power, caprice, ambiguity and fallacy of construction. The instrument is very concise, though perhaps nothing of a similar nature was ever more explicit and intelligible. The political tactician, however, can easily demonstrate, that no system of law or form of government can be couched in such language, as to be beyond the reach of sophistry. The clearest, most forcible and positive expressions, are liable to constructions, glosses, colorings and perversions. It is remarkable, that some of the greatest and most important political disputes in this country, have arisen respecting the intent and meaning of the constitution.

The first page of the Constitution.

Congress may by general Laws prescribe the Manner in which such Acts, Records and Proceedings shall be proved, and the Effect thereof.

Section. 2. The Citizens of each State shall be entitled to all Privileges and Immunities of Citizens in the several States.

A Person charged in any State with Treason, Felony, or other Crime, who shall flee from Justice, and be found in another State, shall on Demand of the executive Authority of the State from which he fled, be delivered up, to be removed to the State having Jurisdiction of the Crime.

No Person held to Service or Labour in one State, under the Laws thereof, escaping into another, shall, in Consequence of any Law or Regulation therein, be discharged from such Service or Labour, but shall be delivered up on Claim of the Party to whom such Service or Labour may be due.

Section. 3. New States may be admitted by the Congress into this Union; but no new State shall be formed or erected within the Jurisdiction of any other State; nor any State be formed by the Junction of two or more States, or Parts of States, without the Consent of the Legislatures of the States concerned as well as of the Congress.

The Congress shall have Power to dispose of and make all needful Rules and Regulations respecting the Territory or other Property belonging to the United States; and nothing in this Constitution shall be so construed as to Prejudice any Claims of the United States, or of any particular State.

Section. 4. The United States shall guarantee to every State in this Union a Republican Form of Government, and shall protect each of them against Invasion; and on Application of the Legislature, or of the Executive (when the Legislature cannot be convened) against domestic Violence.

Article. V.

The Congress, whenever two thirds of both Houses shall deem it necessary, shall propose Amendments to this Constitution, or, on the Application of the Legislatures of two thirds of the several States, shall call a Convention for proposing Amendments, which, in either Case, shall be valid to all Intents and Purposes, as Part of this Constitution, when ratified by the Legislatures of three fourths of the several States, or by Conventions in three fourths thereof, as the one or the other Mode of Ratification may be proposed by the Congress; Provided that no Amendment which may be made prior to the Year One thousand eight hundred and eight shall in any Manner affect the first and fourth Clauses in the Ninth Section of the first Article; and that no State, without its Consent, shall be deprived of its equal Suffrage in the Senate.

Article. VI.

All Debts contracted and Engagements entered into, before the Adoption of this Constitution, shall be as valid against the United States under this Constitution, as under the Confederation.

This Constitution, and the Laws of the United States which shall be made in Pursuance thereof; and all Treaties made, or which shall be made, under the Authority of the United States, shall be the supreme Law of the Land; and the Judges in every State shall be bound thereby, any Thing in the Constitution or Laws of any State to the Contrary notwithstanding.

The Senators and Representatives before mentioned, and the Members of the several State Legislatures, and all executive and judicial officers, both of the United States and of the several States, shall be bound by Oath or Affirmation, to support this Constitution; but no religious Test shall ever be required as a Qualification to any Office or public Trust under the United States.

Article. VII.

The Ratification of the Conventions of nine States, shall be sufficient for the Establishment of this Constitution between the States so ratifying the Same.

The Word, the, being interlined between the seventh and eighth Lines of the first Page, The Word "Thirty" being partly written on an Erasure in the fifteenth Line of the first Page. The Word "is" being interlined between the thirty second and thirty third Lines of the first Page and the Word "the" being interlined between the forty third and forty fourth Lines of the second Page.

Attest William Jackson Secretary

done in Convention by the Unanimous Consent of the States present the Seventeenth Day of September in the Year of our Lord one thousand seven hundred and Eighty seven and of the Independance of the United States of America the Twelfth In witness whereof We have hereunto subscribed our Names,

G⁰ Washington—Presid' and deputy from Virginia

Delaware
Geo: Read
Gunning Bedford jun
John Dickinson
Richard Bassett
Jaco: Broom

Maryland
James McHenry
Dan of St Thos Jenifer
Danl Carroll

Virginia
John Blair—
James Madison Jr.

North Carolina
Wm Blount
Richd Dobbs Spaight.
Hu Williamson

South Carolina
J. Rutledge
Charles Cotesworth Pinckney
Charles Pinckney
Pierce Butler.

Georgia
William Few
Abr Baldwin

New Hampshire
John Langdon
Nicholas Gilman

Massachusetts
Nathaniel Gorham
Rufus King

Connecticut
Wm Saml Johnson
Roger Sherman

New York
Alexander Hamilton

New Jersey
Wil: Livingston
David Brearley.
Wm Paterson.
Jona: Dayton

Pennsylvania
B Franklin
Thomas Mifflin
Robt Morris
Geo. Clymer
Thos FitzSimons
Jared Ingersoll
James Wilson
Gouv Morris

The final page of the Constitution.

1791 Bill of Rights

The Constitution set up our system of government but did not address some of the "inalienable rights" that were mentioned in the Declaration of Independence. A clamor to include a bill of rights resulted in the first ten amendments to the Constitution. These ten amendments are the cornerstones of many freedoms we continue to cherish today, yet they are more open to interpretation than perhaps any other part of any of our governing documents. The Supreme Court has seen countless cases pertaining to freedom of speech and religion (First Amendment), the right against search and seizure (Fourth Amendment), the right of privacy and against self-incrimination (Fifth Amendment), and the right to a fair and speedy trial (Sixth Amendment). As times have changed, so has interpretation of these amendments. One notable example is the freedom of religion—in 1940 the Supreme Court ruled against a school child who did not want to salute the flag in school, and in 1943 it reversed that decision in a similar case. The Bill of Rights was passed in Congress in 1789, sent to the states for ratification, and adopted in November 1791. The Eleventh and Twelfth Amendments followed in 1798 and 1804. It was sixty years before the next Amendment was ratified in 1865.

The Conventions of a number of the States, having at the time of adopting the Constitution, expressed a desire, in order to prevent misconstruction or abuse of its powers, that further declaratory and restrictive clauses should be added: And as extending the ground of public confidence in the Government, will best insure the beneficent ends of its institution.

Resolved by the Senate and House of Representatives of the United States of America, in Congress assembled, two thirds of both Houses concurring, that the following Articles be proposed to the Legislatures of the several States, as amendments to the Constitution of the United States, all, or any of which Articles, when ratified by three-fourths of the said Legislatures, to be valid to all intents and purposes as part of the said Constitution; viz . . .

Amendment I
Congress shall make no law respecting an establishment of religion, or prohibiting the free exercise thereof; or abridging the freedom of speech, or of the press; or the right of the people peaceably to assemble, and to petition the Government for a redress of grievances.

Amendment II
A well regulated Militia, being necessary to the security of a free State, the right of the people to keep and bear Arms, shall not be infringed.

Amendment III
No Soldier shall, in time of peace be quartered in any house, without the consent of the Owner, nor in time of war, but in a manner to be prescribed by law.

Amendment IV
The right of the people to be secure in their persons, houses, papers, and effects, against unreasonable searches and seizures, shall not be violated, and no Warrants shall issue, but upon probable cause, supported by Oath or affirmation, and particularly describing the place to be searched, and the persons or things to be seized.

Amendment V
No person shall be held to answer for a capital, or otherwise infamous crime, unless on a presentment or indictment of a Grand Jury, except in cases arising in the land or naval forces, or in the Militia, when in actual service in time of War or public danger; nor shall any person be subject for the same offense to be twice put in jeopardy of life or limb; nor shall be compelled in any criminal case to be a witness against himself, nor be deprived of life, liberty, or property, without due process of law; nor shall private property be taken for public use, without just compensation.

Amendment VI
In all criminal prosecutions, the accused shall enjoy the right to a speedy and public trial, by an impartial jury of the State and district wherein the crime shall have been committed, which district shall have been previously ascertained by law, and to be informed of the nature and cause of the accusation; to be confronted with the witnesses against him; to have compulsory process for obtaining witnesses in his favor, and to have the Assistance of Counsel for his defense.

Amendment VII
In Suits at common law, where the value in controversy shall exceed twenty dollars, the right of trial by jury shall be preserved, and no fact tried by a jury, shall be otherwise re-examined in any Court of the United States, than according to the rules of the common law.

Amendment VIII
Excessive bail shall not be required, nor excessive fines imposed, nor cruel and unusual punishments inflicted.

Amendment IX
The enumeration in the Constitution, of certain rights, shall not be construed to deny or disparage others retained by the people.

Amendment X
The powers not delegated to the United States by the Constitution, nor prohibited by it to the States, are reserved to the States respectively, or to the people.

# What They Were Saying

from remarks by James Wilson, 1787:

I cannot say . . . what were the reasons, of every member of that [constitutional] Convention, for not adding a bill of rights. I believe the truth is, that such an idea never entered the mind of many of them. I do not recollect to have heard the subject mentioned till within about three days of the time of our rising; and even then, there was no direct motion offered for any thing of this kind. I may be mistaken in this; but as far as my memory serves me, I believe it was the case. A proposition to adopt a measure that would have supposed that we were throwing into the general government every power not expressly reserved by the people, would have been spurned at, in that house, with the greatest indignation. Even in a single government, if the powers of the people rest on the same establishment as is expressed in this Constitution, a bill of rights is by no means a necessary measure.

In a government possessed of enumerated powers, such a measure would be not only unnecessary, but preposterous and dangerous. Whence comes this notion, that in the United States there is no security without a bill of rights? Have the citizens of South Carolina no security for their liberties? They have no bill of rights. . . . The state of New-Jersey has no bill of rights. The state of New-York has no bill of rights. The states of Connecticut and Rhode-Island have no bill of rights. I know not whether I have exactly enumerated the states who have thought it unnecessary to add a bill of rights to their constitutions: but this enumeration will serve to show by experience, as well as principle, that even in single governments, a bill of rights is not an essential or necessary measure. But in a government, confining of enumerated powers, such as is adopted by the United States, a bill of rights would not only be unnecessary, but, in my humble judgment, highly imprudent. In all societies, there are many powers and rights which cannot be particularly enumerated. A bill of rights annexed to a constitution is an enumeration of the powers reserved. If we attempt an enumeration, every thing that is not enumerated is presumed to be given. The consequence is, that an imperfect enumeration would throw all implied power into the scale of the government, and the rights of the people would be rendered incomplete. On the other hand, an imperfect enumeration of the powers of government reserves all implied power to the people; and by that means the constitution becomes incomplete. But of the two, it is much safer to run the risk on the side of the constitution; for an omission in the enumeration of the powers of government, is neither so dangerous nor important as an omission in the enumeration of the rights of the people.

3

Young Republic

★★★

The young republic emerged from the 1780s with a strong Constitution and then enjoyed the benefit of eight years of leadership from the retired war hero, George Washington. Yet division lurked within; serious differences between the two major political parties of the time (Federalists and Democrats) began to emerge over how the country should be governed and how much influence the federal government should exercise over the states.

The young United States was not alone in America. Much of what is now our country was controlled by the Spanish (Florida and the Southwest), British (the Pacific Northwest; Washington and Oregon), and France (Louisiana and states along the lower Mississippi). As the United States grew in experience, it added territory and one by one removed foreign influence from its immediate presence. The first notable addition was the Louisiana Purchase in 1803. With the addition of this new land came the struggle between the North and the South over slavery—should slavery be allowed or banned in those new territories?

1793 Fugitive Slave Law

The Fugitive Slave Law of 1793 put it into no uncertain terms: slaves had no rights and escaped slaves could be captured and returned as if they were simply property. Despite the law, the tide was already turning in some places. In 1791 Vermont entered the union as a free state; slavery had been abolished there back in 1779. In 1799 New York provided for the gradual (over a course of years) emancipation of its slaves, and in 1804 New Jersey abolished slavery. Yet there was no sign of any change in policy in the Southern states; and as is evident from the Fugitive Slave Law, the federal government was willing to make concessions to the Southern states on the issue of slavery. The rights of slaves who lived in free states would be argued and disputed more than sixty years later in the famous *Dred Scott* case that went before the Supreme Court.

Holy Bible.
Thou shalt not deliver unto the master his servant which has escaped from his master unto thee. He shall dwell with thee. Even among you in that place which he shall choose in one of thy gates where it liketh him best. Thou shalt not oppress him
Deut. XXIII 15.16

Effects of the Fugitive-Slave-Law.

Declaration of independence.
We hold that all men are created equal, that they are endowed by their Creator with certain unalienable rights, that among these are life, liberty, and the pursuit of happiness.

The Fugitive Slave Law of 1793 was the first, but not the last, such law. This lithograph expresses Northern outrage at the Fugitive Slave Law of 1850, showing a posse of white men chasing and shooting at black men. It cites passages from the Bible and Declaration of Independence.

Section 1

Be it enacted by the Senate and House of Representatives of the United States of America in Congress assembled, That whenever the executive authority of any state in the Union, or of either of the territories northwest or south of the river Ohio, shall demand any person as a fugitive from justice, of the executive authority of any such state or territory to which such person shall have fled, and shall moreover produce the copy of an indictment found, or an affidavit made before a magistrate of any state or territory as aforesaid, charging the person so demanded, with having committed treason, felony or other crime, certified as authentic by the governor or chief magistrate of the state or territory from whence the person so charged fled, it shall be the duty of the executive authority of the state or territory to which such person shall have fled, to cause him or her to be arrested and secured, and notice of the arrest to be given to the executive authority making such demand, or to the agent of such authority appointed to receive the fugitive, and to cause the fugitive to be delivered to such agent when he shall appear: But if no such agent shall appear within six months from the time of the arrest, the prisoner may be discharged. . . .

Section 2

And be it further enacted, That any agent, appointed as aforesaid, who shall receive the fugitive into his custody, shall be empowered to transport him or her to the state or territory from which he or she shall have fled. And if any person or persons shall by force set at liberty, or rescue the fugitive from such agent while transporting, as aforesaid, the person or persons so offending shall, on conviction, be fined not exceeding five hundred dollars, and be imprisoned not exceeding one year.

Section 3

And it be also enacted, That when a person held to labour in any of the United States, or in either of the territories on the northwest or south of the river Ohio, under the laws thereof, shall escape into any other of the said states or territory, the person to whom such labour or service may be due, his agent or attorney, is hereby empowered to seize or arrest such fugitive from labour. . . .

Section 4

And it be further enacted, That any person who shall knowingly and willingly obstruct or hinder such claimant, his agent or attorney in so seizing or arresting such fugitive from labour, or shall rescue such fugitive from such claimant, his agent or attorney when so arrested pursuant to the authority herein given or declared; or shall harbor or conceal such person after notice that he or she was a fugitive from labour, as aforesaid, shall for either of the said offences, forfeit and pay the sum of five hundred dollars.

What They Were Saying

from "An Act for the Better Ordering and Governing Negroes and other Slaves in this Province [South Carolina]" 1740:

And forasmuch as for want of knowing or finding the owner of any fugitive slave, to be delivered to him as aforesaid, the said warden may not be obliged to keep such slave in his custody, and find and provide provisions for such slave over and beyond a reasonable time; Be it therefore enacted, In what case That if the owner or owners of such fugitive slaves, shall not the warden within the space of eighteen months from the time of commitment, make his, her or their claim or claims, or it shall not be otherwise made known to the said warden, within the time aforesaid, to whom such committed slave shall belong; it shall and may be lawful for the said warden to sell such slave at public outcry, in Charlestown . . .

from *The Works of William E. Channing* (a Unitarian minister), 1840:

The Free States ought to say to the South, "Slavery is yours, not ours, and on you the whole responsibility of it must fall. We wash our hands of it wholly. We shall exert no power against it; but do not call on us to put forth the least power in its behalf. We cannot, directly or indirectly, become accessories to this wrong. We cannot become jailers, or a patrol, or a watch, to keep your slaves under the yoke. You must guard them yourselves. If they escape, we cannot send them back. Our soil makes whoever touches it free. On this point you must manage your own concerns. You must guard your own frontier. In case of insurrection, we cannot come to you, save as friends alike of bond and free. Neither in our separate legislatures, nor in the national legislature, can we touch slavery to sustain it. On this point you are foreign communities. You have often said that you need not our protection; and we must take you at your word. In so doing we have no thought of acting on your fears. We think only of our duty, and this, in all circumstances, and at all hazards, must be done.

President Washington's Farewell Address 1796

After eight years as president, George Washington announced in 1796 that he would not be seeking a third term in office. He used his address to outline his hopes and fears for the future of the young republic, notably the dangers of our government becoming enmeshed in foreign disputes and giving in to the "insidious wiles of foreign influence." The president also urged harmony within the United States and expressed fears over regional interests winning out over the overall welfare of the country. The address is an excellent insight into Washington's political genius. Revered as a Revolutionary War general and as our nation's first president, the Farewell Address presents a picture of Washington as a political philosopher on par with Jefferson or Paine. Washington's fears of regional jealousies came true as the nineteenth century progressed. His words on foreign influence were echoed in the words of President Monroe more than twenty-five years later. Alexander Hamilton had a strong hand in drafting and editing the address, at Washington's request. The address was never given in public; it was printed in a newspaper called the *American Daily Advertiser* in Philadelphia on September 19, 1796.

The death of our country's first president in 1799 marked the end of an era and also the beginning of a heightened reverence for Washington and the founding fathers that still exists today. As time passed, Washington's reputation and stature grew, more so after the deaths of the remaining founding fathers. His contributions as general and as president were equally admired, and whatever flaws he may have had fell away as he acquired cult status.

The period for a new election of a citizen to administer the executive government of the United States being not far distant, and the time actually arrived when your thoughts must be employed in designating the person who is to be clothed with that important trust, it appears to me proper, especially as it may conduce to a more distinct expression of the public voice, that I should now apprise you of the resolution I have formed, to decline being considered among the number of those out of whom a choice is to be made. . . .

In contemplating the causes which may disturb our Union, it occurs as matter of serious concern that any ground should have been furnished for characterizing parties by geographical discriminations, Northern and Southern, Atlantic and Western; whence designing men may endeavor to excite a belief that there is a real difference of local interests and views. One of the expedients of party to acquire influence within particular districts is to misrepresent the opinions and aims of other districts. You cannot shield yourselves too much against the jealousies and heartburnings which spring from these misrepresentations; they tend to render alien to each other those who ought to be bound together by fraternal affection. . . .

Towards the preservation of your government, and the permanency of your present happy state, it is requisite, not only that you steadily discountenance irregular oppositions to its acknowledged authority, but also that you resist with care the spirit of innovation upon its principles, however specious the pretexts. One method of assault may be to effect, in the forms of the Constitution, alterations which will impair the energy of the system, and thus to undermine what cannot be directly overthrown. In all the changes to which you may be invited, remember that time and habit are at least as necessary to fix the true character of governments as of other human institutions; that experience is the surest standard by which to test the real tendency of the existing constitution of a country; that facility in changes, upon the credit of mere hypothesis and opinion, exposes to perpetual change, from the endless variety of hypothesis and opinion; and remember, especially, that for the efficient management of your common interests, in a country so extensive as ours, a government of as much vigor as is consistent with the perfect security of liberty is indispensable. Liberty itself will find in such a government, with powers properly distributed and adjusted, its surest guardian. It is, indeed, little else than a name, where the government is too feeble to withstand the enterprises of faction, to confine each member of the society within the limits prescribed by the laws, and to maintain all in the secure and tranquil enjoyment of the rights of person and property. . . .

So likewise, a passionate attachment of one nation for another produces a variety of evils. Sympathy for the favorite nation, facilitating the illusion of an imaginary common interest in cases where no real common interest exists, and infusing into one the enmities of the other, betrays the former into a participation in the quarrels and wars of the latter without adequate inducement or justification. It leads also to concessions to the favorite nation of privileges denied to others which is apt doubly to injure the nation making the concessions; by unnecessarily parting with what ought to have been retained, and by exciting jealousy, ill-will, and a disposition to retaliate, in the parties from whom equal privileges are withheld. And it gives to ambitious, corrupted, or deluded citizens (who devote themselves to the favorite nation), facility to betray or sacrifice the interests of their own country, without odium, sometimes even with popularity; gilding, with the appearances of a virtuous sense of obligation, a commendable deference for public opinion, or a laudable zeal for public good, the base or foolish compliances of ambition, corruption, or infatuation. . . .

Against the insidious wiles of foreign influence (I conjure you to believe me, fellow-citizens) the jealousy of a free people ought to be constantly awake, since history and experience prove that foreign influence is one of the most baneful foes of republican government.

But that jealousy to be useful must be impartial; else it becomes the instrument of the very influence to be avoided, instead of a defense against it. Excessive partiality for one foreign nation and excessive dislike of another cause those whom they actuate to see danger only on one side, and serve to veil and even second the arts of influence on the other. Real patriots who may resist the intrigues of the favorite are liable to become suspected and odious, while its tools and dupes usurp the applause and confidence of the people, to surrender their interests.

The great rule of conduct for us in regard to foreign nations is in extending our commercial relations, to have with them as little political connection as possible. So far as we have already formed engagements, let them be fulfilled with perfect good faith. Here let us stop. Europe has a set of primary interests which to us have none; or a very remote relation. Hence she must be engaged in frequent controversies, the causes of which are essentially foreign to our concerns. Hence, therefore, it must be unwise in us to implicate ourselves by artificial ties in the ordinary vicissitudes of her politics, or the ordinary combinations and collisions of her friendships or enmities.

Our detached and distant situation invites and enables us to pursue a different course. If we remain one people under an efficient government, the period is not far off when we may defy material injury from external annoyance; when we may take such an attitude as will cause the neutrality we may at any time resolve upon to be scrupulously respected; when belligerent nations, under the impossibility of making acquisitions upon us, will not lightly hazard the giving us provocation; when we may choose peace or war, as our interest, guided by justice, shall counsel.

Why forego the advantages of so peculiar a situation? Why quit our own to stand upon foreign ground? Why, by interweaving our destiny with that of any part of Europe, entangle our peace and prosperity in the toils of European ambition, rivalship, interest, humor or caprice? . . .

Though, in reviewing the incidents of my administration, I am unconscious of intentional error, I am nevertheless too sensible of my defects not to think it probable that I may have committed many errors. Whatever they may be, I fervently beseech the Almighty to avert or mitigate the evils to which they may tend. . . .

Relying on its kindness in this as in other things, and actuated by that fervent love towards it, which is so natural to a man who views in it the native soil of himself and his progenitors for several generations, I anticipate with pleasing expectation that retreat in which I promise myself to realize, without alloy, the sweet enjoyment of partaking, in the midst of my fellow-citizens, the benign influence of good laws under a free government—the ever-favorite object of my heart, and the happy reward, as I trust, of our mutual cares, labors, and dangers.

What They Were Saying

from *Analytical Review*, 1796:

This year General Washington, the greatest of contemporary men, as Catharine was of contemporary sovereigns, resigned the presidency of the American States. Having rescued his country from the tyranny of the English government, and restored it, by a commercial treaty, to an amicable connection with the British nation, he voluntarily retired from power, after giving the most profound instruction and advice respecting Union, Virtue, Liberty and Happiness, between all of which there was a close connection, with, the most ardent prayers for the prosperity and peace of America. There is nothing in profane history to which this sublime address can be compared. In our sacred scriptures we find a parallel in that recapitulation of the divine instructions and commands, which the legislator of the Jews made, in the hearing of Israel, when they were about to pass the Jordan.

from a poem by J. G. C. Brainard on the birthday of Washington, 1822:

Mourn Washington's death, when ye think of his birth.
And far from your thoughts be the lightness of mirth,
And far from your cheek be its smile.
To-day he was born—'twas a loan—not a gift;
The dust of his body is all that is left,
To hallow his funeral pile.

Flow gently, Potomac! Thou washest away
The sands where he trod, and the turf where he lay,
When youth brushed his cheek with her wing;
Breathe softly, ye wild winds, that circle around
That dearest, and purest, and holiest ground
Ever pressed by the foot-prints of Spring.

from *The Religious Tradesman: Or, Plain and Serious Hints of Advice for the Tradesman's Prudent and Pious Conduct . . .*, 1823:

The farewell address of General Washington, should be cherished as a legacy of inestimable value, bequeathed to us by the Father of his country; and, indeed, every thing of a public nature, which ever proceeded from his pen, should be sought after, as fraught with the counsels of wisdom and experience.

from *A Compend of History*, 1828:

George Washington, if any mortal man ever merited the appellation of Father of his country, surely merits that name. He, by united voice of his country, led her armies. He trained them to the art of war. He fixed their wavering resolution; confirmed their dubious virtue; inspired them with invincible courage; taught them to be cool, intrepid, and firm in every danger—to exercise the utmost fortitude in adversity, and to be temperate, magnanimous, mild, and merciful in the moment of victory.

Alien and Sedition Acts 1798

Relations between revolutionary France and the United States were rocky during the late 1790s. The Federalists feared war, French sympathizers, and Republican critics. The federalist-controlled Congress passed the Alien and Sedition Acts to suppress their critics. The laws included a Naturalization Act that changed the residency requirements of an alien from five years to fourteen years. The Alien Act gave the federal government authority to deport aliens of any foreign government with whom the United States happened to be at war. The Sedition Act allowed for the arrest of any person whose writings were seen as scandalous; twenty-five people were arrested under this law, mainly newspaper editors critical of the Federalists.

In response to this legislation, the states of Virginia and Kentucky issued resolutions—Kentucky's was penned by Jefferson and Virginia's primarily by Madison—condemning the Alien and Sedition Acts as unconstitutional. In reaction, northern states such as New York, Connecticut, Massachusetts, New Hampshire, Rhode Island, and Delaware issued counter-resolutions condemning the Virginia and Kentucky resolutions. In this little crisis were the beginnings of real disagreement and division between American political parties, between those who believed in states' rights and those who viewed the federal government as supreme, as well as the seeds of disputes between the North and the South. After the Republican Thomas Jefferson took office in 1801, the controversial laws were not renewed. The Supreme Court ruling in *Marbury v. Madison* (1803; it arose out of a dispute over a Federalist judge appointed at the last minute by the outgoing President Adams whose commission was rejected by incoming President Jefferson) affirmed that the federal government had authority over the states.

from the Alien Enemies Act

Section 1

Be it enacted by the Senate and House of Representatives of the United States of America in Congress assembled, That whenever there shall be a declared war between the United States and any foreign nation or government, or any invasion or predatory incursion shall be perpetrated, attempted, or threatened against the territory of the United States, by any foreign nation or government, and the President of the United States shall make public proclamation of the event, all natives, citizens, denizens, or subjects of the hostile nation or government, being males of the age of fourteen years and upwards, who shall be within the United States, and not actually naturalized, shall be liable to be apprehended, restrained, secured and removed, as alien enemies.

from the Sedition Act

Section 1

Be it enacted by the Senate and House of Representatives of the United States of America, in Congress assembled, That if any persons shall unlawfully combine or conspire together, with intent to oppose any measure or measures of the government of the United States, which are or shall be directed by proper authority, or to impede the operation of any law of the United States, or to intimidate or prevent any person holding a place or office in or under the government of the United States, from undertaking, performing or executing his trust or duty, and if any person or persons, with intent as aforesaid, shall counsel, advise or attempt to procure any insurrection, riot, unlawful assembly, or combination, whether such conspiracy, threatening, counsel, advice, or attempt shall have the proposed effect or not, he or they shall be deemed guilty of a high misdemeanor, and on conviction, before any court of the United States having jurisdiction thereof, shall be punished by a fine not exceeding five thousand dollars, and by imprisonment during a term not less than six months nor exceeding five years. . . .

Section 2

And be it farther enacted, That if any person shall write, print, utter or publish, or shall cause or procure to be written, printed, uttered or published, or shall knowingly and willingly assist or aid in writing, printing, uttering or publishing any false, scandalous and malicious writing or writings against the government of the United States, or either house of the Congress of the United States, or the President of the United States, with intent to defame the said government, or either house of the said Congress, or the said President, or to bring them, or either of them, into contempt or disrepute; or to excite against them, or either or any of them, the hatred of the good people of the United States, or to stir up sedition within the United States, or to excite any unlawful combinations therein, for opposing or resisting any law of the United States, or any act of the President of the United States, done in pursuance of any such law, or of the powers in him vested by the constitution of the United States, or to resist, oppose, or defeat any such law or act, or to aid, encourage or abet any hostile designs of any foreign nation against United States, their people or government, then such person, being thereof convicted before any court of the United States having jurisdiction thereof, shall be punished by a fine not exceeding two thousand dollars, and by imprisonment not exceeding two years. . . .

Section 4

That this act shall continue to be in force until March 3, 1801 and no longer . . .

from the Kentucky Resolution

4. Resolved, That alien friends are under the jurisdiction and protection of the laws of the State wherein they are; that no power over them has been delegated to the United States, nor prohibited to the individual States distinct from their power over citizens. And it being true as a general principle, and one of the amendments to the Constitution having also declared that "the powers not delegated to the United States by the Constitution, nor prohibited to the states, are reserved to the states respectively, or to the people," the act of the Congress of the United States, passed on the 22d day of June, 1798, entitled "An Act concerning Aliens," which assumes power over alien friends not delegated by the Constitution, is not law, but is altogether void and of no force. . . .

6. Resolved, That the imprisonment of a person under the protection of the laws of this commonwealth, on his failure to obey the simple order of the President to depart out of the United States, as is undertaken by the said act, entitled "An Act concerning Aliens," is contrary to the Constitution, one amendment to which has provided, that "no person shall be deprived of liberty without due process of law," and that another having provided, "that in all criminal prosecutions, the accused shall enjoy the right to a public trial by an impartial jury, to be informed of the nature and cause of the accusation, to be confronted with the witnesses against him, to have compulsory process for obtaining witnesses in his favour, and to have the assistance of counsel for his defence," the same act undertaking to authorize the President to remove a person out of the United States, who is under the protection of the law, on his own suspicion, without accusation, without jury, without public trial, without confrontation of the witnesses against him, without having witnesses in his favour, without defence, without counsel, is contrary to these provisions also of the Constitution, is therefore not law, but utterly void and of no force.

 What They Were Saying

from the *Olive Branch*, 1817:

A candid review of the so-styled sedition law, at the present hour, when the public ferment to which it gave rise has wholly subsided, will satisfy any reasonable man, that so far from being an outrageous infringement of liberty, as was asserted, it was a measure not merely defensible, but absolutely necessary and indispensable towards the support of government . . . Laudable and necessary as it was, and guarded, so far as a law can be guarded, against abuse, the opposition to it was so violent, and it excited as much horror and indignation, as if it had wholly destroyed the liberty of the press . . .

1803 Louisiana Purchase

Owned by the Spanish after France ceded it in 1763, the land along the Mississippi River was returned to France under Napoleon's strong-arm tactics in 1800. The United States was anxious about the fate of New Orleans in particular because, as Jefferson wrote, "it is . . . through which the produce of three-eighths of our territory must pass to market." Luckily for America, French ambitions for an empire in the New World were put aside when war loomed between France and England; suddenly, Napoleon was willing to sell the land to the United States to fund his army. Thanks to the Louisiana Purchase in 1803, the United States was able to expand westward uninhibited. This strategic land purchase from France increased the size and resources of the United States dramatically (by more than 925,000 square miles) for a price of fifteen million dollars (worth a lot more at the time than it is now, but still a tremendous bargain). Though it may seem like an obvious and wise choice now, at the time it was hard for some to justify the expense and necessity of such a purchase. The next important land purchase came in 1819, when the United States bought Florida from Spain for five million dollars.

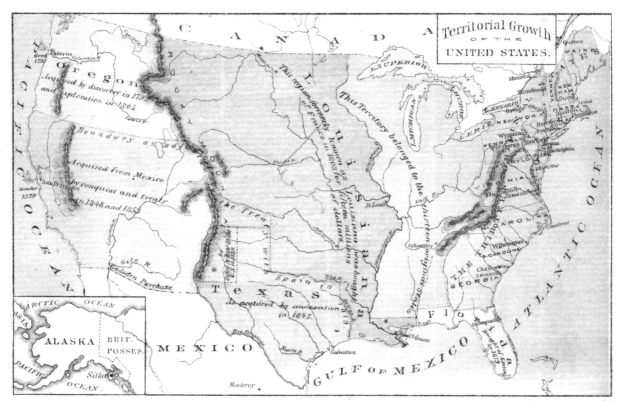

Nineteenth-century map showing land acquisitions including the Louisiana Purchase.

The President of the United States of America and the First Consul of the French Republic in the name of the French People . . . have agreed to the following Articles.

Article I

Whereas by the Article the third of the Treaty concluded at St Ildefonso the 9th Vendé miaire an 9/1st October 1800 between the First Consul of the French Republic and his Catholic Majesty it was agreed as follows.

"His Catholic Majesty promises and engages on his part to cede to the French Republic six months after the full and entire execution of the conditions and Stipulations herein relative to his Royal Highness the Duke of Parma, the Colony or Province of Louisiana with the Same extent that it now has in the hand of Spain, & that it had when France possessed it; and Such as it Should be after the Treaties subsequently entered into between Spain and other States."

And whereas in pursuance of the Treaty and particularly of the third article the French Republic has an incontestible title to the domain and to the possession of the said Territory—The First Consul of the French Republic desiring to give to the United States a strong proof of his friendship doth hereby cede to the United States in the name of the French Republic for ever and in full Sovereignty the said territory with all its rights and appurtenances as fully and in the Same manner as they have been acquired by the French Republic in virtue of the above mentioned Treaty concluded with his Catholic Majesty.

Article II

In the cession made by the preceeding article are included the adjacent Islands belonging to Louisiana all public lots and Squares, vacant lands and all public buildings, fortifications, barracks and other edifices which are not private property.—The Archives, papers & documents relative to the domain and Sovereignty of Louisiana and its dependances will be left in the possession of the Commissaries of the United States, and copies will be afterwards given in due form to the Magistrates and Municipal officers of such of the said papers and documents as may be necessary to them.

Article III

The inhabitants of the ceded territory shall be incorporated in the Union of the United States and admitted as soon as possible according to the principles of the federal Constitution to the enjoyment of all these rights, advantages and immunities of citizens of the United States, and in the mean time they shall be maintained and protected in the free enjoyment of their liberty, property and the Religion which they profess.

Article IV

There Shall be Sent by the Government of France a Commissary to Louisiana to the end that he do every act necessary as well to receive from the Officers of his Catholic Majesty the Said country and its dependances in the name of the French Republic if it has not been already done as to transmit it in the name of the French Republic to the Commissary or agent of the United States.

Article V

Immediately after the ratification of the present Treaty . . . the commissary of the French Republic shall remit all military posts of New Orleans and other parts of the ceded territory to the Commissary or Commissaries named by the President to take possession—the troops whether of France or Spain who may be there shall cease to occupy any military post from the time of taking possession and shall be embarked as soon as possible in the course of three months after the ratification of this treaty.

What They Were Saying

from a letter by Thomas Jefferson to Robert Livingston, 1802:

Every eye in the United States is now fixed on the affairs of Louisiana. Perhaps nothing since the revolutionary war has produced more uneasy sensations through the body of the nation.

from an editorial the *Columbian Centinel and Massachusetts Federalist*, 1803:

At length we hear Louisiana is bought. For what? . . . We are to give money of which we have too little for land of which we already have too much—We expose our want of spirit, and aggravate our want of strength.

There ought to be some balance in the Union; as before hinted, this unexplored empire, of the size of four or five European kingdoms will destroy that—will drain our people away from the pursuit of a better husbandry, and from our manufactures and commerce.

Can an Empire so unwieldy, so nearly uncivilized, that will for a century or two require such heavy charge and contribute so little towards defraying any part of it, will it be, can it be subject to one Government? . . . The inhabitants who will cost most to the United States Treasury, are those who live West from Pennsylvania. Our are the burdens, theirs are the benefits.

from a petition adopted by Deerfield, Massachusetts and presented to the state legislature, 1814:

Should the present administration, with their adherents in the southern states, still persist in . . . unconstitutionally creating new states in the mud of Louisiana, (the inhabitants of which country are as ignorant of republicanism as the alligators of their swamps) much as we deprecate the separation of the union, we deem it an evil much less to be dreaded than a co-operation with them in these nefarious projects.

The Louisiana Purchase treaty.

Treaty of Ghent 1814

Relations between the United States and Great Britain grew tense after 1800. One sore point was Britain claiming the "right of search" to find English-born sailors on American ships and force them into service for Britain; more than fifteen hundred Americans were taken for this reason. In 1807 a British frigate fired on an American ship that refused to be boarded, and twenty-one Americans were killed or wounded. Britain also implemented a naval blockade against France during their conflict, preventing Americans from trading with France. "War hawks" in the southern and western states pushed for war with England. On June 18, 1812, the United States declared war upon Great Britain, just thirty years after the end of the Revolution. The low point of the two-year-long struggle was the burning of Washington, D.C., by the British. Support for the war was by no means unanimous. In fact, Federalists in a few New England states were so opposed to the war that they held the Hartford Convention and discussed the possible dissolution of the Union. At last news came from Europe that a peace treaty had been signed in Belgium in December 1814. The Treaty of Ghent marked the end of the hostilities between the United States and England. Interestingly, Article Ten expresses the hopes that both countries not engage in slavery.

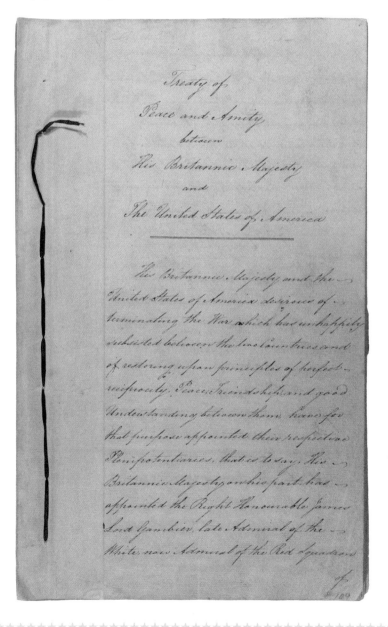

His Britannic Majesty and the United States of America desirous of terminating the war which has unhappily subsisted between the two Countries, and of restoring upon principles of perfect reciprocity, Peace, Friendship, and good Understanding between them, have . . . agreed upon the following Articles.

Article the First
There shall be a firm and universal Peace between His Britannic Majesty and the United States, and between their respective Countries, Territories, Cities, Towns, and People of every degree without exception of places or persons. All hostilities both by sea and land shall cease as soon as this Treaty shall have been ratified by both parties as hereinafter mentioned. All territory, places, and possessions whatsoever taken by either party from the other during the war, or which may be taken after the signing of this Treaty, excepting only the Islands hereinafter mentioned, shall be restored without delay and without causing any destruction or carrying away any of the Artillery or other public property originally captured in the said forts or places, and which shall remain therein upon the Exchange of the Ratifications of this Treaty, or any Slaves or other private property; . . .

Article the Second
Immediately after the ratifications of this Treaty by both parties as hereinafter mentioned, orders shall be sent to the Armies, Squadrons, Officers, Subjects, and Citizens of the two Powers to cease from all hostilities: and to prevent all causes of complaint which might arise on account of the prizes which may be taken at sea after the said Ratifications of this Treaty, it is reciprocally agreed that all vessels and effects which may be taken after the space of twelve days from the said Ratifications . . . shall be restored on each side . . .

Article the Third
All Prisoners of war taken on either side as well by land as by sea shall be restored as soon as practicable after the Ratifications of this Treaty . . .

Article the Ninth
The United States of America engage to put an end immediately after the Ratification of the present Treaty to hostilities with all the Tribes or Nations of Indians with whom they may be at war at the time of such Ratification, and forthwith to restore to such Tribes or Nations respectively all the possessions, rights, and privileges which they may have enjoyed or been entitled to in one thousand eight hundred and eleven previous to such hostilities. . . . And His Britannic Majesty engages on his part to put an end immediately after the Ratification of the present Treaty to hostilities with all the Tribes or Nations of Indians with whom He may be at war at the time of such Ratification. . . .

Article the Tenth
Whereas the Traffic in Slaves is irreconcilable with the principles of humanity and Justice, and whereas both His Majesty and the United States are desirous of continuing their efforts to promote its entire abolition, it is hereby agreed that both the contracting parties shall use their best endeavours to accomplish so desirable an object.

What They Were Saying

Governor Plumer of New Hampshire, 1812:

[Great Britain] has for a series of years by her conduct evinced a deadly hostility to our national rights, to our commerce, peace, and prosperity. She has wantonly impressed thousands of our unoffending seamen . . . she has violated the rights and peace of our coasts; wantonly shed the blood of our citizens in our harbours . . .

from the *Philadelphia Gazette*, 1812:

They [the leaders of congress] have already gone far enough in war. They are conscious they cannot commence, prosecute, and terminate a war; that the hands which begin will never finish it. They shrink from it. They already stagger under the weight.

from the *Olive Branch*, 1817:

The enemies of the administration were lavish of their reproaches, in the early stages of the war, on its ill success, which to many of them was a subject of as much triumph, as if they belonged to a hostile nation . . . The blindness and perversity of many of our citizens on this topic, were utterly astonishing. If . . . we so harassed and crippled the trade of the enemy Great Britain would in that case have been weary of the war in twelve months. She would have given us an early and honourable peace. Millions of debts and taxes would have been saved—thousands of lives on both sides preserved . . .

The burning of Washington in 1814 by the British.

1820 Missouri Compromise

By 1820 slavery was already shaping up to be a major political issue in the young country. With the United States continually expanding in size, the allowance of slavery in new territories and states was a topic of contention. The addition of the Louisiana Purchase land to the United States caused serious concern among the members of Congress from the Northern states. Not only were they opposed to slavery, they also did not wish slavery states to gain too much power in Congress. On the other hand, congressmen and senators from the Southern states felt that restrictions upon slavery in new territories and states went against the Constitution and against the terms of the Louisiana Purchase treaty. The result of much debate and discussion was the Missouri Compromise (authored by Senator Henry Clay, "the Great Peacemaker"), an act that allowed Missouri to enter the Union with no restrictions on slavery imposed in its constitution. In return for this political favor, Maine was to be admitted as a free state. The details of the measure said that, other than Missouri, slavery would be prohibited in any part of the Louisiana Purchase territory that lay north of 36 degrees and 30 minutes latitude.

Senator Henry Clay was the man behind the Missouri Compromise, as well as the Compromise of 1850, thirty years later.

An Act to authorize the people of the Missouri territory to form a constitution and state government, and for the admission of such state into the Union on an equal footing with the original states, and to prohibit slavery in certain territories.

Be it enacted by the Senate and House of Representatives of the United States of America, in Congress assembled, That the inhabitants of that portion of the Missouri territory included within the boundaries herein after designated, be, and they are hereby, authorized to form for themselves a constitution and state government, and to assume such name as they shall deem proper; and the said state, when formed, shall be admitted into the Union, upon an equal footing with the original states, in all respects whatsoever. . . .

Section 8

And be it further enacted. That in all that territory ceded by France to the United States, under the name of Louisiana, which lies north of thirty-six degrees and thirty minutes north latitude, not included within the limits of the state, contemplated by this act, slavery and involuntary servitude, otherwise than in the punishment of crimes, whereof the parties shall have been duly convicted, shall be, and is hereby, forever prohibited: Provided always, That any person escaping into the same, from whom labour or service is lawfully claimed, in any state or territory of the United States, such fugitive may be lawfully reclaimed and conveyed to the person claiming his or her labour or service as aforesaid.

 What They Were Saying

Thomas Jefferson, 1820:

The Missouri question is the most portentous one that ever threatened our Union. In the gloomiest moments of the Revolutionary War, I never had any apprehensions equal to what I feel from this source. . . .But this momentous question, like a fire-bell in the night, awakened and filled me with terror. I considered it at once as the knell of the Union. It is hushed indeed for the moment. But this is a reprieve only, not a final sentence. A geographical line, coinciding with a marked principle, moral and political, once conceived and held up to the angry passions of men, will never be obliterated, and every new irritation will mark it deeper and deeper.

from the *United States Magazine and Democratic Review*, 1847:

The constitution does not prohibit slavery in any of the states, and yet through the Missouri compromise, it is sought to usurp for congress the power to prohibit it in a number of states that will hereafter grow up. When these new states come into the Union they are controlled by the constitution only; and as that instrument permits slavery in all the states that are parties to it, how can congress prevent it? To attempt it, is clearly such a departure from the spirit of the constitution as is at war with the whole course of the democratic party, and as such cannot have a prosperous issue.

1823 Monroe Doctrine

Outgoing President George Washington's farewell words in 1796 were heeded by his successors. Washington's thoughts were further crystallized in a policy document written by President James Monroe in 1823 and delivered in his annual message to Congress. In the years preceding the doctrine, several states in Central and South America had gained their independence from Spain (Colombia, Chile, Mexico) and Portugal (Brazil). While wishing to avoid conflict with European affairs, Monroe warned of European interference in the Americas.

The United States' adherence to the so-called Monroe Doctrine continued long after 1823. For example, in President Zachary Taylor's inaugural address of 1848, he said: "We are warned by the admonitions of history and the voice of our own beloved Washington to abstain from entangling alliances with foreign nations. In all disputes between conflicting governments, it is our interest not less than our duty to remain strictly neutral. . . . It is to be hoped that no international question can now arise which a government, confident in its own strength, and resolved to protect its own just rights, may not settle by wise negotiation." Our neutrality over the course of much of the nineteenth century may have played a role in the immigration of so many Europeans—by not playing a part in the political disturbances of their countries, the United States became more appealing as a refuge.

At the proposal of the Russian Imperial Government, made through the minister of the Emperor residing here, a full power and instructions have been transmitted to the minister of the United States at St. Petersburg to arrange by amicable negotiation the respective rights and interests of the two nations on the northwest coast of this continent. A similar proposal had been made by His Imperial Majesty to the Government of Great Britain, which has likewise been acceded to. The Government of the United States has been desirous by this friendly proceeding of manifesting the great value which they have invariably attached to the friendship of the Emperor and their solicitude to cultivate the best understanding with his Government. In the discussions to which this interest has given rise and in the arrangements by which they may terminate the occasion has been judged proper for asserting, as a principle in which the rights and interests of the United States are involved, that the American continents, by the free and independent condition which they have assumed and maintain, are henceforth not to be considered as subjects for future colonization by any European powers. . . .

It was stated at the commencement of the last session that a great effort was then making in Spain and Portugal to improve the condition of the people of those countries, and that it appeared to be conducted with extraordinary moderation. It need scarcely be remarked that the result has been so far very different from what was then anticipated. Of events in that quarter of the globe, with which we have so much intercourse and from which we derive our origin, we have always been anxious and interested spectators. The citizens of the United States cherish sentiments the most friendly in favor of the liberty and happiness of their fellowmen on that side of the Atlantic. In the wars of the European powers in matters relating to themselves we have never taken any part, nor does it comport with our policy so to do. It is only when our rights are invaded or seriously menaced that we resent injuries or make preparation for our defense. With the movements in this hemisphere we are of necessity more immediately connected, and by causes which must be obvious to all enlightened and impartial observers. The political system of the allied powers is essentially different in this respect from that of America. This difference proceeds from that which exists in their respective Governments; and to the defense of

our own, which has been achieved by the loss of so much blood and treasure, and matured by the wisdom of their most enlightened citizens, and under which we have enjoyed unexampled felicity, this whole nation is devoted. We owe it, therefore, to candor and to the amicable relations existing between the United States and those powers to declare that we should consider any attempt on their part to extend their system to any portion of this hemisphere as dangerous to our peace and safety. With the existing colonies or dependencies of any European power we have not interfered and shall not interfere. But with the Governments who have declared their independence and maintained it, and whose independence we have, on great consideration and on just principles, acknowledged, we could not view any interposition for the purpose of oppressing them, or controlling in any other manner their destiny, by any European power in any other light than as the manifestation of an unfriendly disposition toward the United States. In the war between those new Governments and Spain we declared our neutrality at the time of their recognition, and to this we have adhered, and shall continue to adhere, provided no change shall occur which, in the judgment of the competent authorities of this Government, shall make a corresponding change on the part of the United States indispensable to their security.

The late events in Spain and Portugal show that Europe is still unsettled. Of this important fact no stronger proof can be adduced than that the allied powers should have thought it proper, on any principle satisfactory to themselves, to have interposed by force in the internal concerns of Spain. To what extent such interposition may be carried, on the same principle, is a question in which all independent powers whose governments differ from theirs are interested, even those most remote, and surely none more so than the United States. Our policy in regard to Europe, which was adopted at an early stage of the wars which have so long agitated that quarter of the globe, nevertheless remains the same, which is, not to interfere in the internal concerns of any of its powers; to consider the government de facto as the legitimate government for us; to cultivate friendly relations with it, and to preserve those relations by a frank, firm, and manly policy, meeting in all instances the just claims of every power, submitting to injuries from none. But in regard to those continents circumstances are eminently and conspicuously different. It is impossible that the allied powers should extend their political system to any portion of either continent without endangering our peace and happiness; nor can anyone believe that our southern brethren, if left to themselves, would adopt it of their own accord. It is equally impossible, therefore, that we should behold such interposition in any form with indifference. If we look to the comparative strength and resources of Spain and those new Governments, and their distance from each other, it must be obvious that she can never subdue them. It is still the true policy of the United States to leave the parties to themselves, in the hope that other powers will pursue the same course.

What They Were Saying

from *A Sketch of the Politics, Relations, and Statistics, of the Western World*, 1827:

The posture of affairs, in the winter of 1814–15, was equivalent to an alliance between us and France, it was nothing short of a diversion by her in our favour; and whether this diversion was made in consequence of a written agreement between us and France, or in consequence of a peculiar contingency abroad, it amounted to the same effect . . . What has happened may again occur; and we may again be placed in a situation which will equally require the abrogation of the doctrine to "avoid entangling alliances;" it was adapted to a position of the world widely different from the present, and to the present it does not apply. Can any one in his sober senses believe that the rule ought to be observed if England would now attempt to take possession of Cuba?

from the Democratic Party Platform, 1900:

We insist on the strict maintenance of the Monroe Doctrine, in all its integrity, both in letter and in spirit.

The Seeds of Trouble

★★

The crisis that was averted in 1820 with the Missouri Compromise did not vanish. As the United States continued to acquire new territory, the question of slavery still gnawed at the nation. Further compromises were necessary. The Compromise of 1850 and the Kansas-Nebraska Act were both attempts to avoid conflict. In allowing Kansas and Nebraska residents to decide for themselves whether slavery should be allowed, the Kansas-Nebraska Act only increased tension between pro-slavery and antislavery forces in government. Confrontation with Mexico over Texas came to a head in 1836 and again in 1848 with the Mexican War. A women's rights convention was held in 1848, and abolitionists in the Northern states continued to push for an end to slavery. Beginning in the 1830s, the railroad became a viable means of transportation and led to increased settlement in the central portion of the nation.

1832 Nullification Crisis

Tariffs, or duties on imported goods, were the subject of much debate throughout the nineteenth century. Some people favored high tariffs to protect American manufacturers and stimulate the economy. Others were strongly opposed to tariffs, declaring them to be anti–free trade and bad for American consumers. In 1828, an especially damaging tariff was introduced. It placed a heavy duty on imports of wool and cotton. Southerners feared that Great Britain, a trading partner to whom twenty-four million dollars of Southern products such as rice and tobacco were exported every year, would retaliate with a duty of their own. The Southern states did not want to see their trade with England disintegrate. In 1829 South Carolina protested the Tariff of 1828, also known as the Tariff of Abominations, in a report issued by the state legislature known as the South Carolina Exposition. The Tariff Bill of 1832 modified the original bill of 1828, but did not satisfy Southerners. In November of 1832, the South Carolina legislature issued an Ordinance of Nullification that declared the tariffs of 1828 and 1832 unconstitutional and null and void in that state. South Carolina went so far as to threaten to secede, but President Jackson did not back down. "The laws of the United States must be executed," Jackson said. "Those who told you that you might peaceably prevent their execution deceived you." He declared South Carolina's behavior as treason and Congress gave him the authority to act further if necessary. A compromise bill was passed in March 1833 that promised a reduction in the tariffs and South Carolina soon repealed its Ordinance of Nullification.

President Jackson refused to back down when confronted with the threats of South Carolina in 1832.

from the Ordinance of Nullification

An Ordinance to Nullify certain acts of the Congress of the United States, purporting to be laws laying duties and imposts on the importation of foreign commodities.

Whereas the Congress of the United States, by various acts, purporting to be acts laying duties and imposts on foreign imports, but in reality intended for the protection of domestic manufactures and the giving of bounties to classes and individuals engaged in particular employments, at the expense and to the injury and oppression of other classes and individuals, and by wholly exempting from taxation certain foreign commodities, such as are not produced or manufactured in the United States, to afford a pretext for imposing higher and excessive duties on articles similar to those intended to be protected, hath exceeded its just powers under the Constitution, which confers on it no authority to afford such protection, and hath violated the true meaning and intent of the Constitution, which provides for equality in imposing the burdens of taxation upon the several States and portions of the confederacy: And whereas the said Congress, exceeding its just power to impose taxes and collect revenue for the purpose of effecting and accomplishing the specific objects and purposes which the Constitution of the United States authorizes it to effect and accomplish, hath raised and collected unnecessary revenue for objects unauthorized by the Constitution.

We, therefore, the people of the State of South Carolina in Convention assembled, to declare and ordain, and it is hereby declared and ordained, that the several acts and parts of acts of the Congress of the United States, purporting to be laws for the imposing of duties and imposts on the importation of foreign commodities, and now having actual operation and effect within the United States, and, more especially, an act entitled "An act in alteration of the several acts imposing duties on imports," approved on the nineteenth day of May, one thousand eight hundred and twenty-eight and also an act entitled "An act to alter and amend the several acts imposing duties on imports," approved on the fourteenth day of July, one thousand eight hundred and thirty-two, are unauthorized by the Constitution of the United States, and violate the true meaning and intent thereof, and are null, void, and no law, nor binding upon this State, its officers or citizens; and all promises, contracts, and obligations, made or entered into, or to be made or entered into, with purpose to secure the duties imposed by the said acts, and all judicial proceedings which shall be hereafter had in affirmance thereof, are and shall be held utterly null and void.

And it is further ordained, that it shall not be lawful for any of the constituted authorities, whether of this State or of the United States, to enforce the payment of duties imposed by the said acts within the limits of this State; but it shall be the duty of the legislature to adopt such measures and pass such acts as may be necessary to give full effect to this ordinance, and to prevent the enforcement and arrest the operation of the said acts and parts of acts of the Congress of the United States within the limits of this State, from and after the first day of February next, and the duties of all other constituted authorities, and of all persons residing or being within the limits of this State, and they are hereby required and enjoined to obey and give effect to this ordinance, and such acts and measures of the legislature as may be passed or adopted in obedience thereto.

And it is further ordained, that in no case of law or equity, decided in the courts of this State, wherein shall be drawn in question the authority of this ordinance, or the validity of such act or acts of the legislature as may be passed for the purpose of giving effect thereto, or the validity of the aforesaid acts of Congress, imposing duties, shall any appeal be taken or allowed to the Supreme Court of the United States, nor shall any copy of the record be permitted or allowed for that purpose; and if any such appeal shall be attempted to be taken, the courts of this State shall proceed to execute and enforce their judgments according to the laws and usages of the State, without reference to such attempted appeal, and the person or persons attempting to take such appeal may be dealt with as for a contempt of the court. . . .

And we, the people of South Carolina, to the end that it may be fully understood by the Government of the United States, and the people of the co-States, that we are determined to maintain this our ordinance and declaration, at every hazard, do further declare that we will not submit to the application of force on the part of the federal government, to reduce this State to obedience, but that we will consider the passage, by Congress, of any act authorizing the employment of a military or naval force against the State of South Carolina, her constituted authorities or citizens; or any act abolishing or closing the ports of this State, or any of them, or otherwise obstructing the free ingress and egress of vessels to and from the said ports, or any other act on the part of the federal government, to coerce the State, shut up her ports, destroy or harrass her commerce or to enforce the acts hereby declared to be null and void, otherwise than through the civil tribunals of the country, as inconsistent with the longer continuance of South Carolina in the Union: and that the people of this State will thenceforth hold themselves absolved from all further obligation to maintain or preserve their political connection with the people of the other States; and will forthwith proceed to organize a separate government, and do all other acts and things which sovereign and independent States may of

What They Were Saying

from *Society, Manners and Politics in the United States*, 1839:

In proportion as the territory of the Confederacy has been extended, the Federal bond has been weakened. It was nearly snapped asunder during the Nullification crisis, occasioned by the resistance of South Carolina to the tariff adopted under the influence of New England, in order to protect her growing manufactures. If Congress had not satisfied the demands of South Carolina, Virginia would have made common cause with the latter, and her example would have carried the whole South. The patriotic eloquence of Mr. Webster, the moderation of Mr. Clay and his prodigies of parliamentary strategy, the efforts of Mr. Livingston, then Secretary of State, the firm, and, at the same time, conciliatory conduct of the President, who, for the first time, heard a bold defiance with patience, and the calm attitude of the Northern States, prevented for the moment a general dissolution of the Union; but the germ of mischief remains; the charm is broken; the ear has become familiar with the ominous word SEPARATION.

The Wilmot Proviso was a controversial rider (proposed by Representative David Wilmot of Pennsylvania) on an otherwise harmless bill that was to allot thirty thousand dollars to the president for his use in negotiating a treaty with Mexico. The Wilmot Proviso proposed that slavery should not be allowed in any land acquired from Mexico. Though it was the subject of much discussion and disagreement in Congress over a period of several years, the Wilmot Proviso never actually became law.

Political cartoon from 1850 showing President Zachary Taylor trying to balance the demands of pro- and antislavery factions in Congress.

> Provided that, as an express and fundamental condition to the acquisition of any territory from the Republic of Mexico by the United States, by virtue of any treaty which may be negotiated between them, and to the use by the Executive of the moneys herein appropriated, neither slavery nor involuntary servitude shall ever exist in any part of said territory, except for crime, whereof the party shall first be duly convicted.

 What They Were Saying

from Senate Committee Report (chaired by Senator Henry Clay), 1850:

That proviso has been the fruitful source of distraction and agitation. If it were adopted and applied to any Territory, it would cease to have any obligatory force as soon as such Territory were admitted as a State into the Union. There was never any occasion for it to accomplish the professed object with which it was originally offered. This has been clearly demonstrated by the current of events. California, of all the recent territorial acquisitions from Mexico, was that in which, if anywhere within them, the introduction of Slavery was most likely to take place; and the constitution of California, by the unanimous vote of her convention, has expressly interdicted it. There is the highest decree of probability that Utah and New-Mexico will, when they come to be admitted as States, follow the example. The proviso is, as to all those regions in common, a mere abstraction. Why should it be any longer insisted on? Totally destitute as it is of any practical import, it has, nevertheless, had the pernicious effect to excite serious, if not alarming, consequences. It is high time that the wounds which it has inflicted should be healed up and closed. And, to avoid, in all future time, the agitations which must be produced by the conflict of opinion on the Slavery question, existing as this institution does in some of the States, and prohibited as it is in others, the true principle which ought to regulate the action of Congress in forming Territorial Governments for each newly-acquired domain, is to refrain from all legislation on the subject in the Territory acquired, so long as it retains the Territorial form of Government—leaving it to the people of such Territory, when they have attained to the condition which entitles them to admission as a State, to decide for themselves the question of the allowance or prohibition of domestic Slavery.

Declaration of Sentiments 1848

The women's rights movement in America gathered steam at a convention held at the Wesleyan Methodist Church in Seneca Falls, New York, in July 1848. Suffragists such Lucretia Mott (1793–1880) and Elizabeth Cady Stanton (1815–1902) were present, as well as several prominent male supporters, former slave Frederick Douglass and Lucretia Mott's husband, James, among them. The eloquent Declaration of Sentiments notably revised the language of the Declaration of Independence to include the word women. It also seized upon the structure of the Declaration by listing complaints of women against the male-centric society. However, the uphill battle for equal rights for women did not achieve its main milestone of voting rights for women until 1920. Notably, Susan B. Anthony was arrested and tried for voting in the 1872 election. The women of Seneca Falls were under no illusions, for they acknowledged the "misconception, misrepresentation, and ridicule" they would be subjected to during their struggle. In fact, even after the ratification of the Nineteenth Amendment in 1920, women continued to struggle to be treated as equals in the workplace and elsewhere.

When, in the course of human events, it becomes necessary for one portion of the family of man to assume among the people of the earth a position different from that which they have hitherto occupied, but one to which the laws of nature and of nature's God entitle them, a decent respect to the opinions of mankind requires that they should declare the causes that impel them to such a course.

We hold these truths to be self-evident: that all men and women are created equal; that they are endowed by their Creator with certain inalienable rights; that among these are life, liberty, and the pursuit of happiness; that to secure these rights governments are instituted, deriving their just powers from the consent of the governed. Whenever any form of government becomes destructive of these ends, it is the right of those who suffer from it to refuse allegiance to it, and to insist upon the institution of a new government, laying its foundation on such principles, and organizing its powers in such form, as to them shall seem most likely to effect their safety and happiness. Prudence, indeed, will dictate that governments long established should not be changed for light and transient causes; and accordingly all experience hath shown that mankind are more disposed to suffer, while evils are sufferable, than to right themselves by abolishing the forms to which they were accustomed. But when a long train of abuses and usurpations, pursuing invariably the same object, evinces a design to reduce them under absolute despotism, it is their duty to throw off such government, and to provide new guards for their future security. Such has been the patient sufferance of the women under this government, and such is now the necessity which constrains them to demand the equal station to which they are entitled.

The history of mankind is a history of repeated injuries and usurpations on the part of man toward woman, having in direct object the establishment of an absolute tyranny over her. To prove this, let facts be submitted to a candid world.

He has never permitted her to exercise her inalienable right to the elective franchise.

He has compelled her to submit to laws, in the formation of which she had no voice.

He has withheld from her rights which are given to the most ignorant and degraded men—both natives and foreigners.

Having deprived her of this first right of a citizen, the elective franchise, thereby leaving her without representation in the halls of legislation, he has oppressed her on all sides.

He has made her, if married, in the eye of the law, civilly dead.

He has taken from her all right in property, even to the wages she earns.

He has made her, morally, an irresponsible being, as she can commit many crimes with impunity, provided they be done in the presence of her husband. In the covenant of marriage, she is compelled to promise obedience to her husband, he becoming, to all intents and purposes, her master—the law giving him power to deprive her of her liberty, and to administer chastisement.

He has so framed the laws of divorce, as to what shall be the proper causes, and in case of separation, to whom the guardianship of the children shall be given, as to be wholly regardless of the happiness of women—the law, in all cases, going upon a false supposition of the supremacy of man, and giving all power into his hands.

After depriving her of all rights as a married woman, if single, and the owner of property, he has taxed her to support a government which recognizes her only when her property can be made profitable to it.

He has monopolized nearly all the profitable employments, and from those she is permitted to follow, she receives but a scanty remuneration. He closes against her all the avenues to wealth and distinction which he considers most honorable to himself. As a teacher of theology, medicine, or law, she is not known.

He has denied her the facilities for obtaining a thorough education, all colleges being closed against her.

He allows her in Church, as well as State, but a subordinate position, claiming Apostolic authority for her exclusion from the ministry, and, with some exceptions, from any public participation in the affairs of the Church.

He has created a false public sentiment by giving to the world a different code of morals for men and women, by which moral delinquencies which exclude women from society, are not only tolerated, but deemed of little account in man.

He has usurped the prerogative of Jehovah himself, claiming it as his right to assign for her a sphere of action, when that belongs to her conscience and to her God.

He has endeavored, in every way that he could, to destroy her confidence in her own powers, to lessen her self-respect, and to make her willing to lead a dependent and abject life.

Now, in view of this entire disfranchisement of one-half the people of this country, their social and religious degradation—in view of the unjust laws above mentioned, and because women do feel themselves aggrieved, oppressed, and fraudulently deprived of their most sacred rights, we insist that they have immediate admission to all the rights and privileges which belong to them as citizens of the United States.

In entering upon the great work before us, we anticipate no small amount of misconception, misrepresentation, and ridicule; but we shall use every instrumentality within our power to effect our object. We shall employ agents, circulate tracts, petition the State and National legislatures, and endeavor to enlist the pulpit and the press in our behalf. We hope this Convention will be followed by a series of Conventions embracing every part of the country.

# What They Were Saying

from the *Lowell Courier* (Massachusetts), 1848:

"Progress," is the grand bubble which is now blown up to balloon bulk by the windy philosophers of the age. The women folks have just held a Convention up in New York State, and passed a sort of "bill of rights," affirming it their right to vote, to become teachers, legislators, lawyers, divines, and do all and sundries the "lords" may, and of right now do. They should have resolved at the same time, that it was obligatory also upon the "lords" aforesaid, to wash dishes, scour up, be put to the tub, handle the broom, darn stockings, patch breeches, scold the servants, dress in the latest fashion, wear trinkets, look beautiful, and be as fascinating as those blessed morsels of humanity whom God gave to preserve that rough animal man, in something like a reasonable civilization. "Progress!" Progress, forever!

from the *Rochester Advertiser* (New York), 1848:

To us they [the women of the Convention] appear extremely dull and uninteresting, and, aside from their novelty, hardly worth notice.

from the *Worcester Telegraph* (Massachusetts), 1848:

Insurrection Among the Women—A female Convention has just been held at Seneca Falls, N.Y., at which was adopted a "declaration of rights," setting forth, among other things, that "all men and women are created equal, and endowed by their Creator with certain inalienable rights." The list of grievances which the Amazons exhibit, concludes by expressing a determination to insist that woman shall have "immediate admission to all the rights and privileges which belong to them as citizens of the United States." It is stated that they design, in spite of all misrepresentations and ridicule, to employ agents, circulate tracts, petition the State and National Legislatures, and endeavor to enlist the pulpit and the press in their behalf. This is boiling with a vengeance.

1850 Compromise of 1850

As the United States continued to expand, the disagreement over slavery grew only fiercer. As each new territory became large enough in population for statehood, debate inevitably centered on the issue of slavery. A careful balance was needed between free states and slavery states to keep most citizens happy. By the late 1840s the discovery of gold in the California Territory sent thousands to seek their fortunes there. This influx meant that the territory was rapidly eligible to become a state. With an equal number of slavery and free states in the Union at the time, California's antislavery constitution was seen by some in Congress as a roadblock to its admittance into the Union. One notable opponent of California's admission as a free state was Senator John C. Calhoun of South Carolina. A great debate ensued in Congress. Under the complex Compromise of 1850, authored by Senator Henry Clay of Kentucky, there were concessions to both North and South. California would be admitted to the Union as a free state, provided that fugitive slaves found in free states would be returned to their owners. The compromise also banned the slave trade (but not slavery) in the District of Columbia and provided for the land acquired from Mexico, Utah, and New Mexico to become territories without limitation on whether they eventually entered the Union as free or slavery states.

from Clay's Resolutions

It being desirable, for the peace, concord, and harmony of the Union of these States, to settle and adjust amicably all existing questions of controversy between them arising out of the institution of slavery upon a fair, equitable and just basis: therefore,

1. Resolved, That California, with suitable boundaries, ought, upon her application to be admitted as one of the States of this Union, without the imposition by Congress of any restriction in respect to the exclusion or introduction of slavery within those boundaries.

2. Resolved, That as slavery does not exist by law, and is not likely to be introduced into any of the territory acquired by the United States from the republic of Mexico, it is inexpedient for Congress to provide by law either for its introduction into, or exclusion from, any part of the said territory; and that appropriate territorial governments ought to be established by Congress in all of the said territory, not assigned as the boundaries of the proposed State of California, without the adoption of any restriction or condition on the subject of slavery. . . .

4. Resolved, That it be proposed to the State of Texas, that the United States will provide for the payment of all that portion of the legitimate and bona fide public debt of that State contracted prior to its annexation to the United States, and for which the duties on foreign imports were pledged by the said State to its creditors, not exceeding the sum of [blank] dollars, in consideration of the said duties so pledged having been no longer applicable to that object after the said annexation, but having thenceforward become payable to the United States; and upon the condition, also, that the said State of Texas shall, by some solemn and authentic act of her legislature or of a convention, relinquish to the United States any claim which it has to any part of New Mexico.

5. Resolved, That it is inexpedient to abolish slavery in the District of Columbia whilst that institution continues to exist in the State of Maryland, without the consent of that State, without the consent of the people of the District, and without just compensation to the owners of slaves within the District.

6. But, resolved, That it is expedient to prohibit, within the District, the slave trade in slaves brought into it from States or places beyond the limits of the District, either to be sold therein as merchandise, or to be transported to other markets without the District of Columbia.

7. Resolved, That more effectual provision ought to be made by law, according to the requirement of the constitution, for the restitution and delivery of persons bound to service or labor in any State, who may escape into any other State or Territory in the Union. And,

8. Resolved, That Congress has no power to promote or obstruct the trade in slaves between the slaveholding States; but that the admission or exclusion of slaves brought from one into another of them, depends exclusively upon their own particular laws.

from An Act for the Admission of the State of California into the Union.

Whereas the people of California have presented a constitution and asked admission into the Union, which constitution was submitted to Congress by the President of the United States, by message dated February thirteenth, eighteen hundred and fifty, and which, on due examination, is found to be republican in its form of government:

Be it enacted by the Senate and House of Representatives of the United States of America in Congress assembled, That the State of California shall be one, and is hereby declared to be one, of the United States of America, and admitted into the Union on an equal footing with the original States in all respects whatever.

Section 2
And be it further enacted, That, until the representatives in Congress shall be apportioned according to an actual enumeration of the inhabitants of the United States, the State of California shall be entitled to two representatives in Congress.

Section 3
And be it further enacted, That the said State of California is admitted into the Union upon the express condition that the people of said State, through their legislature or otherwise, shall never interfere with the primary disposal of the public lands within its limits, and shall pass no law and do no act whereby the title of the United States to, and right to dispose of, the same shall be impaired or questioned.

from An Act to Establish a Territorial Government for Utah

Be it enacted by the Senate and House of Representatives of the United States of America in Congress assembled, That all that part of the territory of the United States included within the following limits, to wit: bounded on the west by the State of California, on the north by the Territory of Oregon, and on the east by the summit of the Rocky Mountains, and on the south by the thirty-seventh parallel of north latitude, be, and the same is hereby, created into a temporary government, by the name of the Territory of Utah; and, when admitted as a State, the said Territory, or any portion of the same, shall be received into the Union, with or without slavery, as their constitution may prescribe at the time of their admission . . .

from An Act to Suppress the Slave Trade in the District of Columbia

Be it enacted by the Senate and House of Representatives of the United States of America in Congress assembled, That from and after the first day of January, eighteen hundred and fifty-one, it shall not be lawful to bring into the District of Columbia any slave whatever, for the purpose of being sold, or for the purpose of being placed in depot, to be subsequently transferred to any other State or place to be sold as merchandize. And if any slave shall be brought into the said District by its owner, or by the authority or consent of its owner, contrary to the provisions of this act, such slave shall thereupon become liberated and free.

from An Act to Amend, and Supplementary to, the Act Entitled "An Act Respecting Fugitives from Justice, and Persons Escaping from the Service of Their Masters"

Be it enacted by the Senate and House of Representatives of the United States of America in congress assembled, That the persons who have been, or may hereafter be, appointed commissioners, in virtue of any act of Congress, by the Circuit Courts of the United States and who, in consequence of such appointment, are authorized to exercise the powers that any justice of the peace, or other magistrate of any of the United States, may exercise in respect to offenders for any crime or offence against the United States, by arresting, imprisoning, or bailing the same under and by virtue of the thirty-third section of the act of the twenty-fourth of September seventeen hundred and eighty-nine, entitled "An Act to establish the Judicial courts of the United States," shall be, and are hereby, authorized and required to exercise and discharge all the powers and duties conferred by this act. . . .

Section 6

And be it further enacted, That when a person held to service or labor in any State or Territory of the United States, has heretofore or shall hereafter escape into another State or Territory of the United States, the person or persons to whom such service or labor may be due, or his, her, or their agent or attorney, duly authorized, by power of attorney, in writing, acknowledged and certified under the seal of some legal officer or court of the State or Territory in which the same may be executed, may pursue and reclaim such fugitive person, either by procuring a warrant from some one of the courts, judges, or commissioners aforesaid, of the proper circuit, district, or county, for the apprehension of such fugitive from service or labor, or by seizing and arresting such fugitive . . .

Section 10

And be it further enacted, That when any person held to service or labor in any State or Territory, or in the District of Columbia, shall escape therefrom, the party to whom such service or labor shall be due, his, her, or their agent or attorney, may apply to any court of record therein, or judge thereof in vacation, and make satisfactory proof to such court, or judge in vacation, of the escape aforesaid, and that the person escaping owed service or labor to such party. Whereupon the court shall cause a record to be made of the matters so proved, and also a general description of the person so escaping, with such convenient certainty as may be; and a transcript of such record, authenticated by the attestation of the clerk and of the seal of the said court, being produced in any other State, Territory, or district in which the person so escaping may be found, and being exhibited to any judge, commissioner, or other officer authorized by the law of the United States to cause persons escaping from service or labor to be delivered up, shall be held and taken to be full and conclusive evidence of the fact of escape, and that the service or labor of the person escaping is due to the party in such record mentioned. And upon the production by the said party of other and further evidence if necessary, either oral or by affidavit, in addition to what is contained in the said record of the identity of the person escaping, he or she shall be delivered up to the claimant.

 What They Were Saying

from the *Whig Almanac,* 1850:

Involving as it did the question, whether slavery should be planted on the banks of the Pacific ocean, as it has been in Texas, so that slaves might be carried to New Mexico and California as an article of traffic, and they and their posterity held in perpetual bondage, to the discouragement of free labor, but with a federal representation which should be the badge of freedom, the subject of a government for California and New Mexico occupied much of the time of the 30th Congress . . . The majority in the House struggled manfully for freedom to the great West, while several pretended Democrats from free States worked insidiously to plant slavery on the Pacific, and absorb New Mexico in Texas.

from a speech by John C. Calhoun in Congress, 1850:

The plan of the Administration cannot save the Union, because it can have no effect whatever towards satisfying the States composing the Southern section of the Union. It is, in fact, but a modification of the Wilmot Proviso. It proposes to effect the same object—to exclude the South from all territory acquired by the Mexican treaty. It is well known that the South is united against the Wilmot Proviso, and has committed itself by solemn resolution to resist, should it be adopted. Its opposition is not to the name, but that which it proposes to effect. That, the Southern States hold to be unconstitutional, unjust, inconsistent with their equality as members of the common Union, and calculated to destroy irretrievably the equilibrium between the two sections. These objections equally apply to what, for brevity, I will call the Executive Proviso. There is no difference between it and the Wilmot, except in the mode of effecting the object; and in that respect, I must say, that the latter is much the least objectionable. It goes to its object openly, boldly, and distinctly. It claims for Congress unlimited power over the Territories, and proposes to exert it over the Territories acquired from Mexico by a positive prohibition of slavery. Not so the Executive Proviso. It takes an indirect course, and, in order to elude the Wilmot Proviso and thereby avoid encountering the united and determined resistance of the South, denies, by implication, the authority of Congress to legislate for the Territories, and claims the right as belonging exclusively to the inhabitants of the Territories.

Treaty of Guadalupe Hidalgo 1848

Gadsden Purchase 1853

The Mexican War (1846–1848) began because of a disagreement between Mexico and the United States over the southern boundary of Texas. After skirmishes along the border, the United States declared war on Mexico in 1846. When the war ended, the victorious United States agreed to pay eighteen million dollars for more than five hundred thousand square miles of land (including much of what is now California and the Southwest) as part of the Treaty of Guadalupe Hidalgo. In 1853 the purchase of additional land was negotiated. Combined with the land acquired from Mexico in 1848, the border of the United States extended farther south (encompassing the bottom of present-day New Mexico and Arizona). The United States paid ten million dollars for this additional land, bringing the total amount of land gained as a result of the war with Mexico to nearly six hundred thousand square miles.

American General Winfield Scott on his triumphant entry into Mexico City, 1848.

from the Treaty of Guadalupe Hidalgo

The United States of America and the United Mexican States animated by a sincere desire to put an end to the calamities of the war which unhappily exists between the two Republics and to establish Upon a solid basis relations of peace and friendship . . .

Article I

There shall be firm and universal peace between the United States of America and the Mexican Republic, and between their respective countries, territories, cities, towns, and people, without exception of places or persons.

Article II

Immediately upon the signature of this treaty, a convention shall be entered into between a commissioner or commissioners appointed by the General-in-chief of the forces of the United States, and such as may be appointed by the Mexican Government, to the end that a provisional suspension of hostilities shall take place, and that, in the places occupied by the said forces, constitutional order may be reestablished, as regards the political, administrative, and judicial branches, so far as this shall be permitted by the circumstances of military occupation.

Article III

Immediately upon the ratification of the present treaty by the Government of the United States, orders shall be transmitted to the commanders of their land and naval forces, requiring the latter (provided this treaty shall then have been ratified by the Government of the Mexican Republic, and the ratifications exchanged) immediately to desist from blockading any Mexican ports and requiring the former (under the same condition) to commence, at the earliest moment practicable, withdrawing all troops of the United States then in the interior of the Mexican Republic . . .

Article V

The boundary line established by this article shall be religiously respected by each of the two republics, and no change shall ever be made therein, except by the express and free consent of both nations, lawfully given by the General Government of each, in conformity with its own constitution. . . .

Article VIII

Mexicans now established in territories previously belonging to Mexico, and which remain for the future within the limits of the United States, as defined by the present treaty, shall be free to continue where they now reside, or to remove at any time to the Mexican Republic, retaining the property which they possess in the said territories, or disposing thereof, and removing the proceeds wherever they please, without their being subjected, on this account, to any contribution, tax, or charge whatever.

Those who shall prefer to remain in the said territories may either retain the title and rights of Mexican citizens, or acquire those of citizens of the United States. But they shall be under the obligation to make their election within one year from the date of the exchange of ratifications of this treaty; and those who shall remain in the said territories after the expiration of that year, without having declared their intention to retain the character of Mexicans, shall be considered to have elected to become citizens of the United States . . .

Article XII

In consideration of the extension acquired by the boundaries of the United States, as defined in the fifth article of the present treaty, the Government of the United States engages to pay to that of the Mexican Republic the sum of fifteen millions of dollars . . .

Article XXIII

This treaty shall be ratified by the President of the United States of America, by and with the advice and consent of the Senate thereof; and by the President of the Mexican Republic, with the previous approbation of its general Congress.

from the Gadsden Purchase

The Republic of Mexico and the United States of America desiring to remove every cause of disagreement which might interfere in any manner with the better friendship and intercourse between the two countries . . . have agreed upon the articles following:

Article I

The Mexican Republic agrees to designate the following as her true limits with the United States for the future: retaining the same dividing line between the two Californias as already defined and established, according to the 5th article of the treaty of Guadalupe Hidalgo, the limits between the two republics shall be as follows: Beginning in the Gulf of Mexico, three leagues from land, opposite the mouth of the Rio Grande, as provided in the 5th article of the treaty of Guadalupe Hidalgo; thence, as defined in the said article, up the middle of that river to the point where the parallel of 31° 47' north latitude crosses the same; thence due west one hundred miles; thence south to the parallel of 31° 20' north latitude; thence along the said parallel of 31° 20' to the 111th meridian of longitude west of Greenwich; thence in a straight line to a point on the Colorado River twenty English miles below the junction of the Gila and Colorado rivers; thence up the middle of the said river Colorado until it intersects the present line between the United States and Mexico . . .

Article III

In consideration of the foregoing stipulations, the Government of the United States agrees to pay to the government of Mexico, in the city of New York, the sum of ten millions of dollars, of which seven millions shall be paid immediately upon the exchange of the ratifications of this treaty, and the remaining three millions as soon as the boundary line shall be surveyed, marked, and established.

Article VII

Should there at any future period (which God forbid) occur any disagreement between the two nations which might lead to a rupture of their relations and reciprocal peace, they bind themselves in like manner to procure by every possible method the adjustment of every difference.

What They Were Saying

from *The Mexican War*, 1849:

By this war the United States acquired an immense extent of territory, of which the value and consequence are yet to be developed. It is too soon to tell the effect to be produced by the acquisition. Such consequences as have followed it immediately could in no manner have been imagined or foretold. Difficulties have followed as they invariably follow the consummation of all human desires, either personal or national. Party strife has found abundant aliment in the various questions which have arisen concerning the disposition of the conquest. The discovery of the astonishing amount of gold within its limits has already given scope for the exercise of human avarice, which may prove, as in other days and under other circumstances, most eminently disastrous. But the effects remain to be seen, for the wisest statesmen are seldom aright in their predictions of consequences which are to flow from such causes as already have existence.

from *Travels on the Western Slope of Mexican Cordillera*, 1857:

The Gadsden Purchase, in the northern portion of the Republic of Mexico, produced at the time of its transfer quite a sensation of discontent, especially among a class of politicians then

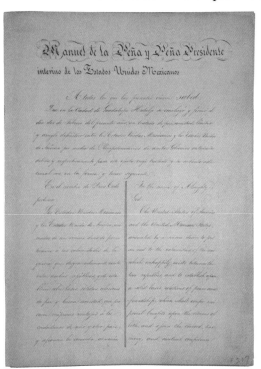

opposed to the conceding administration, and also in the more northern States of the Republic . . . This territory is reputed to abound in rich mines of gold and silver; and also of copper . . . Much has been said with reference to the bad taste and policy of the United States government making and endorsing the Gadsden Purchase, and perhaps the amount paid for it may, to a casual observer, seem extravagant. However, in the consummation of this national acquisition, there were two great and prominent objects in view. The first and paramount, was to obtain . . . a release from an obligation entered into at the confirmation of the Hidalgo treaty with Mexico, stipulating that the United States should protect the northern borders of this Republic from the inroads and depredations of the Indian hordes living north of the boundary line. And the second was the acquirement of a territory which, viewed in every light and consideration, should, the seasons round, most promote the interest and commerce of the United States and the world at large.

The Treaty of Guadalupe Hidalgo.

Kansas-Nebraska Act 1854

Senator Stephen Douglas of Illinois brought forth a bill in Congress that would have settlers in Kansas and Nebraska decide if slavery would be allowed when these states entered the Union (similar to what was proposed for Utah and New Mexico under the Compromise of 1850). This controversial bill contradicted the Missouri Compromise of 1820, which had banned slavery north of Missouri. Despite much opposition, the bill passed. It was at this time that some Northern Democrats broke away from their party and formed the Republican Party with an antislavery platform.

Next followed a long struggle over Kansas between pro-slavery and antislavery forces, both in Congress and in Kansas itself. In 1856, Congressman Brooks of South Carolina physically attacked Senator Charles Sumner of Massachusetts while the Congress was in session. Brooks smashed Sumner three times on the head with a cane, saying, "I have come over from the House to chastise you for the remarks that you made. I have read your speech [about Kansas], it is a libel on South Carolina and against my relative Senator Butler." The Kansas-Nebraska Bill promoted what became known as "squatter sovereignty"; pro- and antislavery supporters each tried to entice people to settle in Kansas. The side that gained the majority might prevail in the vote for or against slavery. Kansas was finally admitted as a free state in January 1861—three months before the Civil War began but after four states had seceded (and taken with them their representation in Congress). By the time Nebraska was admitted in 1867 the war was over and slavery had been abolished.

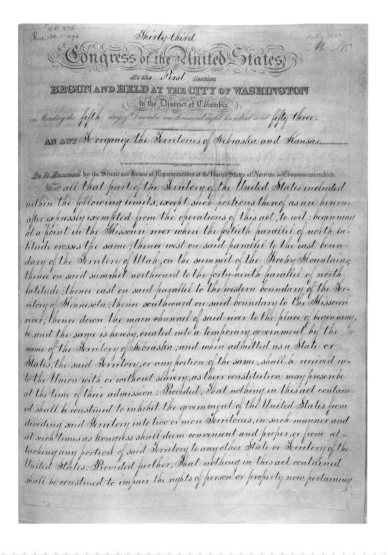

Be it enacted by the Senate and House of Representatives of the United States of America in Congress assembled, That all that part of the territory of the United States included within the following limits, except such portions thereof as are hereinafter expressly exempted from the operations of this act, to wit: beginning at a point in the Missouri River where the fortieth parallel of north latitude crosses the same; then west on said parallel to the east boundary of the Territory of Utah, the summit of the Rocky Mountains; thence on said summit northwest to the forty-ninth parallel of north latitude; thence east on said parallel to the western boundary of the territory of Minnesota; thence southward on said boundary to the Missouri River; thence down the main channel of said river to the place of beginning, be, and the same is hereby, created into a temporary government by the name of the Territory Nebraska; and when admitted as a State or States, the said Territory or any portion of the same, shall be received into the Union with without slavery, as their constitution may prescribe at the time of the admission . . .

Section 10

And be it further enacted, That the provisions of an act entitled "An act respecting fugitives from justice, and persons escaping from the service of their masters," approved February twelve, seventeen hundred and ninety-three, and the provisions of the act entitled "An act to amend, and supplementary to, the aforesaid act," approved September eighteen, eighteen hundred and fifty, be, and the same are hereby, declared to extend to and be in full force within the limits of said Territory of Nebraska. . . .

Section 14

And be it further enacted . . . That the Constitution, and all Laws of the United States which are not locally inapplicable, shall have the same force and effect within the said Territory of Nebraska as elsewhere within the United States, except the eighth section of the act preparatory to the admission of Missouri into the Union approved March sixth, eighteen hundred and twenty, which, being inconsistent with the principle of non-intervention by Congress with slaves in the States and Territories, as recognized by the legislation of eighteen hundred and fifty, commonly called the Compromise Measures, is hereby declared inoperative and void; it being the true intent and meaning of this act not to legislate slavery into any Territory or State, nor to exclude it therefrom, but to leave the people thereof perfectly free to form an regulate their domestic institutions in their own way, subject only to the Constitution of the United States: Provided, That nothing herein contained shall be construed to revive or put in force any law or regulation which may have existed prior to the act of sixth March, eighteen hundred and twenty, either protecting, establishing, prohibiting, or abolishing slavery. . . .

Section 19

And be it further enacted, That all that part of the Territory of the United States included within the following limits. . . . be, and the same is hereby, created into a temporary government by the name of the Territory of Kansas; and when admitted as a State or States, the said Territory, or any portion of the same, shall be received into the Union with or without slavery, as their Constitution may prescribe at the time of their admission . . .

Section 28

And be it further enacted, That the provisions of the act entitled "An act respecting fugitives from justice, and persons escaping from, the service of their masters," approved February twelfth, seventeen hundred and ninety-three, and the provisions of the act entitled "An act to amend, and supplementary to, the aforesaid act," approved September eighteenth, eighteen hundred and fifty, be, and the same are hereby, declared to extend to and be in full force within the limits of the said Territory of Kansas. . . .

> *Section 32*
>
> And be it further enacted . . . That the Constitution, and all laws of the United States which are not locally inapplicable, shall have the same force and effect within the said Territory of Kansas as elsewhere within the United States, except the eighth section of the act preparatory to the admission of Missouri into the Union, approved March sixth, eighteen hundred and twenty, which, being inconsistent with the principle of non-intervention by Congress with slavery in the States and Territories, as recognized by the legislation of eighteen hundred and fifty, commonly called the Compromise Measures, is hereby declared inoperative and void; it being the true intent and meaning of this act not to legislate slavery into any Territory or State, nor to exclude it therefrom, but to leave the people thereof perfectly free to form and regulate their domestic institutions in their own way, subject only to the Constitution of the United States.

 What They Were Saying

from the Republican Party Platform, 1856:

We demand, and shall attempt to secure the repeal of all laws which allow the introduction of slavery into Territories once consecrated to freedom, and will resist, by every Constitutional means, the existence of Slavery in any of the Territories of the United States. We will support, by every lawful means, our brethren in Kansas, in their Constitutional and manly resistance to the usurped authority of their lawless invaders, and will give the full weight of our political power in favor of the immediate admission of Kansas into the Union, as a free, sovereign State. Believing that the present National Administration has shown itself to be weak and faithless, and that its continuance in power is identified with the progress of the slave power to national supremacy, with the exclusion of freedom from the Territories, and with increasing civil discord, it is a leading purpose in our organization to oppose and overthrow it.

from a speech by J. M. Quarles, Senator from Tennessee, on the admission of Kansas, 1860:

I had hoped . . . when this subject, so fruitful of strife, both within the borders of Kansas and throughout the entire land, came again before the American Congress, it would be under such circumstances as to preclude debate; that we might in silence, if not with a smile of approval, seat this, our youngest sister, at our council board . . .

1857 Dred Scott Decision

The *Dred Scott* case (*Dred Scott v. Sandford*) ranks as one of the most important and one of the most controversial Supreme Court decisions in our nation's history. It came at a time when the nation was seriously divided on the slavery issue and only a few years away from a costly civil war. Dred Scott was a slave from the slave state of Missouri who had lived for years with his master in free states and territories. He believed living in a free state had nullified his status as a slave. He first sued for his freedom in 1846, but it took ten years for the case to make its way to the nation's highest court. The case dealt with such thorny issues as whether a slave had the same rights as another human being or should be considered as property. The majority decision declared that it was up to each individual state what rights to confer upon its residents. Unfortunately, for that reason, "He may have all of the rights and privileges of the citizen of a State, and yet not be entitled to the rights and privileges of a citizen in any other State." In handing down this decision, the Supreme Court also declared the Missouri Compromise to be unconstitutional. Ironically, in 1857 the woman who owned Dred Scott married a man who was opposed to slavery. Dred Scott was returned to a family who had owned him before 1830, and that family granted him his freedom.

Though slavery was abolished once and for all when the war ended in 1865, the Supreme Court's *Plessy v. Ferguson* decision of 1896 was another setback for the rights of African Americans. In that case, a man who was one-eighth black was found guilty of refusing to leave a whites-only train car. The Court's ruling said that the state could consider Plessy to be African American if it wished, and it also said that segregation was not unconstitutional.

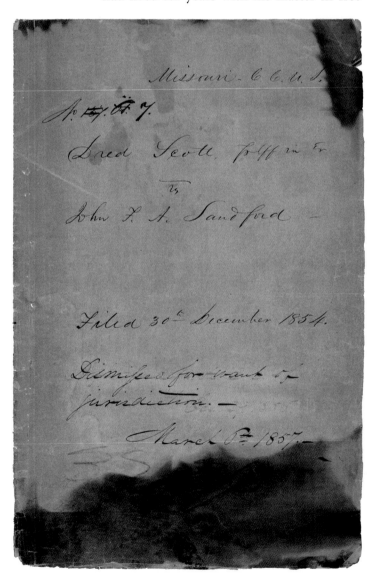

The question is simply this: Can a negro, whose ancestors were imported into this country, and sold as slaves, become a member of the political community formed and brought into existence by the Constitution of the United States, and as such become entitled to all the rights, and privileges, and immunities, guarantied by that instrument to the citizen? One of which rights is the privilege of suing in a court of the United States in the cases specified in the Constitution. . . .

It is not the province of the court to decide upon the justice or injustice, the policy or impolicy, of these laws. The decision of that question belonged to the political or lawmaking power; to those who formed the sovereignty and framed the Constitution. The duty of the court is to interpret the instrument they have framed, with the best lights we can obtain on the subject, and to administer it as we find it, according to its true intent and meaning when it was adopted.

In discussing this question, we must not confound the rights of citizenship which a State may confer within its own limits and the rights of citizenship as a member of the Union. It does not by any means follow, because he has all the rights and privileges of a citizen of a State, that he must be a citizen of the United States. He may have all of the rights and privileges of the citizen of a State, and yet not be entitled to the rights and privileges of a citizen in any other State. For, previous to the adoption of the Constitution of the United States, every State had the undoubted right to confer on whomsoever it pleased the character of citizen, and to endow him with all its rights. But this character of course was confined to the boundaries of the State, and gave him no rights or privileges in other States beyond those secured to him by the laws of nations and the comity of States. Nor have the several States surrendered the power of conferring these rights and privileges by adopting the Constitution of the United States. Each State may still confer them upon an alien, or any one it thinks proper, or upon any class or description of persons; yet he would not be a citizen in the sense in which that word is used in the Constitution of the United States, nor entitled to sue as such in one of its courts, nor to the privileges and immunities of a citizen in the other States. The rights which he would acquire would be restricted to the State which gave them. . . .

The question then arises, whether the provisions of the Constitution, in relation to the personal rights and privileges to which the citizen of a State should be entitled, embraced the negro African race, at that time in this country, or who might afterwards be imported, who had then or should afterwards be made free in any State; and to put it in the power of a single State to make him a citizen of the United States, and endue him with the full rights of citizenship in every other State without their consent? Does the Constitution of the United States act upon him whenever he shall be made free under the laws of a State, and raised there to the rank of a citizen, and immediately clothe him with all the privileges of a citizen in every other State, and in its own courts?

The court think the affirmative of these propositions cannot be maintained. And if it cannot, the plaintiff in error could not be a citizen of the State of Missouri, within the meaning of the Constitution of the United States, and, consequently, was not entitled to sue in its courts. . . .

In the opinion of the court, the legislation and histories of the times, and the language used in the Declaration of Independence, show that neither the class of persons who had been imported as slaves, nor their descendants, whether they had become free or not, were then acknowledged as a part of the people, nor intended to be included in the general words used in that memorable instrument. . . .

The language of the Declaration of Independence . . . proceeds to say: "We hold these truths to be self-evident: that all men are created equal; that they are endowed by their Creator with certain unalienable rights; that among them is life, liberty, and the pursuit of happiness; that to secure these rights, Governments are instituted, deriving their just powers from the consent of the governed."

The general words above quoted would seem to embrace the whole human family, and if they were used in a similar instrument at this day would be so understood. But it is too clear for dispute that the enslaved African race were not intended to be included, and formed no part of the people who framed and adopted this declaration . . .

And upon a full and careful consideration of the subject, the court is of opinion, that, upon the facts stated in the plea in abatement, Dred Scott was not a citizen of Missouri within the meaning of the Constitution of the United States, and not entitled as such to sue in its courts; and, consequently, that the Circuit Court had no jurisdiction of the case, and that the judgment on the plea in abatement is erroneous. . . .

And an act of Congress which deprives a citizen of the United States of his liberty or property, merely because he came himself or brought his property into a particular Territory of the United States, and who had committed no offence against the laws, could hardly be dignified with the name of due process of law . . .

It seems, however, to be supposed that there is a difference between property in a slave and other property, and that different rules may be applied to it in expounding the Constitution of the United States. . . . if the Constitution recognizes the right of property of the master in a slave, and makes no distinction between that description of property and other property owned by a citizen, no tribunal, acting under the authority of the United States, whether it be legislative, executive, or judicial, has a right to draw such a distinction, or deny to it the benefit of the provisions and guarantees which have been provided for the protection of private property against the encroachments of the Government.

Now, as we have already said in an earlier part of this opinion, upon a different point, the right of property in a slave is distinctly and expressly affirmed in the Constitution. The right to traffic in it, like an ordinary article of merchandise and property, was guarantied to the citizens of the United States, in every State that might desire it, for twenty years. And the Government in express terms is pledged to protect it in all future time, if the slave escapes from his owner. This is done in plain words too plain to be misunderstood.

And no word can be found in the Constitution which gives Congress a greater power over slave property, or which entitles property of that kind to less protection that property of any other description. The only power conferred is the power coupled with the duty of guarding and protecting the owner in his rights.

Upon these considerations, it is the opinion of the court that the act of Congress which prohibited a citizen from holding and owning property of this kind in the territory of the United States north of the line therein mentioned, is not warranted by the Constitution, and is therefore void; and that neither Dred Scott himself, nor any of his family, were made free by being carried into this territory; even if they had been carried there by the owner, with the intention of becoming a permanent resident. . . .

As Scott was a slave when taken into the State of Illinois by his owner, and was there held as such, and brought back in that character, his status, as free or slave, depended on the laws of Missouri, and not of Illinois. . . .

Upon the whole, therefore, it is the judgment of this court, that it appears by the record before us that the plaintiff in error is not a citizen of Missouri, in the sense in which that word is used in the Constitution; and that the Circuit Court of the United States, for that reason, had no jurisdiction in the case, and could give no judgment in it. Its judgment for the defendant must, consequently, be reversed, and a mandate issued, directing the suit to be dismissed for want of jurisdiction.

What They Were Saying

from a speech by Abraham Lincoln, 1858:

"A house divided against itself cannot stand." I believe this government cannot endure, permanently half slave and half free.

I do not expect the Union to be dissolved—I do not expect the house to fall—but I do expect it will cease to be divided. It will become all one thing or all the other. Either the opponents of slavery will arrest the further spread of it, and place it where the public mind shall rest in the belief that it is in the course of ultimate extinction; or its advocates will push it forward, till it shall become alike lawful in all the States, old as well as new—North as well as South. Have we no tendency to the latter condition?

Let any one who doubts, carefully contemplate that now almost complete legal combination—piece of machinery so to speak—compounded of the Nebraska doctrine, and the Dred Scott decision.

from *The Slave Power: Its Character, Career, and Probable Designs*, 1863:

Such was the momentous decision in the Dred Scott case. Its effect was to reverse the fundamental assumption upon which up to that time society in the Union had been based; and, whereas formerly freedom had been regarded as the rule and slavery the exception, to make slavery in future the rule of the Constitution. According to the law, as expounded by the Chief Justice of the Supreme Court, it was now competent to a slaveholder to carry his slaves not merely into any portion of the Territories, but, if it pleased him, into any of the Free States, to establish himself with his slave retinue in Ohio or Massachusetts, in Pennsylvania or New York, and to hold his slaves in bondage there, the regulations of Congress or the laws of the particular state to the contrary notwithstanding. The Union, if this doctrine were to be accepted, was henceforth a single slave-holding domain, in every part of which property in human beings was equally sacred. So sweeping were the consequences involved in the Dred Scott decision . . . The Slave Power had thus accomplished its first object. The Constitution had been turned against itself, and . . . the right to extend slavery over the whole area of the Union was declared by the highest tribunal in the Republic to be good in constitutional law.

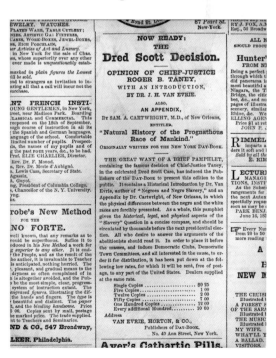

Advertisement for a pamphlet on the
Dred Scott *Decision, 1859.*

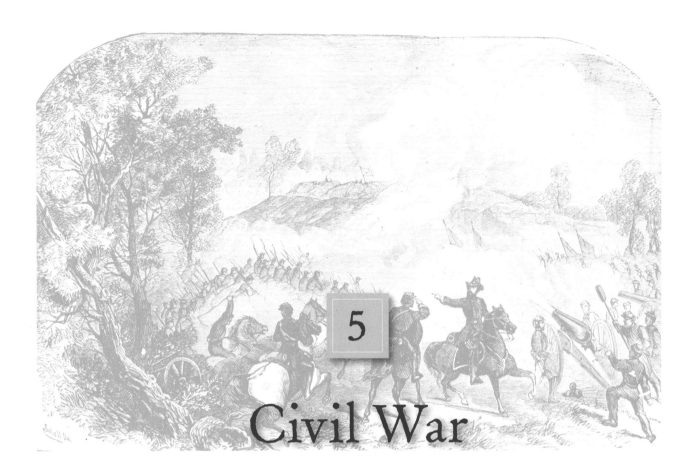

5

Civil War

★★

When the Civil War finally began in 1861, many in government had been expecting it despite their fervent hope that it would never happen. The four-year-long conflict mightily taxed the resources of both the North and the South, yet Lincoln's government was nonetheless productive and able to pass major legislation aimed at expanding the nation westward. The Homestead Act provided government land to settlers, the Pacific Railway Act provided for an expansion of the rail transportation network all the way to the West Coast, and the Morrill Act provided land for agricultural colleges. As the war continued, Lincoln's eloquence on the battlefield at Gettysburg, Pennsylvania, reflected his stature as a wartime leader. Lincoln's assassination just as the war ended proved to be an omen for the difficult years of Reconstruction that lay ahead.

1861 Constitution of the Confederate States of America

By the time the Confederate Constitution was created, several states had already seceded from the Union. The fact that the Southern states adopted their own Constitution was a sign of the gravity of the crisis facing the country. It was the South's attempt to legitimize its secession and organize its own government. In actuality, the Confederate Constitution was a moderately edited version of the United States' Constitution. Much of it was identical, except a few key places—slavery was allowed in all states and territories of the Confederacy, and term limits would be imposed for the president, for example. Among other edits, the words "invoking the favor and guidance of Almighty God" were added.

We, the People of the Confederated States, each State acting in its sovereign and independent character, in order to form a permanent Federal government, establish Justice, insure domestic Tranquillity, and secure the Blessings of Liberty to ourselves and our Posterity, invoking the favor and guidance of Almighty God, do ordain and establish this Constitution for the Confederate States of America. . . .

Article II, Section I
The executive power shall be vested in a President of the Confederate States of America. He and the Vice President shall hold their offices for the term of six years; but the President shall not be re-eligible. The President and Vice President shall be elected as follows . . .

Article IV, Section III
Other States may be admitted into this Confederacy by a vote of two-thirds of the whole House of Representatives and two-thirds of the Senate, the Senate voting by States; but no new State shall be formed or erected within the Jurisdiction of any other State; nor any State be formed by the Junction of two or more States, or Parts of States, without the Consent of the Legislatures of the States concerned as well as of the Congress.

The Congress shall have Power to dispose of and make all needful Rules and Regulations concerning the property of the Confederate States, including the lands thereof.

The Confederate States may acquire new territory, and Congress shall have power to legislate and provide governments for the inhabitants of all territory belonging to the Confederate States lying without the limits of the several States, and may permit them, at such times and in such manner as it may by law provide, to form States to be admitted into the Confederacy. In all such territory the institution of negro slavery as it now exists in the Confederate States shall be recognized and protected by Congress and by the territorial government, and the inhabitants of the several Confederate States and territories shall have the right to take to such territory any slaves lawfully held by them in any of the States or Territories of the Confederate States.

 What They Were Saying

from a speech by Alexander Stephens, soon-to-be vice president of the Confederacy, 1861:

We are in the midst of one of the greatest epochs in our history. The last ninety days will mark one of the most interesting eras in the history of modern civilization.

Seven States have in the last three months thrown off an old government and formed a new. This revolution has been signally marked, up to this time, by the fact of its having been accomplished without the loss of a single drop of blood. This new constitution, or form of government . . . amply secures all our ancient rights, franchises, and liberties. All the great principles of Magna Charta are retained in it. No citizen is deprived of life, liberty, or property, but by the judgment of his peers under the laws of the land. The great principle of religious liberty, which was the honor and pride of the old Constitution, is still maintained and secured. All the essentials of the old Constitution, which have endeared it to the hearts of the American people, have been preserved and perpetuated. Some changes have been made. Some of these I should prefer not to have seen made; but other important changes do meet my cordial approbation. They form great improvements upon the old Constitution. So, taking the whole new constitution, I have no hesitancy in giving it as my judgment that it is decidedly better than the old. . . .

The Constitution, it is true, secured every essential guarantee to the institution while it should last, and hence no argument can be justly urged against the constitutional guaranties thus secured, because of the common sentiment of the day. Those ideas, however, were fundamentally wrong. They rested upon the assumption of the equality of races. This was an error. It was a sandy foundation, and the government built upon it fell when "the storm came and the wind blew."

Our new government is founded upon exactly the opposite idea; its foundations are laid, its corner-stone rests, upon the great truth that the negro is not equal to the white man, that slavery—subordination to the superior race—is his natural and normal condition.

from a speech by Abraham Lincoln, 1861:

The States have their status in the Union, and they have no other legal status. If they break from this, they can only do so against law and by revolution. The Union, and not themselves separately, procured their independence and their liberty. By conquest or purchase the Union gave each of them whatever of independence or liberty it has. The Union is older than any of the States, and, in fact, it created them as States. Originally some dependent colonies made the Union, and, in turn, the Union threw off their old dependence for them, and made them States, such as they are. Not one of them ever had a State constitution independent of the Union . . .

What is now combated is the position that secession is consistent with the Constitution—is lawful and peaceful. It is not contended that there is any express law for it; and nothing should ever be implied as law which leads to unjust or absurd consequences. The nation purchased with money the countries out of which several of these States were formed. Is it just that they shall go off without leave and without refunding? The nation paid very large sums (in aggregate, I believe, nearly a hundred millions) to relieve Florida the aboriginal tribes. Is it just that she shall now be off with-out consent or without making any return! The nation is now in debt for money applied to the benefit of these so-called seceding States in common with the rest. Is it just either that creditors shall go unpaid or the remaining States pay the whole? A part of the present national debt was contracted to pay the old debts of Texas, it just that she shall leave and pay no part of this herself?

Again, if one State may secede, so may another; and when all shall have seceded, none is left to pay the debts. Is this quite just to creditors? Did we notify them of this sage view of ours when we borrowed their money? If we now recognize this doctrine by allowing the seceders to go in peace, it is difficult to see what we do it others choose to go or to extort terms upon which they will promise to remain.

The Confederate States of America issued war bonds to help pay for the Civil War. This one for thirty dollars is dated 1864 and was to be repaid after the war.

Homestead Act 1862

In the early 1860s the American frontier was still wide open. Vast areas of the country between the Mississippi River and the West Coast were still undeveloped. Millions of acres of fertile land owned by the United States government lay unclaimed. According to the 1860 federal census, the population of Oregon was just fifty-two thousand; Washington, eleven thousand five hundred; Colorado, thirty-four thousand; Nevada, less than seven thousand; Nebraska, about twenty-eight thousand; and the Dakota Territory, just five thousand. In 1860, the short-lived Pony Express ran from Missouri to California before it was made obsolete by the telegraph and the railroad. In the decades following the California gold strike of 1848, settlers discovered that silver and copper deposits in Nevada and elsewhere were also quite profitable. They flocked to the rich farmland in the Midwest and later to the wide-open vistas of natural beauty in what would become the states of Colorado, Wyoming, Montana, and Idaho.

In an attempt to encourage the settling of the West, Congress passed the Homestead Act in 1862. President Lincoln signed the act into law on May 20, 1862. This breakthrough legislation proclaimed that heads of families, citizens, or even foreign-born people who had declared their intention to become citizens (over the age of twenty-one) could obtain as many as 160 acres for free, with just a ten dollar fee for the transaction plus a two dollar fee for the land agent. The land was not fully owned by the claimant until he had been on the land for five years, built a house, and made improvements. Another six dollar fee, and the land was permanently granted to the settler. More than one million acres were granted under this act by the time the Civil War ended. In the first two years the Homestead Act was in effect, most of the land was given in Michigan, Minnesota, and Wisconsin. By 1871, the top states had shifted west to Kansas and Nebraska. Most settlers of the American frontier had the drive and the enthusiasm to make their lives a success. This act provided settlers with the land to help them accomplish it—160 acres of the American dream. By the time the act was finally repealed in 1976, a total of 270 million acres of land had been given out.

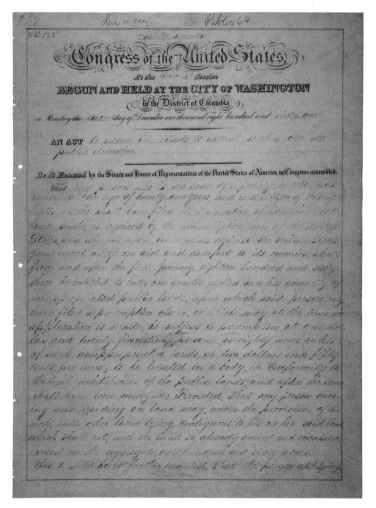

Be it enacted by the Senate and House of Representatives of the United States of America in Congress assembled, That any person who is the head of a family, or who has arrived at the age of twenty-one years, and is a citizen of the United States, or who shall have filed his declaration of intention to become such, as required by the naturalization laws of the United States, and who has never borne arms against the United States Government or given aid and comfort to its enemies, shall, from and after the first January, eighteen hundred and sixty-three, be entitled to enter one quarter section or a less quantity of unappropriated public lands, upon which said person may have filed a preemption claim, or which may, at the time the application is made, be subject to preemption at one dollar and twenty-five cents, or less, per acre; or eighty acres or less of such unappropriated lands, at two dollars and fifty cents per acre, to be located in a body, in conformity to the legal subdivisions of the public lands, and after the same shall have been surveyed: Provided, That any person owning and residing on land may, under the provisions of this act, enter other land lying contiguous to his or her said land, which shall not, with the land so already owned and occupied, exceed in the aggregate one hundred and sixty acres.

Section 2
And be it further enacted, That the person applying for the benefit of this act shall, upon application to the register of the land office in which he or she is about to make such entry, make affidavit before the said register or receiver that he or she is the head of a family, or is twenty-one years or more of age, or shall have performed service in the army or navy of the United States, and that he has never borne arms against the Government of the United States or given aid and comfort to its enemies, and that such application is made for his or her exclusive use and benefit, and that said entry is made for the purpose of actual settlement and cultivation, and not either directly or indirectly for the use or benefit of any other person or persons whomsoever; and upon filing the said affidavit with the register or receiver, and on payment of ten dollars, he or she shall thereupon be permitted to enter the quantity of land specified.

What They Were Saying

President Andrew Johnson, 1865:

The homestead policy was established only after long and earnest resistance. Experience proves its wisdom. The lands in the hands of industrious settlers, whose labor creates wealth and contributes to the public resources, are worth more to the United States than if they had been reserved as a solitude for future purchasers.

from *The Public Domain: Its History With Statistics*, 1881:

The homestead act is now the approved and preferred method of acquiring title to the public lands. It has stood the test of eighteen years, and was the outgrowth of a system extending through nearly eighty years, and now, within the circle of a hundred years since the United States acquired the first of her public lands, the homestead act stands as the concentrated wisdom of legislation for settlement of the public lands. It protects the Government, it fills the States with homes, it builds up communities, and lessens the chances of social and civil disorder by giving ownership of the soil, in small tracts, to the occupants thereof. It was copied from no other nation's system. It was originally and distinctively American, and remains a monument to its originators.

Pacific Railway Act 1862

The California Gold Rush of the late 1840s and the following settlement of the future states of Colorado, Utah, Washington, Nevada, and Oregon made one thing clear—if the nation were to continue its phenomenal growth and fulfill its manifest destiny, transportation had to be improved. While railroads were popping up in various locations across the country, there was no easy way for prospective settlers to reach the West Coast. The trip by wagon was long and dangerous, and best made in groups. Goods and supplies from the east were expensive and hard to come by. The Pacific Railway Act recognized the potential of the railroad to decrease travel time and encourage settlement and commerce. Work on the railroad began in earnest with a Union Pacific Railroad crew starting at San Francisco and a Central Pacific crew working west from Omaha, Nebraska. Two golden spikes were hammered home with much fanfare as the tracks met at Promontory Summit, Utah, on May 10, 1869. Engineers from the Union Pacific and Central Pacific drove their trains upon the last feet of completed track until their trains met, and then the engineers shook hands and smashed champagne bottles upon each other's trains. The good news was instantly telegraphed across the nation.

The effect on further development of railroads was dramatic. Between 1870 and 1880, the number of miles of tracks in the country doubled from forty thousand to eighty thousand miles. Other railroads receiving federal land grants were the Northern Pacific, with tracks from Minnesota to Washington; the Kansas Pacific, from Kansas City to Denver, Colorado; and the South Pacific and Atlantic & Pacific Railroads from California to what would later become Arizona and New Mexico.

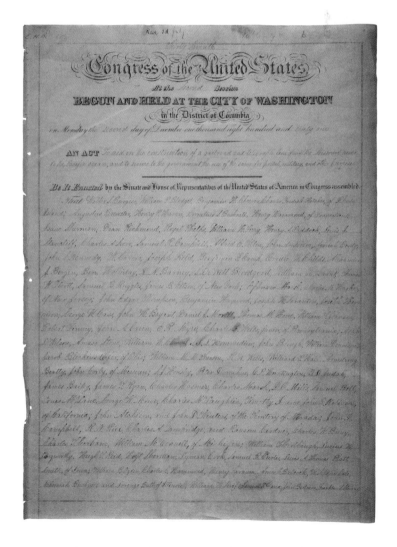

Be it enacted by the Senate and House of Representatives of the United States of America in Congress assembled, That [list of names] together with commissioners to be appointed by the Secretary of the Interior, and all persons who shall or may be associated with them, and their successors, are hereby created and erected into a body corporate and politic in deed and in law, by the name, style, and title of "The Union Pacific Railroad Company;" . . . the said corporation is hereby authorized and empowered to layout, locate, construct, furnish, maintain, and enjoy a continuous railroad and telegraph, with the appurtenances, from a point on the one hundredth meridian of longitude west from Greenwich, between the south margin of the valley of the Republican River and the north margin of the valley of the Platte River, in the Territory of Nebraska, to the western boundary of Nevada Territory . . .

Section 2

And be it further enacted, That the right of way through the public lands be, and the same is hereby, granted to said company for the construction of said railroad and telegraph line; and the right, power, and authority is hereby given to said company to take from the public lands adjacent to the line of said road, earth, stone, timber, and other materials for the construction thereof; said right of way is granted to said railroad to the extent of two hundred feet in width on each side of said railroad where it may pass over the public lands, including all necessary grounds for stations, buildings, workshops, and depots, machine shops, switches, side tracks, turntables, and, water stations. The United States shall extinguish as rapidly as may be the Indian titles to all lands falling under the operation of this act and required for the said right of way and; grants hereinafter made.

Section 3

And be it further enacted, That there be, and is hereby, granted to the said company, for the purpose of aiding in the construction, of said railroad and telegraph line, and to secure the safe and speedy transportation of the mails, troops, munitions of war, and public stores thereon, every alternate section of public land, designated by odd numbers, to the amount of five alternate sections per mile on each side of said railroad, on the line thereof, and within the limits often miles on each side of said road, not sold, reserved, or otherwise disposed of by the United States, and to which a preemption or homestead claim may not have attached, at the time the line of said road is definitely fixed . . .

Section 4

And be it further enacted, That whenever said company shall have completed forty consecutive miles of any portion of said railroad and telegraph line, ready for the service contemplated by this act, and supplied with all necessary drains, culverts, viaducts, crossings, sidings, bridges, turnouts, watering places, depots, equipments, furniture, and all other appurtenances of a first class railroad, the rails and all the other iron used in the construction and equipment of said road to be American manufacture of the best quality, the President of the United States shall appoint three commissioners to examine the same and report to him in relation thereto; and if it shall appear to him that forty consecutive miles of said railroad and telegraph line have been completed and equipped in all respects as required by this act, then, upon certificate of said commissioners to that effect, patents shall issue conveying the right and title to said lands to said company, on each side of the road as far as the same is completed, to the amount aforesaid; and patents shall in like manner issue as each forty miles of said railroad and telegraph line are completed, upon certificate of said commissioners. . . .

Section 9

And be it further enacted, That the Leavenworth, Pawnee, and Western Railroad Company of Kansas are hereby authorized to construct a railroad and telegraph line, from the Missouri River, at the mouth of the Kansas River, on the south side thereof, so as to connect with the Pacific railroad of Missouri, to the aforesaid point, on the one hundredth meridian of longitude west from Greenwich. . . . The Central Pacific Railroad Company of California, a corporation existing under the laws of the State of California, are hereby authorized to construct a railroad and telegraph line from the Pacific coast, at or near San Francisco, or the navigable waters of the Sacramento River, to the eastern boundary of California . . . to meet and connect with the first mentioned railroad and telegraph line on the eastern boundary of California. . . .

Section 11

And be it further enacted, That for three hundred miles of said road most mountainous and difficult of construction, to wit: one hundred and fifty miles westwardly from the eastern base of the Rocky Mountains, and one hundred and fifty miles eastwardly from the western, base of the Sierra Nevada mountains, said points to be fixed by the President of the United States, the bonds to be issued to aid in the construction thereof shall be treble the number per mile hereinbefore provided. . . .

Section 15

And be it further enacted, That any other railroad company now incorporated, or hereafter to be incorporated, shall have the right to connect their road with the road and branches provided for by this act.

What They Were Saying

from *The History of the Great Republic*, 1868:

This vast work [the transcontinental railroad] was boldly commenced by the United States in the midst of our gigantic civil war. . . . This immense undertaking is now (fall of 1867) more than half completed. The cars will doubtless pass from ocean to ocean early in the year 1870. In the mean time, American genius has rapidly improved the comfort of railroad traveling. We may now at our pleasure enjoy our saloons and refreshments in the splendid cars fitting up for this and other roads; and, when weary, at night we can retire to our state-rooms, and enjoy our repose, and wake in the morning to find that we have moved as rapidly and safely in the hours of sleep as in the day.

During the 1840s, '50s, and '60s, railroad construction was booming throughout the country. Shown are the operating expenses for the Northern Railroad for the month of November 1848.

The population of the United States was more than thirty million in 1860, and growing fast. Farming was the way of life for most Americans who lived in rural areas. In 1862 the government established the cabinet-level Department of Agriculture in recognition of the growing need to regulate, control, and support farming on a national level. The Morrill Act was another step in that direction. It provided land to each state for the purpose of establishing a new college, one that would focus mainly on agriculture and the mechanical arts (such as civil and mechanical engineering). Introduced by Justin Morrill, a congressman from Vermont, the act was a recognition by the government that agriculture was every bit as much a science as physics or biology and that its serious study would result in advances in technology and improved crops.

The agricultural studies at the schools were designed to help farmers understand farming technology and get more out of their land. Efficiency was important in the closing years of the nineteenth century because the growing urban population meant that more and more people in cities depended on farmers to grow their food. Most farmers were no longer growing food just for themselves and a small group of people living nearby. Ensuring a large crop and getting it properly stored and processed was an important step in making sure the crops eventually found their way to the city folk.

The Morrill Act was originally introduced in 1857 and passed by Congress in 1860, but was vetoed by President James Buchanan. The Senate failed to override the veto, but the bill was reintroduced after Abraham Lincoln took office. It passed in Congress again and Lincoln finally signed a modified version of the act into law in 1862. Notably, it excluded any states that were in a "condition of rebellion."

An Act Donating Public Lands to the several States and Territories which may provide Colleges for the Benefit of Agriculture and Mechanic Arts.

Be it enacted by the Senate and House of Representatives of the United States of America in Congress assembled, That there be granted to the several States, for the purpose hereinafter mentioned, an amount of public land, to be apportioned to each State a quantity equal to thirty thousand acres for each senator and representative in Congress to which the States are respectively entitled by the apportionment under the census of eighteen hundred and sixty: Provided, That no mineral lands shall be selected or purchased under the provisions of this Act. . . .

Section 2

And be it further enacted, That the land aforesaid, after being surveyed, shall be apportioned to the several States in sections or subdivisions of sections, not less than one quarter of a section; and whenever there are public lands in a State subject to sale at private entry at one dollar and twenty-five cents per acre, the quantity to which said State shall be entitled shall be selected from such lands within the limits of such State, and the Secretary of the Interior is hereby directed to issue to each of the States in which there is not the quantity of public lands subject to sale at private entry at one dollar and twenty-five cents per acre, to which said State may be entitled under the provisions of this act, land scrip to the amount in acres for the deficiency of its distributive share: said scrip to be sold by said States and the proceeds thereof applied to the uses and purposes prescribed in this Act, and for no other purpose whatsoever: Provided, That in no case shall any State to which land scrip may thus be issued be allowed to locate the same within the limits of any other State, or of any Territory of the United States, but their assignees may thus locate said land scrip upon any of the unappropriated lands of the United States subject to the sale at private entry at one dollar and twenty-five cents, or less, per acre: And provided, further, That not more than one million acres shall be located by such assignees in any one of the States: And provided, further, That no such location shall be made before one year from the passage of this Act. . . .

Section 5

Third. Any State which may take and claim the benefit of the provisions of this act shall provide, within five years from the time of its acceptance as provided in subdivision seven of this section, at least not less than one college, as described in the fourth section of this act, or the grant to such State shall cease; and said State shall be bound to pay the United States the amount received of any lands previously sold; and that the title to purchasers under the State shall be valid.

Fourth. An annual report shall be made regarding the progress of each college, recording any improvements and experiments made, with their cost and results, and such other matters, including State industrial and economical statistics, as may be supposed useful; one copy of which shall be transmitted by mail [free] by each, to all the other colleges which may be endowed under the provisions of this act, and also one copy to the Secretary of the Interior.

Fifth. When lands shall be selected from those which have been raised to double the minimum price, in consequence of railroad grants, they shall be computed to the States at the maximum price, and the number of acres proportionally diminished.

Sixth. No State while in a condition of rebellion or insurrection against the government of the United States shall be entitled to the benefit of this act.

Seventh. No State shall be entitled to the benefits of this act unless it shall express its acceptance thereof by its legislature within three years from July 23, 1866: Provided, That when any Territory shall become a State and be admitted to the Union, such a new State shall be entitled to the benefits of the said act of July two, eighteen hundred and sixty-two, by expressing the acceptance therein required within three years from the date of its admission into the Union, and providing the college or colleges within five years after such acceptance, as prescribed in this act.

What They Were Saying

from a report of the Sheffield Scientific School, Connecticut, 1872:

This institution, in common with many others of kindred character in different parts of the country, owes its present position largely to the land grant bestowed by Congress in the enactment of July 2, 1862. From this source a fund of $135,000 was received, but this was only one result of the grant. Its bestowal secured the maintenance of this School, strengthened the confidence of the instructors and the public, and elicited the generous contributions of many individuals in Connecticut and at a distance. Every year gives new evidence of the wisdom of the Congressional enactment which secured (a) local responsibility under national aid; (b) scientific education without the disparagement of literary culture; (c) scientific schools rather than simple agricultural schools; and (d) instruction funds instead of bricks and mortar.

Emancipation Proclamation

The Emancipation Proclamation, the groundbreaking document that freed all the slaves in the states that had seceded, was a long time coming. A great deal of tension during the previous few decades emanated from the central issue of slavery. With the Civil War raging, President Lincoln decided that the time was right to draft this proclamation. Though he despised slavery, the decision was still a momentous one for Lincoln. He realized that it would be in direct contradiction with the text of the Constitution that allowed slavery to exist, but he believed it was a necessary step to preserve the Union, "a fit and necessary war measure for suppressing said rebellion." On September 22, 1862, he presented to his cabinet a final draft of the proclamation that declared that as of January 1, 1863, slaves in the rebel states would be free.

At one point during the war, someone brought a petition to Lincoln asking that he pardon a man who had been convicted as a slave trader. After reading it, he said: "My friend, that is a very touching appeal to our feelings. You know my weakness is to be, if possible, too easily moved by appeals to mercy. If this man were guilty of the foulest murder that the arm of man could perpetrate, I could forgive him on such an appeal; but the man who could go to Africa, and rob her of her children, and sell them into interminable bondage, with no other motive than that which is furnished by dollars and cents, is so much worse than the most depraved murderer, that he can never receive pardon at my hands."

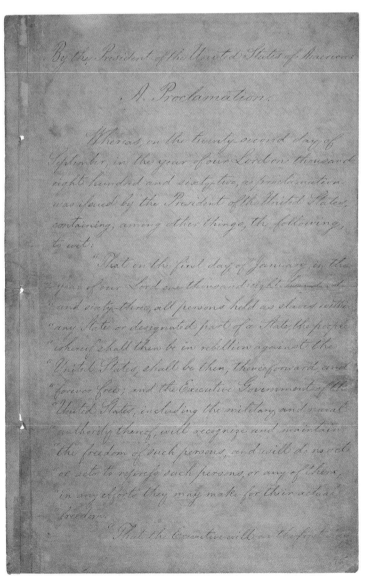

Whereas, on the twenty-second day of September, in the year of our Lord one thousand eight hundred and sixty-two, a proclamation was issued by the President of the United States, containing, among other things, the following, to wit:

"That on the first day of January, in the year of our Lord one thousand eight hundred and sixty-three, all persons held as slaves within any State or designated part of a State, the people whereof shall then be in rebellion against the United States, shall be then, thenceforward, and forever free; and the Executive Government of the United States, including the military and naval authority thereof, will recognize and maintain the freedom of such persons, and will do no act or acts to repress such persons, or any of them, in any efforts they may make for their actual freedom.

"That the Executive will, on the first day of January aforesaid, by proclamation, designate the States and parts of States, if any, in which the people thereof, respectively, shall then be in rebellion against the United States; and the fact that any State, or the people thereof, shall on that day be, in good faith, represented in the Congress of the United States by members chosen thereto at elections wherein a majority of the qualified voters of such State shall have participated, shall, in the absence of strong countervailing testimony, be deemed conclusive evidence that such State, and the people thereof, are not then in rebellion against the United States."

Now, therefore I, Abraham Lincoln, President of the United States, by virtue of the power in me vested as Commander-in-Chief, of the Army and Navy of the United States in time of actual armed rebellion against the authority and government of the United States, and as a fit and necessary war measure for suppressing said rebellion, do, on this first day of January, in the year of our Lord one thousand eight hundred and sixty-three, and in accordance with my purpose so to do publicly proclaimed for the full period of one hundred days, from the day first above mentioned, order and designate as the States and parts of States wherein the people thereof respectively, are this day in rebellion against the United States, the following, to wit:

Arkansas, Texas, Louisiana, (except the Parishes of St. Bernard, Plaquemines, Jefferson, St. John, St. Charles, St. James Ascension, Assumption, Terrebonne, Lafourche, St. Mary, St. Martin, and Orleans, including the City of New Orleans) Mississippi, Alabama, Florida, Georgia, South Carolina, North Carolina, and Virginia, (except the forty-eight counties designated as West Virginia, and also the counties of Berkley, Accomac, Northampton, Elizabeth City, York, Princess Ann, and Norfolk, including the cities of Norfolk and Portsmouth), and which excepted parts, are for the present, left precisely as if this proclamation were not issued.

And by virtue of the power, and for the purpose aforesaid, I do order and declare that all persons held as slaves within said designated States, and parts of States, are, and henceforward shall be free; and that the Executive government of the United States, including the military and naval authorities thereof, will recognize and maintain the freedom of said persons.

And I hereby enjoin upon the people so declared to be free to abstain from all violence, unless in necessary self-defence; and I recommend to them that, in all cases when allowed, they labor faithfully for reasonable wages.

And I further declare and make known, that such persons of suitable condition, will be received into the armed service of the United States to garrison forts, positions, stations, and other places, and to man vessels of all sorts in said service.

And upon this act, sincerely believed to be an act of justice, warranted by the Constitution, upon military necessity, I invoke the considerate judgment of mankind, and the gracious favor of Almighty God.

 What They Were Saying

Abraham Lincoln, 1864:

I am naturally antislavery. If slavery is not wrong, nothing is wrong. I cannot remember when I did not so think and feel. And yet I have never understood that the Presidency conferred upon me an unrestricted right to act officially upon this judgment and feeling. It was in the oath that I took, that I would, to the best of my ability, preserve, protect, and defend the Constitution of the United States . . . this oath forbade me to practically indulge my primary, abstract judgment on the moral question of slavery . . . I did understand, however, that my oath to preserve the Constitution to the best of my ability imposed upon me the duty of preserving, by every indispensable means, that government, that nation, of which the Constitution was the organic law. Was it possible to lose the nation, and yet preserve the Constitution? By general law, life and limb must be protected; yet often a limb must be amputated to save a life; but a life is never given to save a limb. I feel that measures, otherwise unconstitutional, might become lawful, by being indispensable to the preservation of the Constitution, through the preservation of the nation. Right or wrong, I assumed this ground, and now avow it.

from President Ulysses Grant's memoirs, 1885:

There was no time during the rebellion when I did not think, and often say, that the South was more to be benefited by its defeat than the North. The latter had the people, the institutions, and the territory to make a great and prosperous nation. The former was burdened with an institution abhorrent to all civilised people not brought up under it, and one which degraded labor, kept it in ignorance, and enervated the governing class.

Abraham Lincoln signs the Emancipation Proclamation.

1863 Gettysburg Address

National Cemetery Gettysburg Pa.

The bloody Battle of Gettysburg (Pennsylvania) was very costly for both the North and the South. Altogether, more than fifty-one thousand soldiers were killed or wounded between July 1 and July 3, 1863, at Gettysburg. Within months, a seventeen-acre portion of the site was set aside as the Gettysburg National Cemetery so the Union soldiers who died in the battle could receive a proper burial. On November 19, President Lincoln arrived at Gettysburg for the dedication of the cemetery and spoke only after the two-hour oration of the main speaker, Edward Everett. The first five words of this very short speech are perhaps among the most famous of any American speech ever made. Lincoln's inspirational wartime words were filled not with anger, but with thoughts of hope.

A nineteenth-century photograph of the cemetery at the Gettysburg battlefield.

Four score and seven years ago our fathers brought forth, upon this continent, a new nation, conceived in Liberty and dedicated to the proposition that all men are created equal.

Now we are engaged in a great civil war, testing whether that nation, or any nation, so conceived and so dedicated, can long endure. We are met here on a great battlefield of that war. We have come to dedicate a portion of it as a final resting place for those who here gave their lives that that nation might live. It is altogether fitting and proper that we should do this.

But in a larger sense we cannot dedicate—we cannot consecrate—we cannot hallow this ground. The brave men, living and dead, who struggled here, have consecrated it far above our poor power to add or detract. The world will little note, nor long remember, what we say here, but can never forget what they did here. It is for us, the living, rather to be dedicated here to the unfinished work which they have, thus far, so nobly carried on. It is rather for us to be here dedicated to the great task remaining before us—that from these honored dead we take increased devotion to that cause for which they gave the last full measure of devotion—that we here highly resolve that these dead shall not have died in vain; that this nation under God shall have a new birth of freedom; and that government of the people, by the people, for the people, shall not perish from the earth.

 What They Were Saying

from Edward Everett's speech at Gettysburg, November 19, 1863:

We have assembled, friends, fellow-citizens, at the invitation of the Executive of the great central State of Pennsylvania, seconded by the Governors of seventeen other loyal States of the Union, to pay the last tribute of respect to the brave men, who, in the hard-fought battles of the first, second, and third days of July last, laid down their lives for the country on these hill sides and the plains before us, and whose remains have been gathered into the cemetery which we consecrate this day.

    As my eye ranges over the fields whose sods were so lately moistened by the blood of gallant and loyal men, I feel, as never before, how truly it was said of old that it is sweet and becoming to die for one's country. I feel, as never before, how justly, from the dawn of history to the present time, men have paid the homage of their gratitude and admiration to the memory of those who nobly sacrifice their lives, that their fellow-men may live in safety and in honor. And if this tribute were, ever due, when, to whom, could it be more justly paid than to those whose last resting-place we this day commend to the blessing of Heaven and of men?

from *The Life of Abraham Lincoln*, 1866:

The brief remarks of Mr. Lincoln, though brought into immediate comparison with the elaborate eloquence of the venerable Massachusetts orator [Edward Everett], were very effective, and betrayed a degree of literary ability quite unexpected to those who had read only his formal state papers.

from *Life of Abraham Lincoln: For the Young Man and the Sabbath School*, 1868:

That "the world will little note nor long remember" what Lincoln said there, was a mistaken prophecy. It will be read and admired so long as Gettysburg is remembered as a battlefield of freedom.

Executive Mansion.

Washington, , 186

Four score and seven years ago our fathers brought forth, upon this continent, a new nation, conceived in liberty, and dedicated to the proposition that "all men are created equal"

Now we are engaged in a great civil war, testing whether that nation, or any nation so conceived, and so dedicated, can long endure. We are met on a great battle field of that war. We have come to dedicate a portion of it, as a final resting place for those who died here, that the nation might live. This we may, in all propriety do. But, in a larger sense, we can not dedicate — we can not consecrate — we can not hallow, this ground — The brave men, living and dead, who struggled here, have hallowed it, far above our poor power to add or detract. The world will little note, nor long remember what we say here; while it can never forget what they did here.

It is rather for us, the living, to stand here,

---

ted to the great task remaining before us — that, from these honored dead we take increased devotion to that cause for which they here, gave the last full measure of devotion — that we here highly resolve these dead shall not have died in vain; that the nation, shall have a new birth of freedom, and that government of the people by the people for the people, shall not perish from the earth.

Thirteenth Amendment

The outcry against slavery was not universal and hard feelings persisted after the war. The Republicans, party of Abraham Lincoln, were all for abolition. Among the Democrats, however, the feeling was somewhat different. In the Democratic Almanac for 1869, for example, the Constitution and first twelve Amendments were faithfully printed. This was followed by the headline "Amendments Claimed by the Mongrels to have been Legally Added to the Constitution" printed above the Thirteenth and Fourteenth Amendments. Nonetheless, whether they liked it or not, the days of slavery were over. The Emancipation Proclamation and Thirteenth Amendment, together abolishing and prohibiting slavery, were only the beginning. The amendment also gave Congress the authority to provide for the passage of any future laws that would help to enforce the ban on slavery. Though slavery was now legally outlawed, its legacy made life for African Americans difficult for many years to come. Slavery was illegal, but racism was not. Bias against former slaves translated to economic hardship and often violence.

An article about the Thirteenth Amendment from a Massachusetts newspaper, February 1, 1865.

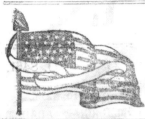

THE DAILY COURIER.

Wednesday, February 1, 1865.

PASSAGE OF THE CONSTITUTIONAL AMENDMENT TO ABOLISH SLAVERY. Yesterday the House of Representatives of the United States took a step that will render the 31st of January a memorable day in American history. By a vote of 119 to 56 —seven more than the two-thirds required by the Constitution—the House passed the proposed amendment to the Constitution, which if adopted by three-fourths of the States, forever abolishes slavery in the United States. The proposed amendment is in the following words :—

"That the following article be proposed to the Legislatures of the several States as an amendment to the Constitution of the United States, which, when ratified by three-fourths of said Legislatures, shall be valid to all intents and purposes, as a part of the said Constitution, namely :

ARTICLE XIII.

Sec. 1. Neither slavery nor involuntary servitude except as a punishment for crime, whereof the party shall have been duly convicted, shall exist within the United States, or any place subject to their jurisdiction.

Sec. 2. Congress shall have power to enforce this article by appropriate legislation."

The Senate passed the amendment last year by vote of nearly three to one, but it was rejected in the House by 94 to 63. As the House is composed of 103 Union men or Republicans, to 80 Democrats, at least 16 Democrats must have voted for the proposed bill, if all the Union members were present. English of Connecticut, and Ganson of New York, are known to have voted in its favor, and no doubt Odell of New York, voted the same way.

There was a large attendance of spectators, and when the result was known the hall rang with applause, and the ladies waved their handkerchiefs in token of approval. A salute of one hundred guns was fired in the evening in honor of the great event. Should it be necessary to go back to the Senate for the action of that body, it will there pass, and after receiving the signature of the President, immediately go the Legislatures for their action.

The bill will be adopted without delay by the following State Legislatures, which are now in session :—California, Illinois, Indiana, Iowa, Kansas, Maine, Maryland, Massachusetts, Michigan, Minnesota, Missouri, Nevada, New York, Ohio, Pennsylvania, Rhode Island, West Virginia, and Wisconsin—eighteen in all. In addition

THE PI

In the b the manufa try, Lowell position. was tried scale, with millions of of labor, w dence of th for many ki ing many k considerabl ed, the effe interests wa ferent view equal judg who had th Lowell ge adopted tl shortening the greatl works. Th was greatly ell, but it g dends with those mana the plan of most compl instant resu times shoul other cours adopted wi ful; and wh resumed, L ter conditio country, re mills in the disaster wo no disaster With capit best order, career of about enter our mills nc

Middling cents. If ed with a fu from its hig of the capit of existenc works, to s holders in c come upon in *our city*, resume wor and *works* It is not qu have so mu Lowell cor not some thank these serving the which are s perity of o cotton incr price dimin perfected operation market for think we a

> *Section 1.* Neither slavery nor involuntary servitude, except as a punishment for crime whereof the party shall have been duly convicted, shall exist within the United States, or any place subject to their jurisdiction.
>
> *Section 2.* Congress shall have power to enforce this article by appropriate legislation. . . .

What They Were Saying

from the *Lowell Daily Courier* (Massachusetts), February 1, 1865:

Yesterday the House of Representatives of the United States took a step that will render the 31st of January a memorable day in American history. By a vote of 119 to 56—seven more than the two-thirds required by the Constitution—the House passed the proposed amendment, which if adopted by three-fourths of the States, forever abolishes slavery in the United States . . . There was a large attendance of spectators, and when the result was known the hall rang with applause, and the ladies waved their handkerchiefs in token of approval. A salute of one hundred guns was fired in the evening in honor of the great event . . . Under any circumstance, the amendment may be considered as secured beyond question, and universal freedom will hereafter be the destiny of the great American Republic.

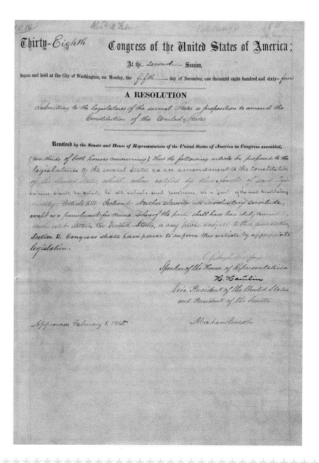

1865 Lincoln's Second Inaugural Address

Four long years of war marked Abraham Lincoln's first presidency. His other domestic accomplishments were largely overshadowed by his war-related decisions. The election of 1864 was held in a smaller United States, one that had been shorn in half by the secession of the Southern states. His opponent was the Democrat and war hero General George B. McClellan, whose platform was an immediate cessation of hostilities with the Confederate States. Though it was not looking good for Lincoln early in 1864, his reelection in the autumn of 1864 came at a time when the tides were finally turning for the Union. Sherman's march on the South was encouraging news, and it looked as though there might be hope for a Union victory.

Lincoln won by five hundred thousand popular votes and crushed McClellan in the electoral count, 212 to 21. The people had spoken and it seemed that they wanted to see the war to its conclusion rather than have a cease-fire. By the time of Lincoln's inauguration in March 1865, the end of the war seemed still nearer. He dared not make any predictions but expressed his sincere hope that the end would come soon.

He acknowledged that the war was quite simply about slavery and that the war was dragging on longer than anyone anticipated. Importantly, Lincoln proclaimed that there should be "malice toward none" and "charity for all." He offered a reconciliatory speech where he spoke of healing the wounds of a nation. Lincoln knew that in order for the Union to be whole again there would have to be a "just and lasting peace." His speech laid the groundwork for the postwar period that he would not live long enough to see.

In April 1865, just as the war was ending, Lincoln was assassinated. It was a shock to the nation and a setback at a time of crisis. It was also the first time a president had been killed. Abraham Lincoln received a fatal gunshot wound to the head while watching a play in a Washington, D.C., theater. His assassin, John Wilkes Booth, was an actor and Confederate sympathizer who had, a month before, plotted to kidnap the president. The murder was a sign of the strife that would seize the country over the next several years. The war was over but the bad feelings between North and South, Democrats and Republicans, continued through the rest of the decade.

Fellow-Countrymen: At this second appearing to take the oath of the Presidential office there is less occasion for an extended address than there was at the first. Then a statement somewhat in detail of a course to be pursued seemed fitting and proper. Now, at the expiration of four years, during which public declarations have been constantly called forth on every point and phase of the great contest which still absorbs the attention and engrosses the energies of the nation, little that is new could be presented. The progress of our arms, upon which all else chiefly depends, is as well known to the public as to myself, and it is, I trust, reasonably satisfactory and encouraging to all. With high hope for the future, no prediction in regard to it is ventured.

On the occasion corresponding to this four years ago all thoughts were anxiously directed to an impending civil war. All dreaded it, all sought to avert it. While the inaugural address was being delivered from this place, devoted altogether to saving the Union without war, insurgent agents were in the city seeking to *destroy* it without war—seeking to dissolve the Union and divide effects by negotiation. Both parties deprecated war, but one of them would make war rather than let the nation survive, and the other would accept war rather than let it perish, and the war came.

One-eighth of the whole population were colored slaves, not distributed generally over the Union, but localized in the southern part of it. These slaves constituted a peculiar and powerful interest. All knew that this interest was somehow the cause of the war. To strengthen, perpetuate, and extend this interest was the object for which the insurgents would rend the Union even by war, while the Government claimed no right to do more than to restrict the territorial enlargement of it. Neither party expected for the war the magnitude or the duration which it has already attained. Neither anticipated that the cause of the conflict might cease with or even before the conflict itself should cease. Each looked for an easier triumph, and a result less fundamental and astounding. Both read the same Bible and pray to the same God, and each invokes His aid against the other. It may seem strange that any men should dare to ask a just God's assistance in wringing their bread from the sweat of other men's faces, but let us judge not, that we be not judged. The prayers of both could not be answered. That of neither has been answered fully. The Almighty has His own purposes.

"Woe unto the world because of offenses; for it must needs be that offenses come, but woe to that man by whom the offense cometh." If we shall suppose that American slavery is one of those offenses which, in the providence of God, must needs come, but which, having continued through His appointed time, He now wills to remove, and that He gives to both North and South this terrible war as the woe due to those by whom the offense came, shall we discern therein any departure from those divine attributes which the believers in a living God always ascribe to Him?

Fondly do we hope, fervently do we pray, that this mighty scourge of war may speedily pass away. Yet, if God wills that it continue until all the wealth piled by the bondsman's two hundred and fifty years of unrequited toil shall be sunk, and until every drop of blood drawn with the lash shall be paid by another drawn with the sword, as was said three thousand years ago, so still it must be said "the judgments of the Lord are true and righteous altogether."

With malice toward none, with charity for all, with firmness in the right as God gives us to see the right, let us strive on to finish the work we are in, to bind up the nation's wounds, to care for him who shall have borne the battle and for his widow and his orphan, to do all which may achieve and cherish a just and lasting peace among ourselves and with all nations.

 What They Were Saying

from the *London Spectator*, 1865:

We cannot read it [Lincoln's inauguration speech] without a renewed Conviction that it is the noblest political document known to history, and should have for the nation, and the statesmen he left behind him, something of a sacred and almost prophetic character. Surely none was ever written under a stronger sense of the reality of God's government; and certainly none written in a period of passionate conflict ever so completely excluded the partiality of victorious faction, and breathed so pure a strain of mingled justice and mercy.

General Ulysses S. Grant to his army, 1865:

Soldiers of the Army of the United States! By your patriotic devotion to your country in the hour of danger and alarm, your magnificent fighting, bravery, and endurance, you have maintained the supremacy of the Union and the Constitution, overthrown all armed opposition to the enforcement of the laws, and of all the proclamations forever abolishing Slavery—the cause and pretext of the Rebellion—and opened the way to the rightful authorities to restore order and inaugurate peace on a permanent and enduring basis on every foot of American soil. Your marches, sieges, and battles, in distance, duration, resolution, and brilliancy of results, dim the luster of the world's past military achievements, and will be the patriot's precedent in defence of Liberty and the right in all time to come. In obedience to your country's call, you left your homes and families and volunteered in her defence.

Victory has crowned your valor, and secured the purpose of your patriotic hearts; and, with the gratitude of your countrymen and the highest honors a great and free nation can accord, you will soon be permitted to return to your homes and families, conscious of having discharged the highest duty of American citizens. To achieve these glorious triumphs, and to secure to yourselves, your fellow-countrymen, and posterity, the blessings of free institutions, tens of thousands of your gallant comrades have fallen and sealed the priceless legacy with their blood. The graves of these a grateful nation bedews with tears, honors their memories, and will ever cherish and support their stricken families.

from *Lives of the Presidents of the United States of America from Washington to the Present Time*, 1884:

Never before, in the history of the world, was a nation plunged into such deep grief by the death of its ruler. Abraham Lincoln had won the affection of all patriot hearts. Strong men met in the streets, and wept in speechless anguish. It is not too much to say that a nation was in tears. As the awful tidings flew along the wires, funeral-bells were tolled in city and in country, flags everywhere were at half-mast, and groups gathered in silent consternation. It was Saturday morning when the murder was announced. On Sunday all the churches were draped in mourning. The atrocious act was the legitimate result of the vile Rebellion, and was in character with its developed ferocity from the beginning to the end.

Abraham Lincoln takes the oath of office on March 4, 1865.

from General Robert E. Lee's farewell to his soldiers, 1865:

After four years of arduous service marked by unsurpassed courage and fortitude, the Army of Northern Virginia has been compelled to yield to overwhelming numbers and resources. I need not tell the survivors of so many hard fought battles, who have remained steadfast to the last, that I have consented to this result from no distrust of them; but feeling that valor and devotion could accomplish nothing that could compensate for the loss that would have attended the continuation of the contest, I have determined to avoid the useless sacrifice of those whose past services have endeared them to their countrymen. By the terms of the agreement, officers and men can return to their homes, and remain there until exchanged. You will take with you the satisfaction that proceeds from the consciousness of duty faithfully performed; and I earnestly pray that a merciful God will extend to you His blessing and protection. With an unceasing admiration of your constancy and devotion to country; and a grateful remembrance of your kind and generous consideration of myself, I bid you an affectionate farewell.

Dr. Phineas Gurley, Lincoln's family pastor, at his funeral, 1865:

Probably no man, since the days of Washington, was ever so deeply and firmly embedded and enshrined in the hearts of the people as Abraham Lincoln. Nor was it a mistaken confidence and love. He deserved it, deserved it well, deserved it all. He merited it by his character, by his acts, and by the tenor and tone and spirit of his life.

6

Progress and Expansion

★★

The forty years following the Civil War were a period of healing, reconstruction, and expansion. Though the rebuilding of infrastructure and physical damage was relatively rapid, political and mental recovery from the Civil War was slow and arduous. Particularly difficult was the issue of how and when the former rebel states should be reincorporated back into the Union. The impeachment of President Lincoln's successor Andrew Johnson did not help heal the nation's wounds. Only after the Fourteenth and Fifteenth Amendments were ratified and the Union was completely restored did the country truly begin to heal, although turmoil followed the contested presidential election of 1876.

Meanwhile, physical growing pains led to the realization that natural resources had to be protected, especially after the purchase of Alaska, the country's last major land acquisition, took place. Rapid growth westward also led to fears about the immigration of tens of thousands of Chinese workers into the country. The increasing dominance of big business led to legislation to protect consumers against monopolies. Despite a tendency to maintain the isolationist policies of the Monroe Doctrine, the United States began to grow into its present role as international superpower, and became involved in more imperial conquests, notably occupation of Cuba and the Philippines following the Spanish-American War.

1867 Reconstruction Act

The end of the Civil War was by no means the end of the rancor between the North and the South. The reconstruction of the Union—the integration of the Confederate states back into the United States of America—was a subject of much disagreement in the nation and within Congress. Setting up the process of reentry of the Confederate states into the Union was not a simple task. The Democrats were in favor of the immediate acceptance of rebel states back into the Union, while the Republicans, Abraham Lincoln's party, favored a slower approach that ensured each state accept the provisions of the new amendments to the Constitution. Though on Lincoln's ticket in 1864 as vice president, President Andrew Johnson was in fact a Democrat; many of those who had voted for Lincoln resented the man they were stuck with after Lincoln was assassinated. Johnson, who had already granted amnesty to some Confederate leaders, devised a plan for the reorganization of the South during the summer of 1865, a plan Republicans saw as too lenient on the Southern states. When ten southern states failed to ratify the Fourteenth Amendment, Congress devised its own, stricter Reconstruction Act. This act made ratification of the Fourteenth Amendment mandatory for a state to be readmitted into the Union. Many Democrats saw the Reconstruction Act as harsh and unnecessary, but there was still enough support in Congress for it to pass.

President Andrew Johnson did not approve of the Reconstruction Act passed by Congress, calling it too harsh.

from the First Reconstruction Act

WHEREAS no legal State governments or adequate protection for life or property now exists in the rebel States of Virginia, North Carolina, South Carolina, Georgia, Mississippi, Alabama, Louisiana, Florida, Texas, and Arkansas; and whereas it is necessary that peace and good order should be enforced in said States until loyal and republican State governments can be legally established: Therefore,

Be it enacted . . . That said rebel States shall be divided into military districts and made subject to the military authority of the United States as hereinafter prescribed, and for that purpose Virginia shall constitute the first district; North Carolina and South Carolina the second district; Georgia, Alabama, and Florida the third district; Mississippi and Arkansas the fourth district; and Louisiana and Texas the fifth district. . . .

Section 2

And be it further enacted, That it shall be the duty of the President to assign to the command of each of said districts an officer of the army, not below the rank of brigadier-general, and to detail a sufficient military force to enable such officer to perform his duties and enforce his authority within the district to which he is assigned.

Section 3

And be it further enacted, That it shall be the duty of each officer assigned as aforesaid, to protect all persons in their rights of person and property, to suppress insurrection, disorder, and violence, and to punish, or cause to be punished, all disturbers of the public peace and criminals; and to this end he may allow local civil tribunals to take jurisdiction of and to try offenders, or, when in his judgment it may be necessary for the trial of offenders, he shall have power to organize military commissions or tribunals for that purpose, and all interference under color of State authority with the exercise of military authority under this act, shall be null and void.

Section 4

And be it further enacted, That all persons put under military arrest by virtue of this act shall be tried without unnecessary delay, and no cruel or unusual punishment shall be inflicted, and no sentence of any military commission or tribunal hereby authorized, affecting the life or liberty of any person, shall be executed until it is approved by the officer in command of the district . . .

Section 5

And be it further enacted, That when the people of any one of said rebel States shall have formed a constitution of government in conformity with the Constitution of the United States in all respects . . . and when such constitution shall provide that the elective franchise shall be enjoyed by all persons as have the qualifications herein stated for electors of delegates, and when such constitution shall be ratified by a majority of the persons voting on the question of ratification who are qualified as electors for delegates, and when such constitution shall have been submitted to Congress for examination and approval, and Congress shall have approved the same, and when said State, by a vote of its legislature elected under said constitution, shall have adopted the amendment to the Constitution of the United States, proposed by the Thirty-ninth Congress, and known as article fourteen and when said article shall have become a part of the Constitution of the United States said State shall be declared entitled to representation in Congress . . .

# What They Were Saying

from President Andrew Johnson's veto message to Congress, 1867:

The bill places all the people of the ten States therein named under the absolute domination of military rulers . . . [the measure] in its whole character, scope, and object, was without precedent and without authority, in palpable conflict with the plainest provisions of the Constitution, and utterly destructive to those great principles of liberty and humanity for which our ancestors on both sides of the Atlantic have shed so much blood and expended so much treasure . . . the purpose and object of the bill, the general intent which pervades it from beginning to end, is to change the entire structure and character of the State governments, and to compel them by force to the adoption of organic laws and regulations which they are unwilling to accept if left to themselves.

from the Democratic Party platform, 1868:

Instead of restoring the Union, it [the Republican Party] has, so far as lay in its power, dissolved it, and subjected ten States in time of profound peace to military despotism and negro supremacy; it has nullified there the right of trial by jury; it has abolished the habeus corpus—the most sacred writ of liberty; it has overthrown the freedom of speech and the press; it has substituted arbitrary seizures and arrests and military trials . . .

from the Republican Party platform, 1868:

We congratulate the country on the assured success of the Reconstruction policy of Congress, as evinced by the adoption, in the majority of the States lately in rebellion, of Constitutions securing equal civil and political rights to all, and it is the duty of the Government to sustain these institutions and to prevent the people of such States from being remitted to a state of anarchy.

from *Harper's Weekly*, 1872:

Since the abolition of slavery in this country there has been no fact so full of encouragement to every man who truly believes in the American principle as this spectacle of the decay of one of the most powerful and perilous of political organizations. Could the Democratic party have remained in power, the struggle between liberty and practical despotism, which was indeed cruel enough, would have been very much desperate and doubtful . . .

Purchase of Alaska 1867

Russian presence in North America dated back to the 1780s, when Russians settled in what is now Alaska. By the 1860s, the Russians were no longer interested in their North American property, and in 1867 they negotiated a purchase treaty with U.S. secretary of state William Seward. Derided at the time as Seward's Folly, the $7.2 million purchase of 586,000 square miles of land added a bounty of natural resources to America. Similar to the reaction after the Louisiana Purchase six decades earlier, it was hard for many average Americans to envision how the purchase could possibly benefit the United States. When the treaty with Russia went before the Senate, it was the subject of considerable debate and passed by only two votes. Despite this, it was a shrewd purchase, if for no other reason than to remove the Russian sphere of influence from North America. By 1884 there were still relatively few white settlers in Alaska. Any talk of folly ended by the time a major gold strike occurred in the Alaskan panhandle area, known as the Klondike, during the 1890s. Thousands of enterprising adventurers made their way north to seek their fortune. Though only a few found gold, the craze nonetheless helped populate the territory.

The canceled check for the purchase of Alaska.

from the Treaty with Russia

Article I

His Majesty the Emperor of all the Russias, agrees to cede to the United States, by this convention, immediately upon the exchange of the ratifications thereof, all the territory and dominion now possessed by his said Majesty on the continent of America and in adjacent islands, the same being contained within the geographical limits herein set forth . . .

Article II

In the cession of territory and dominion made by the preceding article, are included the right of property in all public lots and squares, vacant lands, and all public buildings, fortifications, barracks, and other edifies which are not private individual property. It is, however, understood and agreed, that the churches which have been built in the ceded territory by the Russian Government, shall remain the property of such members of the Greek Oriental Church resident in the territory as may choose to worship therein. . . .

Article III

The inhabitants of the ceded territory, according to their choice, reserving their natural allegiance, may return to Russia within three years; but if they should prefer to remain in the ceded territory, they, with the exception of uncivilized native tribes, shall be admitted to the enjoyment of all the rights, advantages, and immunities of citizens of the United States, and shall be maintained and protected in the free enjoyment of their liberty, property, and religion. The uncivilized tribes will be subject to such laws and regulations as the United States may from time to time adopt in regard to aboriginal tribes of that country. . . .

Article V

Immediately after the exchange of the ratifications of this convention, any fortifications or military posts which may be in the ceded territory shall be delivered to the agent of the United States, and any Russian troops which may be in the territory shall be withdrawn as soon as may be reasonably and conveniently practicable.

Article VI

In consideration of the cession aforesaid, the United States agree to pay at the Treasury in Washington, within ten months after the exchange of the ratifications of this convention, to the diplomatic representative or other agent of His Majesty the Emperor of all the Russias, duly authorized to receive the same, seven million two hundred thousand dollars in gold.

 What They Were Saying

from a speech in Congress by Representative Cadwalader Washburn, 1868:

First, that at the time the treaty for Alaska was negotiated, not a soul in the whole United States asked for it; second, that it was secretly negotiated, and in a manner to prevent the representatives of the people from being heard; third, that by existing treaties we possess every right that is of any value to us, without the responsibility and never-ending expense of governing a nation of savages; fourth, that the country ceded is absolutely without value; fifth, that it is the right and duty of the House to inquire into the treaty, and to vote or not vote the money, according to its best judgment.

from a speech in Congress by Representative Roderick Butler, 1868:

If we are to pay this price as usury on the friendship of Russia, we are paying for it very dear indeed. If we are to pay for her friendship, I desire to give her the seven million two hundred thousand dollars in cash, and let her keep Alaska, because I think it may be a small sum to give for the friendship if we could only get rid of the land, or rather the ice, which we are to get by paying for it.

from a biography of William Seward, 1891:

In the Senate Chamber the treaty with Russia had not met serious opposition. But the purchase of the new territory was not consummated without a storm of raillery in conversation and ridicule in the press. Russian-America was declared to be a "barren, worthless, God-forsaken region," whose only products were "icebergs and polar bears." The ground was frozen six feet deep," and the "streams were glaciers." "Walrussia" was suggested as a fitting name for it, if it deserved to have any. Vegetation was "confined to mosses," and "no useful animals could live there." There might be some few "wretched fish," only fit for "wretched Esquimaux" to eat. But nothing could be raised or dug there. Seven millions of good money was going to be wasted in buying it. Many millions more would have to be spent in holding and defending it, for it was "remote, inhospitable and inaccessible." It was "Seward's folly." It was [President] Johnson's "polar bear garden." It was an "egregious blunder," a "bad bargain," palmed off on a "silly Administration" by the "shrewd Russians," etc., etc., etc.

1868 Impeachment and Trial of President Andrew Johnson

Before the Civil War, Andrew Johnson, then a senator from Tennessee, had voted against Abraham Lincoln. He made a name for himself, however, as strongly opposed to secession of the South. By 1864 he had found favor among the Northern Republicans. He was seen as a political advantage and was nominated to be Lincoln's running mate. His romance with the Republicans soured soon after he became president in 1865, and before long he was despised by many in the North. In 1868 the House of Representatives brought Articles of Impeachment against President Johnson for not following the recently passed Tenure of Office Act. He had attempted to remove Secretary of War Edwin Stanton from office without the approval of the Senate, which was expressly forbidden by the Tenure of Office Act of 1867. Although the impeachment was ostensibly about this particular issue, the broader political problem was that many in Congress disapproved of the way President Johnson was approaching the Reconstruction. The formerly Northern-friendly Johnson was now seen as siding with the South; those who had once burned him in effigy were now pleased with Johnson. Republicans were unhappy with the number of pardons the president issued, calling it an abuse of his powers (though this charge did not appear in the impeachment documents). After a nearly three-month-long trial, the Senate voted thirty-five to nineteen in favor of convicting the president, but that was less than the two-thirds majority needed for conviction. Andrew Johnson was free to continue his presidency, though a heavy cloud hung over it.

The last speech is given in the House of Representatives during the impeachment trial of President Johnson, 1868.

Article I

That said Andrew Johnson, President of the United States, on the 21st day of February, in the year of our Lord, 1868 . . . unmindful of the high duties of his office, of his oath of office, and of the requirement of the Constitution that he should take care that the laws be faithfully executed, did unlawfully and in violation of the Constitution and laws of the United States issue and order in writing for the removal of Edwin M. Stanton from the office of Secretary for the Department of War, said Edwin M. Stanton having been theretofore duly appointed and commissioned, by and with the advice and consent of the Senate of the United States, as such Secretary, and said Andrew Johnson, President of the United States, on the 12th day of August, in the year of our Lord 1867, and during the recess of said Senate, having been suspended by his order Edwin M. Stanton from said office, and within twenty days after the first day of the next meeting of said Senate, that is to say, on the 12th day of December, in the year last aforesaid, having reported to said Senate such suspension, with the evidence and reasons for his action in the case and the name of the person designated to perform the duties of such office temporarily until the next meeting of the Senate, and said Senate thereafterward, on the 13th day of January, in the year of our Lord 1868, having duly considered the evidence and reasons reported by said Andrew Johnson for said suspension, and having been refused to concur in said suspension, whereby and by force of the provisions of an act entitled "An act regulating the tenure of certain civil offices," passed March 2, 1867, said Edwin M. Stanton did forthwith resume the functions of his office, whereof the said Andrew Johnson had then and there due notice, and said Edwin Stanton, by reason of the premises, on said 21st day of February, being lawfully entitled to hold said office of Secretary for the Department of War, which said order for the removal of said Edwin M. Stanton is, in substance, as follows, that is to say:

EXECUTIVE MANSION,
WASHINGTON, D.C., February 21, 1868
SIR: By virtue of the power and authority vested in me, as President by the Constitution and laws of the United States, you are hereby removed from the office of Secretary for the Department of War, and your functions as such will terminate upon receipt of their communication. You will transfer to Brevet Major-General L. Thomas, Adjutant-General of the Army, who has this day been authorized and empowered to act as Secretary of War ad interim, all books, paper and other public property now in your custody and charge.
Respectfully yours, ANDREW JOHNSON.
Hon. E. M. Stanton, Secretary of War

Which order was unlawfully issued, and with intent then are there to violate the act entitled "An act regulating the tenure of certain civil office," passed March 2, 1867; and, with the further intent contrary to the provisions of said act, and in violation thereof, and contrary to the provisions of the Constitution of the United States, and without the advice and consent of the Senate of the United States, the said Senate then and there being in session, to remove said Edwin M. Stanton from the office of Secretary for the Department of War, the said Edwin M. Stanton being then and there Secretary of War, and being then and there in the due and lawful execution of the duties of said office, whereby said Andrew Johnson, President of the United States, did then and there commit, and was guilty of a high misdemeanor in office. . . .

Article X

That said Andrew Johnson, President of the United States, unmindful of the high duties of his office and the dignity and proprieties thereof, and of the harmony and courtesies which ought to exist and be maintained between the executive and legislative branches of the Government of the United States, designing and intending to set aside the rightful authorities and powers of Congress, did attempt to bring into disgrace, ridicule, hatred, contempt and reproach the Congress of the United States, and the several branches thereof, to impair and destroy the regard and respect of all the good people of the United States for the Congress and legislative power thereof, (which all officers of the government ought inviolably to preserve and maintain,) and to excite the odium and resentment of all good people of the United States against Congress and the laws by it duly and constitutionally enacted . . . said Andrew Johnson as the Chief Magistrate of the United States, did, on the 18th day of August, in the year of our Lord 1866, and on divers other days and times, as well before as afterward, make and declare, with a loud voice certain intemperate, inflammatory, and scandalous harangues, and therein utter loud threats and bitter menaces, as well against Congress as the laws of the United States duly enacted thereby, amid the cries, jeers and laughter of the multitudes then assembled in hearing . . .

Article XI

That the said Andrew Johnson, President of the United States, unmindful of the high duties of his office and of his oath of office, and in disregard of the Constitution and laws of the United States, did, heretofore, to wit: On the 18th day of August, 1866, at the city of Washington, and in the District of Columbia, by public speech, declare and affirm in substance, that the Thirty-Ninth Congress of the United States was not a Congress of the United States authorized by the Constitution to exercise legislative power under the same; but, on the contrary, was a Congress of only part of the States, thereby denying and intending to deny, that the legislation of said Congress was valid or obligatory upon him . . . the said Andrew Johnson . . . did then . . . commit and was guilty of a high misdemeanor in office.

 What They Were Saying

Andrew Johnson, 1866:

I care not for their [his Congressional enemies] menaces, the taunts and the jeers. I care not for threats. I do not intend to be bullied by my enemies, nor overawed by my friends; but God willing . . . I will veto their measures whenever they come to me.

from Andrew Johnson's veto of the Tenure of Office Act, 1867:

The bill . . . conflicts in my judgement, with the Constitution of the United States . . . the power of removal is constitutionally vested in the President of the United States . . .

from the Democratic Party Platform, 1868:

The President of the United States, Andrew Johnson, in exercising the powers of his high office in resisting the aggressions of Congress upon the constitutional rights of the States and the people, is entitled to the gratitude of the whole American people, and in behalf of the Democratic party we tender him our thanks for his patriotic efforts in that regard.

from the Republican Party Platform, 1868:

The corruptions which have been so shamefully nursed and fostered by Andrew Johnson call loudly for radical reform . . . We regret the accession of Andrew Johnson to the Presidency, who has acted treacherously to the people who elected him, and the cause he was pledged to support. . . . and who has been justly impeached . . .

from a newspaper editorial, New York, 1868:

The President will be convicted, not because he is guilty of any crime or misdemeanor, but because there is not sufficient manliness, not sufficient self-respect or integrity in the Senate majority, to resist the party or other improper influences that oppress them. To convict is required as a matter of party fidelity, and they dare not be unfaithful to their party. The question of actual guilt or innocence will be wholly foreign to their thoughts.

from *Popular School History of the United States*, 1884:

The President, for the remainder of his term, was but little regarded. He continued, though impotently, his conflict with Congress. His own party did not think it expedient to renominate him for the Presidency . . . Andrew Johnson was forgotten. The bullet of an assassin introduced him to the President's chair. Notwithstanding this, never was there presented to a man a better opportunity to immortalize his name, and to win the gratitude of a nation. He failed utterly.

1868 Fourteenth Amendment

1870 Fifteenth Amendment

As the Reconstruction got underway, Congress passed the Fourteenth Amendment in 1866. The amendment said that African Americans were citizens of their respective states but left it up to the states to decide if

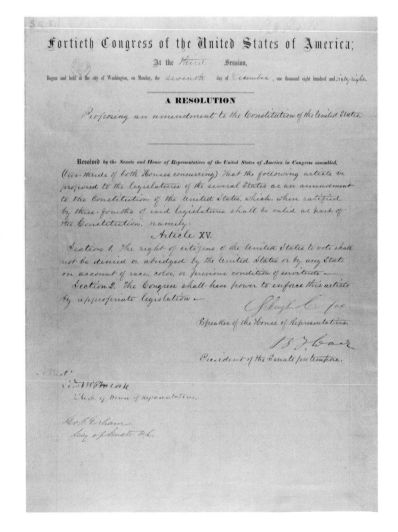

they could vote. If the former slaves were to be denied the vote, however, the representation of that state in Congress would be based solely on the white (voting) population. It also eliminated any hope of Southern plantation owners getting reimbursed for the loss of their slaves. President Johnson opposed the amendment, which was rejected by ten states before Congress mandated in the Reconstruction Act that the Southern states had to accept the amendment before being allowed to reenter the Union. The Fourteenth Amendment was adopted on July 28, 1868.

The Fifteenth Amendment removed uncertainty from the Fourteenth Amendment by mandating that all races be allowed to vote. The Fifteenth Amendment was adopted on March 30, 1870. By early 1871, Congress was once again whole, with all the secession states once again represented.

Fourteenth Amendment

Section 1

All persons born or naturalized in the United States, and subject to the jurisdiction thereof, are citizens of the United States and of the State wherein they reside. No State shall make or enforce any law which shall abridge the privileges or immunities of citizens of the United States; nor shall any State deprive any person of life, liberty, or property, without due process of law; nor deny to any person within its jurisdiction the equal protection of the laws.

Section 2

Representatives shall be apportioned among the several States according to their respective numbers, counting the whole number of persons in each state, excluding Indians not taxed. But when the right to vote at any election for the choice of electors for President and Vice President of the United States, Representatives in Congress, the executive and judicial officers of a state, or the members of the legislature thereof, is denied to any of the male inhabitants of such state, being twenty-one years of age, and citizens of the United States, or in any way abridged, except for participation in rebellion, or other crime, the basis of representation therein shall be reduced in the proportion which the number of such male citizens shall bear to the whole number of male citizens twenty-one years of age in such State.

Section 3

No person shall be a Senator or Representative in Congress, or elector of President and Vice President, or hold any office, civil or military, under the United States, or under any State, who, having previously taken an oath, as a member of Congress, or as an officer of the United States, or as a member of any State Legislature, or as an executive or judicial officer of any State, to support the Constitution of the United States, shall have engaged in insurrection or rebellion against the same, or given aid or comfort to the enemies thereof. But Congress may by a vote of two-thirds of each House, remove such disability.

Section 4

The validity of the public debt of the United States, authorized by law, including debts incurred for payment of pensions and bounties for services in suppressing insurrection or rebellion, shall not be questioned. But neither the United States nor any State shall assume or pay any debt or obligation incurred in aid of insurrection or rebellion against the United States, or any claim for the loss or emancipation of any slave; but all such debts, obligations and claims shall be held illegal and void.

Section 5

The Congress shall have power to enforce, by appropriate legislation, the provisions of this article.

Fifteenth Amendment

Section 1

The right of citizens of the United States to vote shall not be denied or abridged by the United States or by any State on account of race, color, or previous condition of servitude.

Section 2

The Congress shall have power to enforce this article by appropriate legislation.

What They Were Saying

from *Essays on the Progress of Nations in Civilization*, 1868:

The indications now are, that the 14th amendment will be adopted; and it seems impossible for the South to prevent it. The prospects are that all, or nearly all the seceding States will soon be ushered into the Union under new Constitutions, framed and designed to disfranchise a large portion of the white population, and to establish and perpetuate universal negro suffrage, and negro supremacy.

from the *New-York Daily Tribune*, February 18, 1869:

The last Republican National Convention was persuaded to resolve that Suffrage in loyal States was wholly within the rightful control of those States respectively . . . The Democratic journalists and stumpers, but especially those of the outright Rebel variety, instantly seized upon this Chicago declaration as too horrible to be contemplated without shuddering . . . All over the country, we were roundly accused of making the Black a voter in the South out of hatred to her Whites, but denying him the Right of Suffrage at the North, because we despised and detested the Blacks. Congress took hold of the matter at this session, and resolved to remove all cause for just complaint of partiality or sectional indignity.

President Ulysses Grant to Congress, 1870:

I consider the adoption of the 15th Amendment to the Constitution completes the greatest civil change, and constitutes the most important event that has occurred since the nation came to life.

from *The American System of Government*, 1870:

While [the southern states] ratified the 13th amendment to the federal constitution, they ignored and denied some of the most important civil rights of the negro; they employed their wits in forging new chains for him, and refused to ratify the reasonable and important provisions contained in the 14th amendment—to secure the civil rights of the negro, and give peace to the country.

from *Fears for Democracy*, 1875:

It was claimed that 29 States voted for the 14th amendment; 8 against it. In counting generally, dollars for example, 29 is ¾, and more than ¾ of 37, for the dollar can be taken by fractions, halves, quarters, etc., thus $27¾ is ¾ of $37. But a State cannot be divided, like a dollar, to count for the ¾ majority. If this be so, the way to count is to take that number of States of which 4 is a multiple, then take ¾ of that number, then add to the original number the additional State or States; and, without dividing any of them, but taking their number as a whole multiple of 4, add their ¾, thus: of 36 States, the assenting ¾ were 27. The additional State must be one of 4, of which there must be assenting 3, making requisite, for a ¾ majority of the 37 States, 30 assenting States; there were but 29 assenting States.

The presidential election of 1876 pitted the Democrat Samuel J. Tilden against the Republican Rutherford B. Hayes, a Civil War general for the Union. The results on election day were highly contested because the vote in South Carolina, Florida, and Louisiana was uncertain. In South Carolina, for example, two different groups claimed to be the legal state legislature; one giving victory to Tilden and the other to Hayes. A special commission was appointed in January 1877 to review the situation. The composition of the committee was three Republican senators, two Democratic senators, three Democratic representatives, two Republican representatives, and two Republican and two Democratic Supreme Court justices. Those four justices were called upon to name a fifth justice to the commission. Their choice was a Republican,

and so the commission membership was eight Republicans to seven Democrats. Though Samuel J. Tilden received more popular votes, the special commission voted strictly along party lines and declared Rutherford B. Hayes the winner, 185 electoral votes to 184 electoral votes. Shown on page 146 is the text of the announcement in a joint session of Congress of the commission's findings. Wisconsin is mentioned only because it was the last state in the recount of electoral votes.

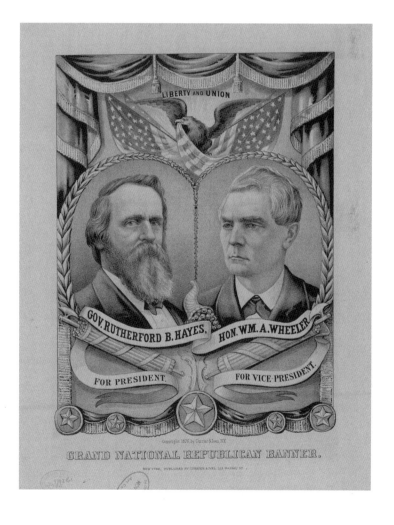

Republicans Hayes and Wheeler won the contested 1876 presidential election.

from *Senate Proceedings* (1877)

The President of the Senate took the Speaker's chair as the presiding officer of the joint meeting of the two houses of Congress, under and in pursuance of the act entitled "An act to provide for and regulate the counting of votes for President and Vice-President, and the decision of questions arising thereon, for the term commencing March 4, A. D. 1877," approved January 29, 1877, and announced that the joint meeting of the two houses of Congress for the counting of the electoral votes for President and Vice-President resumed its session.

The presiding officer further stated that the two houses of Congress separately having considered and determined the objections to the certificates from the State of Wisconsin, their action thereon would now be read.

The Secretary of the Senate thereupon read the decision of the Senate thereon, viz:

That the vote of Daniel L. Downs, as an elector for the State of Wisconsin, be counted, together with the other nine electoral votes of that State, the objections made thereto to the contrary notwithstanding.

The Clerk of the House thereupon read the decision of the House of Representatives thereon, viz:

Resolved, That the vote of Daniel L. Downs, as an elector of the State of Wisconsin, should not be counted, because be held an office of trust and profit under the United States, and therefore was not constitutionally appointed an elector by said State of Wisconsin.

The presiding officer thereupon announced that, the two houses not concurring otherwise, the full electoral vote of the State of Wisconsin would be cast for Rutherford B. Hayes, of Ohio, for President, and William A. Wheeler, of New York, for Vice-President.

The tellers thereupon announced the vote of the State of Wisconsin accordingly.

The presiding officer thereupon announced the conclusion of the counting of the electoral votes of the thirty-eight States of the Union . . .

The whole number of the electors appointed to vote for President and Vice-President of the United States is 369, of which a majority is 185.

The state of the vote for President of the United States as delivered by the tellers, and as determined under the act of Congress approved January 29, 1877, is:

For Rutherford B. Hayes, of Ohio, 185
For Samuel J. Tilden, of New York, 184

The state of the vote for Vice-President of the United States as delivered by the tellers, and as determined under the act of Congress approved January 29, 1877, is:

For William A. Wheeler, of New York, 185
For Thomas A. Hendricks, of Indiana, 184
Wherefore, I do declare—

That Rutherford B. Hayes, of Ohio, having received a majority of the whole number of electoral votes, is duly elected President of the United States for your years, commencing on the 4th day of March, 1877. And that William A. Wheeler, of New York, having received a majority of the whole number of electoral votes, is duly elected Vice-President of the United States for four years, commencing on the 4th day of March, 1877.

 What They Were Saying

from the *Republican Campaign Text Book*, 1882:

The infamous and violent fraud, in the form of an election in 1876, has no parallel in the history of free government. In 1861 the Democratic rebellion was, by force of arms, to destroy the union, to blot out the Republic from the family of nations, and to erect an oligarchy, based upon negro slavery—upon the ruins of American liberty. In 1876 the Confederate Democratic conspiracy was but slightly modified—a rebellion by all malignant agencies, by systematic intimidation and fraud, both organized violence and murder, to disfranchise the legal popular majorities of the States, to subvert the Constitution, to destroy the popular principle underlying it and our laws and substitute for it, in the rule of the government and nation, the old oligarichal tyranny!

from *Lives of the Presidents of the United States*, 1884:

Unfortunately all the questions at issue were decided by party votes, -eight to seven. General Hayes was declared to be elected by one vote over Samuel J. Tilden, the Democratic candidate . . . His administration of the affairs of the government was at first much embarrassed by the fact that many of his political opponents felt that he was not entitled to the office.

from *Great Issues and National Leaders*, 1900:

Perhaps few will believe what is unquestionably the fact, that the most critical period in the history of our country was not in the Revolution, nor yet in the Civil War, but in the autumn of 1876, or more properly, the opening weeks of 1877. The peril was an appalling one, and the most thoughtful patriots trembled for the safety of their beloved land . . . The situation was unparalleled. The peril was of the gravest nature. Some plan must be devised or anarchy and civil war were certain.

1882 Chinese Exclusion Act

The immigration of one hundred thousand Chinese to the United States during the first three decades of the second half of the nineteenth century caused animosity, especially among Californians (three-fourths of the Chinese immigrant population lived in California). Opposition to Chinese immigration was based on the perception that the Chinese were only coming to the United States to work, mainly as laborers, with no intention of bringing their families or becoming citizens.

There was also a fear that their willingness to work for lower wages would take jobs away from Americans. Congress issued a 1,300-page report in 1877 discussing why Chinese immigration should be limited. In a California referendum in 1879, a total of 154,638 people voted against Chinese immigration while only 883 people voted for it (although it was alleged that the ballots were unfairly composed). The Chinese Exclusion Act placed a ten-year moratorium on Chinese immigration, despite a treaty with China a few years earlier. Between 1904 and 1906, forty-five hundred Chinese were arrested for being in the United States illegally. The exclusion policy was renewed and refined by Congress several times, reducing Chinese immigration to a trickle. The policy was not fully reversed until the 1940s. The Chinese Exclusion Act was indicative of a broader fear on the part of Americans about the vast numbers of immigrants arriving every year. The act came during a year in which immigration to the United States reached a new high of nearly 789,000 people. The Chinese were not the only ethnic group singled out—in 1906 the San Francisco school board decided to exclude Japanese children from public school. President Theodore Roosevelt said in December 1907, "To shut them out from the public schools is a wicked absurdity" and pointed out that such behavior went against the United States' treaty with Japan. The Emergency Quota Act of 1921 severely limited all immigration to the country, and the Immigration Quota Act of 1924 further cut the influx of foreigners.

WHEREAS in the opinion of the Government of the United States the coming of Chinese laborers to this country endangers the good order of certain localities within the territory thereof: Therefore,

Be it enacted by the Senate and House of Representatives of the United States of America in Congress assembled, That from and after the expiration of ninety days next after the passage of this act, and until the expiration of ten years next after the passage of this act, the coming of Chinese laborers to the United States . . . is hereby, suspended; and during such suspension it shall not be lawful for any Chinese laborer to come, or having so come after the expiration of said ninety days to remain within the United States.

Section 2
That the master of any vessel who shall knowingly bring within the United States on such vessel, and land or permit to be landed, any Chinese laborer, from any foreign port or place, shall be deemed guilty of a misdemeanor, and on conviction thereof shall be punished by a fine of not more than five hundred dollars for each and every such Chinese laborer so brought, and maybe also imprisoned for a term not exceeding one year. . . .

Section 8
That the master of any vessel arriving in the United States from any foreign port or place shall, at the same time he delivers a manifest of the cargo, and if there be no cargo, then at the time of making a report of the entry of the vessel pursuant to law, in addition to the other matter required to be reported, and before landing, or permitting to land, any Chinese passengers, deliver and report to the collector of customs of the district in which such vessels shall have arrived a separate list of all Chinese passengers taken on board his vessel at any foreign port or place, and all such passengers on board the vessel at that time. Such list shall show the names of such passengers (and if accredited officers of the Chinese Government traveling on the business of that government, or their servants, with a note of such facts), and the names and other particulars, as shown by their respective certificates; and such list shall be sworn to by the master in the manner required by law in relation to the manifest of the cargo.

Section 9
That before any Chinese passengers are landed from any such line vessel, the collector, or his deputy, shall proceed to examine such passenger, comparing the certificate with the list and with the passengers; and no passenger shall be allowed to land in the United States from such vessel in violation of law. . . .

Section 11
That any person who shall knowingly bring into or cause to be brought into the United States . . . shall be deemed guilty of a misdemeanor, and shall, on conviction thereof, be fined in a sum not exceeding one thousand dollars, and imprisoned for a term not exceeding one year.

Section 12
That no Chinese person shall be permitted to enter the United States by land without producing to the proper officer of customs the certificate in this act required of Chinese persons seeking to land from a vessel. And any Chinese person found unlawfully within the United States shall be caused to be removed therefrom to the country from whence he came.

# What They Were Saying

from *A Compend of History*, 1828:

It is not unlikely, however, that the future historian will be compelled to say, that our government, in relation to foreigners, erred through excess of benevolence and urbanity . . . the rapid increase of any nation, by means of an influx of foreigners, is dangerous to the repose of that nation . . .

Secretary of State Hamilton Fish, 1869:

Every month brings thousands of Chinese immigrants to the Pacific coast. Already they have crossed the great mountains and are beginning to be found in the interior of the continent. By their assiduity, patience and fidelity, and by their intelligence, they earn the good will and confidence of those who employ them.

from *Appleton's Journal*, 1870:

The Pacific train from Omaha is crowded with passengers, every one of whom is discussing Chinese labor. At the first station on the Plains, where the Mongolian cue appears, a rush is made for the windows. The visible presence of a Canton female, no matter what she sells, furnishes topic for the day . . . It is safe to say that the chief interest taken by nine persons out of every ten who pass over the Pacific road is expended upon the [Chinese].

Theodore Roosevelt, 1897:

Where immigrants, or the sons of immigrants, do not heartily and in good faith throw in their lot with us, but cling to the speech, the customs, the ways of life, and the habits of thought of the Old World which they have left, they thereby harm both themselves and us. If they remain alien elements, unassimilated, and with interests separate from ours, they are mere obstructions to the current of our national life, and, moreover, can get no good from it themselves.

from the Democratic Party Platform, 1900:

We favor the continuance and strict enforcement of the Chinese Exclusion law and its application to the same classes of all Asiatic races.

from *History of the United States*, 1914:

These swarms of foreigners who come to us each year are causing uneasiness in the minds of the thinking people. Can our foreign population be growing more rapidly than our power to assimilate it? Is this element as dangerous to our civilization as we think? Has criminality increased as a result of increased immigration? . . . Some contend that we are rapidly approaching the limit of our power of assimilation and that we are in constant danger of losing the traits which we call American.

Dawes Act 1887

By 1887 the Native Americans, who had just a few decades earlier flourished in the western half of the country, had been marginalized and their way of life (dating back thousands of years) dangerously threatened. Not only had they been pushed off their land, their numbers had been drastically reduced by diseases introduced by Europeans and by skirmishes with United States forces. The Dawes Act was a recognition that they were entitled to own land outside of reservations. It also granted them instant citizenship once they accepted land through the act. The general attitude toward Native Americans by the 1880s and 1890s was mixed. There was some repentance over all the blood that had been

shed and an acknowledgment of American guilt as the invaders, yet at the same time there was continued referral to the natives as barbarous or uncivilized. Though many Native Americans chose to remain on reservations, between 1904 and 1908 alone, fifteen thousand received 2.5 million acres of government land. The total area of the reservations dropped from 242,000 square miles in 1880 to 122,000 square miles by 1900.

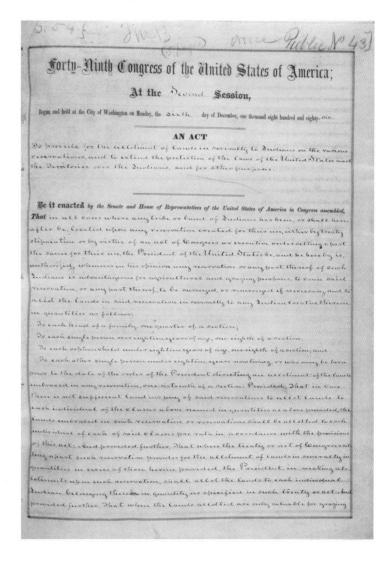

Be it enacted by the Senate and House of Representatives of the United States of America in Congress assembled, That in all cases where any tribe or band of Indians has been, or shall hereafter be, located upon any reservation created for their use, either by treaty stipulation or by virtue of an act of Congress or executive order setting apart the same for their use, the President of the United States be, and he hereby is, authorized, whenever in his opinion any reservation or any part thereof of such Indians is advantageous for agricultural and grazing purposes, to cause said reservation, or any part thereof, to be surveyed, or resurveyed if necessary, and to allot the lands in said reservation in severalty to any Indian located thereon in quantities as follows:

To each head of a family, one-quarter of a section;

To each single person over eighteen years of age, one-eighth of a section;

To each orphan child under eighteen years of age, one-eighth of a section; and

To each other single person under eighteen years now living, or who may be born prior to the date of the order of the President directing an allotment of the lands embraced in any reservation, one-sixteenth of a section: *Provided*, That in case there is not sufficient land in any of said reservations to allot lands to each individual of the classes above named in quantities as above provided, the lands embraced in such reservation or reservations shall be allotted to each individual of each of said classes pro rata in accordance with the provisions of this act: *And provided further*, That where the treaty or act of Congress setting apart such reservation provides for the allotment of lands in severalty in quantities in excess of those herein provided, the President, in making allotments upon such reservation, shall allot the lands to each individual Indian belonging thereon in quantity as specified in such treaty or act: And provided further, That when the lands allotted are only valuable for grazing purposes, an additional allotment of such grazing lands, in quantities as above provided, shall be made to each individual.

Section 2

That all allotments set apart under the provisions of this act shall be selected by the Indians, heads of families selecting for their minor children, and the agents shall select for each orphan child, and in such manner as to embrace the improvements of the Indians making the selection. Where the improvements of two or more Indians have been made on the same legal subdivision of land, unless they shall otherwise agree, a provisional line may be run dividing said lands between them, and the amount to which each is entitled shall be equalized in the assignment of the remainder of the land to which they are entitled under this act . . .

Section 5

That upon the approval of the allotments provided for in this act by the Secretary of the Interior, he shall cause patents to issue therefor in the name of the allottees, which patents shall be of the legal effect, and declare that the United States does and will hold the land thus allotted, for the period of twenty-five years, in trust for the sole use and benefit of the Indian to whom such allotment shall have been made, or, in case of his decease, of his heirs according to the laws of the State or Territory where such land is located, and that at the expiration of said period the United States will convey the same by patent to said Indian, or his heirs as aforesaid, in fee, discharged of said trust and free of all charge or incumbrance whatsoever . . .

Section 6

. . . . And every Indian born within the territorial limits of the United States to whom allotments shall have been made under the provisions of this act, or under any law or treaty, and every Indian born within the territorial limits of the United States who has voluntarily taken up, within said limits, his residence separate and apart from any tribe of Indians therein, and has adopted the habits of civilized life, is hereby declared to be a citizen of the United States, and is entitled to all the rights, privileges, and immunities of such citizens . . .

What They Were Saying

from *History of the United States*, 1898:

In the course of time it is hoped that the individual Indian, like the white man, will have his own land and reap the fruits of his own toil. Individual ownership, along with industrial training and general education, will aid in making him a useful citizen.

from *The History of Our Country*, 1900:

It is well that the young reader, who may take pride in the prowess of the early settlers of his country in ridding it of hostile Indians . . . should remember that much of the Indian blood spilled on this continent was due to the coming of the white man . . . We came to the Indian, not the Indian to us. As it has been the fate of some portions of the race to lapse into barbarism, we should like to think that out of barbarism they will yet emerge. In the philanthropies of a coming day, we trust that forces will continually, and more effectively, be employed to restore the Indian to civilization, and to eradicate from his nature those dispositions and tendencies that drag him backward in the path of progress, or, while imitating bad examples set before him, that civilize him out of existence.

Sherman Antitrust Act

By the late nineteenth century, several industries were falling under the control of single companies. On the one hand, monopolies were seen as having a positive effect because large companies tended to invest great amounts of money in research and infrastructure and that was good for the economy. For example, the Standard Oil Company laid thousands of miles of pipelines and employed thirty thousand people. On the other hand, these monopolies were seen as dangerous because they limited competition and controlled the market by reigning over prices as well as supply. The consumer had no choice but to use that company, and so was at their mercy regarding price and service. The Sherman Antitrust Act was legislation passed by Congress to limit the monopolies, also known as trusts, that controlled certain businesses. At first, the government was slow to enforce the law. In 1895 the Supreme Court ruled in favor of the E. C. Knight Co., a sugar refinery that was challenged for controlling 98 percent of the refining business, saying the Sherman Antitrust Act did not apply to manufacturing of goods, only the selling of goods. Other monopolies were not so lucky. In 1904, the Supreme Court ruled against the Northern Securities Company, a railroad conglomerate, stating that it illegally blocked interstate trade. Several additional monopolies were soon busted, including those in the beef, tobacco, and oil industries.

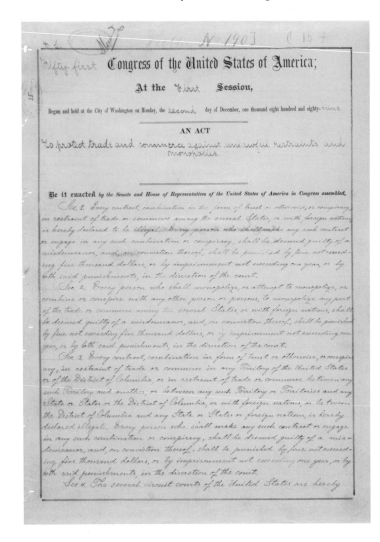

Be it enacted by the Senate and House of Representatives of the United States of America in Congress assembled,

Section 1

Every contract, combination in the form of trust or otherwise, or conspiracy, in restraint of trade or commerce among the several States, or with foreign nations, is hereby declared to be illegal. Every person who shall make any such contract or engage in any such combination or conspiracy, shall be deemed guilty of a misdemeanor, and, on conviction thereof, shall be punished by fine not exceeding five thousand dollars, or by imprisonment not exceeding one year, or by both said punishments, at the discretion of the court.

Section 2

Every person who shall monopolize, or attempt to monopolize, or combine or conspire with any other person or persons, to monopolize any part of the trade or commerce among the several States, or with foreign nations, shall be deemed guilty of a misdemeanor, and, on conviction thereof; shall be punished by fine not exceeding five thousand dollars, or by imprisonment not exceeding one year, or by both said punishments, in the discretion of the court.

Section 3

Every contract, combination in form of trust or otherwise, or conspiracy, in restraint of trade or commerce in any Territory of the United States or of the District of Columbia, or in restraint of trade or commerce between any such Territory and another, or between any such Territory or Territories and any State or States or the District of Columbia, or with foreign nations, or between the District of Columbia and any State or States or foreign nations, is hereby declared illegal. Every person who shall make any such contract or engage in any such combination or conspiracy, shall be deemed guilty of a misdemeanor, and, on conviction thereof, shall be punished by fine not exceeding five thousand dollars, or by imprisonment not exceeding one year, or by both said punishments, in the discretion of the court. . . .

Section 7

Any person who shall be injured in his business or property by any other person or corporation by reason of anything forbidden or declared to be unlawful by this act, may sue therefor in any circuit court of the United States in the district in which the defendant resides or is found, without respect to the amount in controversy, and shall recover threefold the damages by him sustained, and the costs of suit, including a reasonable attorney's fee.

 What They Were Saying

William J. Bryan, Democratic presidential candidate, circa 1890s:

Monopoly in private hands is indefensible from any standpoint and intolerable. I do not divide monopolies. There can be no good monopoly in private hands until the Almighty sends us angels to preside over us. There may be a despot who is better than another despot, but there is no good despotism . . . When a branch of industry is entirely in the hands of one great monopoly, so that every skilled man in that industry has to go to the one man for employment, then that man will fix wages as he pleases, and the laboring man will then share the suffering of the man who sells the raw material.

from *An American Commoner: The Life and Times of Richard Parks Bland*, 1900:

The sugar trust, the Standard Oil trust and the national banks, through millionaire stockholders combined in various other syndicates, political and commercial, had contributed to Mr. Cleveland's campaign fund, but this fact was not decisive in controlling the policies of his administration towards them. The complete failure to enforce the Sherman act . . . is due primarily to the fact that every indictment under it is the indictment of a system, and every punishment under it would be the punishment of a theory of government supported and carried out by the economic laws and the executive machinery of the entire United States.

from *Great Issues and National Leaders*, 1900:

The Standard Oil Company, which practically controls the output of petroleum in this country by owning a large portion of the oil lands is quoted as an illustration of the advantages of trusts. Their investment includes thousands of miles of pipe line, tank capacity for millions of gallons oil . . . and has reduced the price of oil seventy-five per cent since the corporation was organized.

Resolution on Spanish-American War 1898

During the mid-1890s, Cuban independence from Spain became a topic of discussion among the households of America. Sympathy for the plight of the Cubans was strong. The destruction of the battleship USS *Maine* in February 1898 in Havana Harbor led to U.S. involment in a war with Spain in April. Another factor was the so-called DeLome Letter (see illustration), a note written by the Spanish ambassador to the United States. This note, which criticized President McKinley, became public and caused embarrassment to the president. It read, in part, that McKinley was "weak and catering to the rabble, and, besides, a low politician, who desires to leave a door open to me and to stand well with the jingoes of his party."

The Spanish-American War had two main fronts: Cuba and the Philippines. By July 1, there were forty thousand American troops overseas. The United States won the Battle of San Juan in July; Spain had eighteen hundred casualties or prisoners taken and lost six ships. Soon after, American forces over- whelmed the Spanish in the Philippines. Peace came in August, and on December 10, 1898, a peace treaty was signed. As a result of the treaty, America took possession of the Philippines and remained in control until the Japanese occupied it during World War II, though there was fighting on the island between Filipino insurgents and American forces starting in 1899 and lasting for several years. Because of the war's popularity in the United States, one of its chief heroes soon rose to prominence. Theodore Roosevelt became a household name due to his exploits in 1898, which led to his run as McKinley's vice president in 1900.

*J*oint Resolution—*For the recognition of the independence of the people of Cuba, demanding that the Government of Spain relinquish its authority and government in the Island of Cuba, and to withdraw its land and naval forces from Cuba and Cuban waters, and directing the President of the United States to use the land and naval forces of the United States to carry these resolutions into effect.*

Whereas, the abhorrent conditions which have existed for more than three years in the Island of Cuba, so near our own borders, have shocked the moral sense of the people of the United States, have been a disgrace to Christian civilization, culminating, as they have, in the destruction of a United States battleship, with two hundred and sixty-six of its officers and crew, while on a friendly visit in the harbor of Havana, and can not longer be endured, as has been set forth by the President of the United States in his message to Congress of April eleventh, eighteen hundred and ninety-eight, upon which the action of Congress was invited: therefore,

Resolved, By the Senate and House of Representatives of the United States of America in Congress assembled,

1. That the people of the Island of Cuba are, and of right ought to be, free and independent.

2. That it is the duty of the United States to demand, and the Government of the United States does hereby demand, that the Government of Spain at once relinquish its authority and government in the Island of Cuba, and withdraw its land and naval forces from Cuba and Cuban waters.

3. That the President of the United States be, and he hereby is, directed and empowered to use the entire land and naval forces of the United States, and to call into the actual service of the United States, the militia of the several States, to such extent as may be necessary to carry these resolutions into effect.

4. That the United States hereby disclaims any disposition or intention to exercise sovereignty, jurisdiction, or control over said Islands except for the pacification thereof, and asserts its determination, when that is accomplished, to leave the government and control of the Island to its people.

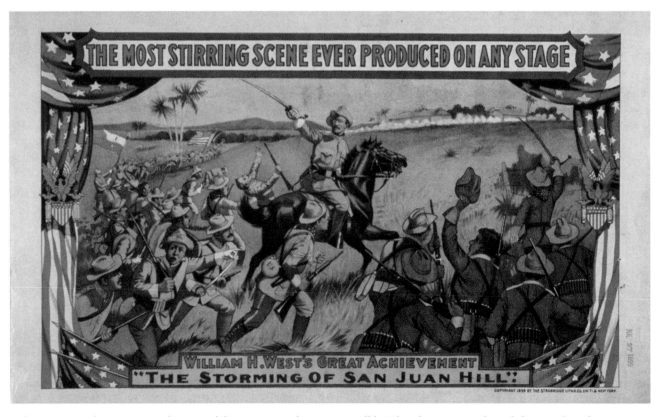

Advertisement for a stage production of the storming of San Juan Hill by Theodore Roosevelt and the Rough Riders, 1898.

What They Were Saying

Theodore Roosevelt, 1899:

During the year preceding the outbreak of the Spanish War, I was Assistant Secretary of the Navy. While my party was in opposition, I had preached, with all the fervor and zeal I possessed, our duty to intervene in Cuba, and to take this opportunity of driving the Spaniard from the Western world. Now that my party had come to power, I felt it incumbent on me, by word and deed, to do all I could to secure the carrying out of the policy in which I so heartily believed . . . if a war came, somehow or other, I was going to the front.

from Senator Albert Beveridge of Indiana, 1899:

The Philippines are ours forever. Let faint hearts anoint their fears with the thought that some day American administration and American duty there may end. But they will never end.

from *Great Men and Famous Women*, 1900:

[McKinley's] conduct during the war . . . was the source of much bitter criticism. It is too soon yet for final judgment. The events are too near at hand, and the conception of them too confused. Success, that generally accepted test of merit, has certainly been his. Never was victory more complete and glorious . . . All the repute, good or bad, that attaches to that [peace] treaty must go to William McKinley.

from *Great Issues and National Leaders*, 1900:

December 10, 1898, was one of the most eventful days in the past decade—one fraught with great interest to the world, and involving the destiny of more than 10,000,000 of people. . . . This treaty transformed the political geography of the world by establishing the United States' authority in both hemispheres, and also in the tropics, where it had never before extended.

from the Democratic Party Platform, 1900:

We condemn and denounce the Philippine policy of the present Administration. It has involved the Republic in an unnecessary war, sacrificed the lives of many of our noblest sons.

from *The History of Our Country*, 1900:

It should be added that the war was the most popular in which our country has ever engaged. It was eagerly advocated everywhere, and it has been shown that it was as easy to obtain a million as a hundred thousand recruits for our army. The reason for this was that it was not solely a war of conquest, but one that appealed to the noblest instincts of humanity . . . The war spirit was everywhere . . . The American military spirit was more aggressive and more general than ever before in the history of the country.

from *The Outlook* magazine, 1909:

The Spanish-American War placed in the coffers of Uncle Sam two jewels of great value—Cuba "The Pearl of the Antilles," and "The Emerald of the Southern Seas," as the Philippines are called . . . When we have really developed the Philippine Islands and handed them over to an independent Philippine people, we shall have accomplished the greatest and proudest task ever undertaken by a nation.

Once the western United States became populated and the frontier was considered "closed," most of the good quality land was already occupied. However, there was still a great deal of semiarid land that was not occupied in places such as Nevada and Utah. The government realized that without some plan for providing water to these territories, it would be impossible for those states to support long-term settlement for the many thousands of people who were drawn there. The Newlands Reclamation Act set aside funds for huge irrigation projects to provide water to farmers in semiarid states and set in motion the construction of a series of dams on western rivers.

Be it enacted by the Senate and House of Representatives of the United States of America in Congress assembled, That all moneys received from the sale and disposal of public lands in Arizona, California, Colorado, Idaho, Kansas, Montana, Nebraska, Nevada, New Mexico, North Dakota, Oklahoma, Oregon, South Dakota, Utah, Washington, and Wyoming . . . shall be . . . appropriated as a special fund in the Treasury to be known as the "reclamation fund," to be used in the examination and survey for and the construction and maintenance of irrigation works for the storage, diversion, and development of waters for the reclamation or arid and semiarid lands in the said States and Territories, and for the payment of all other expenditures provided for in this Act . . .

Section 2
That the Secretary of the Interior is hereby authorized and directed to make examinations and surveys for, and to locate and construct, as herein provided, irrigation works for the storage, diversion, and development of waters, including artesian wells . . .

Section 3
That the Secretary of the Interior shall, before giving the public notice provided for in section four of this Act, withdraw from public entry the lands required for any irrigation works contemplated under the provisions of this Act, and shall restore to public entry any of the lands so withdrawn when, in his judgment, such lands are not required for the purposes of this Act; and the Secretary of the Interior is hereby authorized, at or immediately prior to the time of beginning the surveys for any contemplated irrigation works, to withdraw from entry, except under the homestead laws, any public lands believed to be susceptible of irrigation from said works . . .

Section 4
That upon the determination by the Secretary of the Interior that any irrigation project is practicable, he may cause to be let contracts for the construction of the same, in such portions or sections are available in the reclamation fund, and irrigable under such project, and limit of area per entry which limit shall represent the acreage which, in the opinion of the Secretary, may be reasonably required for the support of a family upon the lands in question . . .

Section 5
That the entryman upon lands to be irrigated by such works shall, in addition to compliance with the homestead laws, reclaim at least one-half of the total irrigable area of his entry for agricultural purposes, and before receiving patent for the lands covered by his entry shall pay to the Government the charges apportioned against such tract, as provided in section four. . . .

Section 6
That the Secretary of the Interior is hereby authorized and directed to use the reclamation fund for the operation and maintenance of all reservoirs and irrigation works constructed under the provisions of this Act . . .

Section 7
That where in carrying out the provisions of this Act it becomes necessary to acquire any rights or property, the Secretary of the Interior is hereby authorized to acquire the same for the United States by purchase or by condemnation under judicial process, and to pay from the reclamation fund the sums which may be needed for that purpose . . .

What They Were Saying

from a resolution by the nation's governors, 1908:

We agree that the land should be so used that erosion and soil-wash shall cease; and that there should be reclamation of arid and semi-arid regions by means of irrigation, and of swamp and overflowed regions by means of drainage; that the waters should be so conserved and used as to promote navigation, to enable the arid regions to be reclaimed by irrigation, and to develop power in the interests of the people: that the forests which regulate our rivers, support our industries, and promote the fertility and productiveness of the soil should be preserved and perpetuated; that the minerals found so abundantly beneath the surface should be so used as to prolong their utility; that the beauty, healthfullness, and habitability of our country should be preserved and increased; that the sources of national wealth exist for the benefit of the People, and that monopoly thereof should not be tolerated.

Theodore Roosevelt, 1908:

It is safe to say that the prosperity of our people depends directly on the energy and intelligence with which our natural resources are used. It is equally clear that these resources are the final basis of national power and perpetuity. Finally, it is ominously evident that these resources are in the course of rapid exhaustion.

from *The American Nation: A History*, 1918:

Serious difficulties appeared. So many costly projects were undertaken that funds became insufficient, and to avert injustice to settlers Congress was obliged, by act of June 25, 1910, to authorize a bond issue in aid of the Service to the amount of twenty million dollars. Embarrassment arose, too, from the slowness of settlers to make entry of the irrigated lands, and from the inability of some to keep up their payments to the government. Early in the administration of President Wilson the conviction that the main need was more intelligent and more intensive farming led to an arrangement whereby each of the fifteen principal projects was provided with an expert agriculturist to advise the settlers and to assist them in growing better crops and finding better markets . . .

1906 Antiquities Act

The written history of the United States extends back to only 1776, and the history of the colonies back to 1607, but North America's prehistoric history goes back much further. Native Americans had been in North America for at least ten thousand years. Through the eighteenth and nineteenth centuries, Americans found remnants of the prehistoric past all across the country, from the deserts to the plains. Cliff dwellings, Native American burial mounds, and other ruins were found and looted by enterprising or curious folk. Even Thomas Jefferson was interested; at one point he excavated an ancient Native American burial mound. The country is filled with unique geologic formations that date back millions of years. From the time of the first explorers, people were aware of these marvels, but until the Antiquities Act was passed in 1906, there was no law to protect archaeological finds or natural wonders.

Not only did the Antiquities Act provide penalties for anyone who injured historic or prehistoric remains on federal lands, it also gave the president the full authority to set aside National Monuments that would be forever protected as national treasures. President Theodore Roosevelt, a big proponent of the Antiquities Act, set aside many thousands of acres of land as National Monuments, including the Muir Woods and Pinnacles National Monument in California, and the Mount Olympus National Monument in Washington. Decades later, presidents are still using the Antiquities Act to preserve federal land for posterity; two new national monuments were created in 2006, the African Burial Ground in New York City and the Northwestern Hawaiian Islands Marine in Hawaii.

Devils Tower in Wyoming, the nation's first National Monument, was preserved under the Antiquities Act of 1906.

Be it enacted by the Senate and House of Representatives of the United States of America in Congress assembled, That any person who shall appropriate, excavate, injure, or destroy any historic or prehistoric ruin or monument, or any object of antiquity, situated on lands owned or controlled by the Government of the United States, without the permission of the Secretary of the Department of the Government having jurisdiction over the lands on which said antiquities are situated, shall, upon conviction, be fined in a sum of not more than five hundred dollars or be imprisoned for a period of not more than ninety days, or shall suffer both fine and imprisonment, in the discretion of the court.

Section 2

That the President of the United States is hereby authorized, in his discretion, to declare by public proclamation historic landmarks, historic and prehistoric structures, and other objects of historic or scientific interest that are situated upon the lands owned or controlled by the Government of the United States to be national monuments, and may reserve as a part thereof parcels of land, the limits of which in all cases shall be confined to the smallest area compatible with proper care and management of the objects to be protected . . .

Section 3

That permits for the examination of ruins, the excavation of archaeological sites, and the gathering of objects of antiquity upon the lands under their respective jurisdictions may be granted by the Secretaries of the Interior, Agriculture, and War to institutions which the may deem properly qualified to conduct such examination, excavation, or gathering, subject to such rules and regulation as they may prescribe: Provided, That the examinations, excavations, and gatherings are undertaken for the benefit of reputable museums, universities, colleges, or other recognized scientific or educational institutions, with a view to increasing the knowledge of such objects, and that the gatherings shall be made for permanent preservation in public museums.

What They Were Saying

from *Preliminary Report on a Visit to the Navajo National Monument, Arizona*, 1911:

Manifestly, the purpose of a national monument is the preservation of important objects contained therein, and a primary object of archeological work should be to attract to it as many visitors and students as possible.

from *Proceedings* of the National Park Conference, 1911:

This is one of the most attractive of the national monuments made possible because of its great scientific interest, although the chief of the objects it protects and preserves are giant redwoods 18 feet in diameter at the base and 300 feet high. It is located about 7 miles northwest of San Francisco and is visited annually by thousands of people, who may almost step over from the crowded streets of a great modern city into a wilderness where nature reigns supreme and appalls with the magnitude of her works. The monument tract embraces 295 acres, covered with a virgin forest of which three-fourths are giant redwoods, with much fir and the common hardwoods of the coast country. . . .This magnificent possession of the people was the gift of a public-spirited citizen of San Francisco and Chicago, William Kent, who placed a market value on the redwoods alone at $150,000, but who believed that as the attractive and impressive feature of a national monument they would be priceless. . . . It is certain in the years to come that this unique and accessible national monument will be visited and appreciated by a growing army of nature-loving people. The custodian estimates that 50,000 people visited it the past year.

7

America at War

★★★

The first half of the twentieth century was punctuated by two world wars. Our entry into the first war was not anticipated, but Germany forced our hand with its aggression in the Atlantic. Although patriotism and cooperation ran high in 1917 and 1918—the years of American involvement in the war—national interest in foreign affairs waned by 1920. Woodrow Wilson's efforts to get the United States to join the League of Nations he helped create failed and the American government retreated into an isolationist policy once again. The three Republican presidents elected after the Democrat Wilson left office were a sign that Americans wanted no further part of European issues. After the Great Depression hit, the Democrat Franklin Roosevelt was elected. He created many new programs aimed at helping the economy and the citizens, including a comprehensive Social Security package. When World War II began, the United States tried to maintain its neutrality. That ended when the Japanese attacked Pearl Harbor in 1941, bringing the United States into the war, consequently sparking the economy and ending the Depression. The relocation of Japanese Americans notwithstanding, Roosevelt proved to be an excellent wartime leader. World War II ended after Roosevelt's death with the surrender of Germany in May 1945, and Japan in August 1945 after the United States dropped atomic bombs on two of its cities.

1917 President Wilson Declares War

At the start of the Great War (later known as World War I) in 1914, President Woodrow Wilson declared the neutrality of the United States, saying, "Every man who really loves America will act and speak in the true spirit of neutrality." However, German submarines in the waters of the Atlantic Ocean soon threatened the safety of all kinds of ships, including those carrying American passengers. On May 7, 1915, the ocean liner *Lusitania* was torpedoed and sunk near Ireland. More than one hundred Americans were killed in that attack. By 1917, the situation had deteriorated further. On March 1, the so-called Zimmerman Note was made public. This intercepted document was a letter written by the German foreign secretary to a German diplomat in Mexico. In it, Secretary Zimmerman proposed trying to keep the United States neutral but failing that, suggested an alliance between Germany and Mexico. On April 2, President Wilson addressed Congress. Four days later, Congress passed a joint resolution stating that "a state of war between the United States and the Imperial German Government, which has been thrust upon the United States, is hereby formally declared."

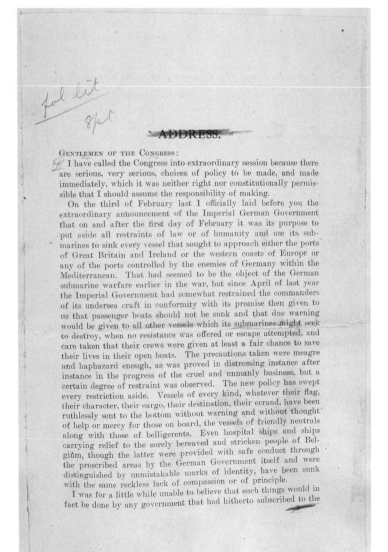

Woodrow Wilson's War Message to Congress

I have called the Congress into extraordinary session because there are serious, very serious, choices of policy to be made, and made immediately, which it was neither right nor constitutionally permissible that I should assume the responsibility of making.

On the 3d of February last I officially laid before you the extraordinary announcement of the Imperial German Government that on and after the 1st day of February it was its purpose to put aside all restraints of law or of humanity and use its submarines to sink every vessel that sought to approach either the ports of Great Britain and Ireland or the western coasts of Europe or any of the ports controlled by the enemies of Germany within the Mediterranean. . . . Vessels of every kind, whatever their flag, their character, their cargo, their destination, their errand, have been ruthlessly sent to the bottom without warning and without thought of help or mercy for those on board, the vessels of friendly neutrals along with those of belligerents. Even hospital ships and ships carrying relief to the sorely bereaved and stricken people of Belgium, though the latter were provided with safe-conduct through the proscribed areas by the German Government itself and were distinguished by unmistakable marks of identity, have been sunk with the same reckless lack of compassion or of principle. . . .

It is a war against all nations. American ships have been sunk, American lives taken, in ways which it has stirred us very deeply to learn of, but the ships and people of other neutral and friendly nations have been sunk and overwhelmed in the waters in the same way. There has been no discrimination. The challenge is to all mankind. Each nation must decide for itself how it will meet it. The choice we make for ourselves must be made with a moderation of counsel and a temperateness of judgment befitting our character and our motives as a nation. We must put excited feeling away. Our motive will not be revenge or the victorious assertion of the physical might of the nation, but only the vindication of right, of human right, of which we are only a single champion.

When I addressed the Congress on the 26th of February last, I thought that it would suffice to assert our neutral rights with arms, our right to use the seas against unlawful interference, our right to keep our people safe against unlawful violence. But armed neutrality, it now appears, is impracticable . . .

With a profound sense of the solemn and even tragical character of the step I am taking and of the grave responsibilities which it involves, but in unhesitating obedience to what I deem my constitutional duty, I advise that the Congress declare the recent course of the Imperial German Government to be in fact nothing less than war against the Government and people of the United States; that it formally accept the status of belligerent which has thus been thrust upon it, and that it take immediate steps not only to put the country in a more thorough state of defense but also to exert all its power and employ all its resources to bring the Government of the German Empire to terms and end the war.

What this will involve is clear. . . . It will involve the organization and mobilization of all the material resources of the country to supply the materials of war and serve the incidental needs of the nation in the most abundant and yet the most economical and efficient way possible. It will involve the immediate full equipment of the Navy in all respects but particularly in supplying it with the best means of dealing with the enemy's submarines. It will involve the immediate addition to the armed forces of the United States already provided for by law in case of war at least 500,000 men . . .

We have no quarrel with the German people. We have no feeling towards them but one of sympathy and friendship. It was not upon their impulse that their Government acted in entering this war. It was not with their previous knowledge or approval. . . .

It is a distressing and oppressive duty, gentlemen of the Congress, which I have performed in thus addressing you. There are, it may be, many months of fiery trial and sacrifice ahead of us. It is a fearful thing to lead this great peaceful people into war, into the most terrible and disastrous of all wars, civilization itself seeming to be in the balance. But the right is more precious than peace, and we shall fight for the things which we have always carried nearest our hearts—for democracy, for the right of those who submit to authority to have a voice in their own governments, for the rights and liberties of small nations, for a universal dominion of right by such a concert of free peoples as shall bring peace and safety to all nations and make the world itself at last free. To such a task we can dedicate our lives and our fortunes, everything that we are and everything that we have, with the pride of those who know that the day has come when America is privileged to spend her blood and her might for the principles that gave her birth and happiness and the peace which she has treasured. God helping her, she can do no other.

 What They Were Saying

from *Americans Defending Democracy*, 1919:

The strong, brave, contending soldiers, however, were not the only sufferers of the war. There were other wounds than those inflicted by shot and shell. The wives, the mothers, the fathers, the brothers, the sisters of the crippled soldiers, and of those who lie in Flanders fields are among the keenest of war sufferers. No comradeship of trench or field, nor music of fife and drum, can steal away their pain of bereavement or soothe their misery.

from *A History of the United States for Schools*, 1920:

The promptness and zeal with which the American people responded to the action of the government was a signal proof of their loyalty and patriotism.

President Wilson asks Congress to declare war on Germany, 1917.

Disorder and unfairness characterized the Civil War draft. During that war, a rich man could pay someone else to take his place on the battlefield. Though many Americans hoped a draft would never again be needed, the American armed forces were not very extensive by the time the United States entered World War I. Without conscription, there simply would not be enough soldiers to fight the Germans and help the Allies (including the French and British) win the war. This time, Congress created a more equitable and orderly draft bill, and on May 18, 1917, they passed the Selective Service Act. The draft was used three times between June 1917 and September 1918. First requiring men between twenty-one and thirty-one years of age to register, the draft was then changed to include those aged eighteen to twenty-one, and thirty-one to forty-five.

Shown on the next page is the text of President Wilson's proclamation on the draft, given ten days after Congress approved the draft bill.

A World War I recruitment poster.

I, Woodrow Wilson, President of the United States... proclaim and give notice to all persons subject to registration in the several states and in the District of Columbia in accordance with the above law, that the time and place of such registration shall be between 7 a. m. and 9 p. m. on the 5th day of June, 1917, at the registration place in the precinct wherein they have their permanent homes.

Those who shall have attained their twenty-first birthday and who shall not have attained their thirty-first birthday on or before the day here named are required to register, excepting only officers and enlisted men of the regular Army, the Navy, the Marine Corps, and the National Guard and Naval Militia while in the service of the United States, and officers in the officers' reserve corps and enlisted men in the enlisted reserve corps while in active service . . .

The power against which we are arrayed has sought to impose its will upon the world by force. To this end it has increased armament until it has changed the face of war. In the sense in which we have been wont to think of armies there are no armies in this struggle. There are entire nations armed. Thus, the men who remain to till the soil and man the factories are no less a part of the army than the men beneath the battle flags. It must be so with us. It is not an army that we must shape and train for war; it is a nation.

To this end our people must draw close in one compact front against a common foe. But this cannot be if each man pursue a private purpose. All must pursue one purpose.

The nation needs all men; but it needs each man, not in the field that will most pleasure him, but in the endeavor that will best serve the common good. Thus, though a sharpshooter pleases to operate a triphammer for the forging of great guns, and an expert machinist desires to march with the flag, the nation is being served only when the sharpshooter marches and the machinist remains at his levers. The whole nation must be a team in which each man shall play the part for which he is best fitted. To this end, Congress has provided that the nation shall be organized for war by selection and that each man shall be classified for service in the place to which it shall best serve the general good to call him.

The significance of this cannot be overstated. It is a new thing in our history and a landmark in our progress. It is a new manner of accepting and vitalizing our duty to give ourselves with thoughtful devotion to the common purpose of us all. It is in no sense a conscription of the unwilling; it is rather selection from a nation which has volunteered in mass. It is no more a choosing of those who shall march with the colors than it is a selection of those who shall serve an equally necessary and devoted purpose in the industries that lie behind the battle line.

The day here named is the time upon which all shall present themselves for assignment to their tasks. It is for that reason destined to be remembered as one of the most conspicuous moments in our history. It is nothing less than the day upon which the manhood of the country shall step forward in one solid rank in defense of the ideals to which this nation is consecrated. It is important to those ideals no less than to the pride of this generation in manifesting its devotion to them that there be no gaps in the ranks.

It is essential that the day be approached in thoughtful apprehension of its significance and that we accord to it the honor and the meaning that it deserves . . .

 # What They Were Saying

from a war bond advertisement in a boys magazine, 1918:

I wish I was old enough to fight. Do you know what "Retreat" is in the Army? I always thought it was something about running away, or getting licked, or something. Only I knew our boys don't run away and I often wondered about it. But last fall Mother and Sis and I were at an Army Camp where my brother is a First-class Private; he's only nineteen and he enlisted when War was declared. Well we were visiting him one evening, and the bugle blew, and the boys "Fell in," and at command they all "Presented Arms," and the sun was just setting and it seemed awful kind of quiet, like a noise had stopped when the sun went down. And the Colonel and his staff were standing there, when "B-o-o-m!" went a gun, and the band began to play "The Star Spangled Banner," and the Color Sergeant and the Color Guard hauled down the Big Beautiful Flag, and there was a lump in my throat, but I didn't want to cry. I was just GLAD, and gee! How I wanted to be old enough to carry a gun and "Present Arms" to the flag when the sun goes down. But I'm busy these days in war gardens and it's easy to earn money. And every cent I get I count up at sunset, and present it to the Flag—in WAR SAVINGS STAMPS. I'll help lick those Germans yet.

from *The World's Work*, 1919:

If all are to participate in the Government, all should defend or be prepared to defend the Government against attack since the Government is the people, is the means by which the voice of the people finds expression. There is as much logic then in the assertion that the defense of the country should be borne by a volunteer soldiery as there would be in the claim that the expense of running the country should be provided by volunteer taxation. Both are ridiculous. The President realized this and realized further the failure which was inherent in the volunteer system when in his war message to Congress in April, 1917, he cast the volunteer idea aside and pleaded for universal service as the only feasible means of putting into the field against Germany the man power of the country.

1918 Wilson's Fourteen Points

President Woodrow Wilson entered World War I begrudgingly only after neutrality was no longer possible. Many months before the war ended in November 1918, Wilson began to play a part in the prospective peace. He drafted "Fourteen Points" to be considered during the peace process. Over the following months (but still before the war ended), he added an additional thirteen points. When Germany surrendered, Wilson's points served as the terms of the armistice.

Twenty-seven nations gathered for the Paris Peace Conference in January 1919 to try to work out the terms of a peace treaty. They discussed Wilson's points and debated the terms and language of the treaty, which was finally signed in June 1919.

Wilson was also very active in promoting the idea of a League of Nations (precursor to the United Nations; see point XIV), an international watchdog and support organization. Negative feelings about the toll of the war, however, led to the election of a Republican president, Warren Harding, and propelled a return to a policy of isolationism. Despite Wilson's continued lobbying for support, the United States did not join the League of Nations. Franklin Roosevelt was the next president to promote American participation in a world organization, more than twenty years later. When the United Nations was founded in 1945, it owed a debt to Woodrow Wilson.

frankness, a largeness of view, a generosity of spirit, and a universal human sympathy which must challenge the admiration of every friend of mankind; and they have refused to compound their ideals or desert others that they themselves may be safe. They call to us to say what it is that we desire, in what, if in anything, our purpose and our spirit differ from theirs; and I believe that the people of the United States would wish me to respond, with utter simplicity and frankness. Whether their present leaders believe it or not, it is our heartfelt desire and hope that some way may be opened whereby we may be privileged to assist the people of Russia to attain their utmost hope of liberty and ordered peace.

It will be our wish and purpose that the processes of peace, when they are begun, shall be absolutely open and that they shall involve and permit henceforth no secret understandings of any kind. The day of conquest and aggrandizement is gone by; so is also the day of secret covenants entered into in the interest of particular governments and likely at some unlooked-for moment to upset the peace of the world. It is this happy fact, now clear to the view of every public man whose thoughts do not still linger in an age that is dead and gone, which makes it possible for every nation whose purposes are consistent with justice and the peace of the world to avow now or at any other time the objects it has in view.

We entered this war because violations of right had occurred which touched us to the quick and made the life of our own people impossible unless they were corrected and the world secured once for all against their recurrence. What we demand in this war, therefore, is nothing peculiar to ourselves. It is that the world be made fit and safe to live in; and particularly that it be made safe for every peace-loving nation which, like our own, wishes to live its own life, determine its own institutions, be assured of justice and fair dealing by the other peoples of the world as against force and selfish aggression. All the peoples of the world are in effect partners in this interest, and for our own part we see very clearly that unless justice be done to others it will not be done to us. The programme of the world's peace, therefore, is our programme; and that programme, the only possible programme, as we see it, is this:

I. Open covenants of peace, openly arrived at, after which there shall be no private international understandings of any kind but diplomacy shall proceed always frankly and in the public view.

II. Absolute freedom of navigation upon the seas, outside territorial waters, alike in peace and in war, except as the seas may be closed in whole or in part by international action for the enforcement of international covenants.

III. The removal, so far as possible, of all economic barriers and the establishment of an equality of trade conditions among all the

We entered this war because violations of right had occurred which touched us to the quick and made the life of our own people impossible unless they were corrected and the world secure once for all against their recurrence. What we demand in this war, therefore, is nothing peculiar to ourselves. It is that the world be made fit and safe to live in; and particularly that it be made safe for every peace-loving nation which, like our own, wishes to live its own life, determine its own institutions, be assured of justice and fair dealing by the other peoples of the world as against force and selfish aggression. All the peoples of the world are in effect partners in this interest, and for our own part we see very clearly that unless justice be done to others it will not be done to us. The programme of the world's peace, therefore, is our programme; and that programme, the only possible programme, as we see it, is this:

I. Open covenants of peace, openly arrived at, after which there shall be no private international understandings of any kind but diplomacy shall proceed always frankly and in the public view.

II. Absolute freedom of navigation upon the seas, outside territorial waters, alike in peace and in war, except as the seas may be closed in whole or in part by international action for the enforcement of international covenants.

III. The removal, so far as possible, of all economic barriers and the establishment of an equality of trade conditions among all the nations consenting to the peace and associating themselves for its maintenance.

IV. Adequate guarantees given and taken that national armaments will be reduced to the lowest point consistent with domestic safety.

V. A free, open-minded, and absolutely impartial adjustment of all colonial claims, based upon a strict observance of the principle that in determining all such questions of sovereignty the interests of the populations concerned must have equal weight with the equitable claims of the government whose title is to be determined.

VI. The evacuation of all Russian territory and such a settlement of all questions affecting Russia as will secure the best and freest cooperation of the other nations of the world in obtaining for her an unhampered and unembarrassed opportunity for the independent determination of her own political development and national policy and assure her of a sincere welcome into the society of free nations under institutions of her own choosing; and, more than a welcome, assistance also of every kind that she may need and may herself desire. The treatment accorded Russia by her sister nations in the months to come will be the acid test of their good will, of their comprehension of her needs as distinguished from their own interests, and of their intelligent and unselfish sympathy.

VII. Belgium, the whole world will agree, must be evacuated and restored, without any attempt to limit the sovereignty which she enjoys in common with all other free nations. No other single act will serve as this will serve to restore confidence among the nations in the laws which they have themselves set and determined for the government of their relations with one another. Without this healing act the whole structure and validity of international law is forever impaired.

VIII. All French territory should be freed and the invaded portions restored, and the wrong done to France by Prussia in 1871 in the matter of Alsace-Lorraine, which has unsettled the peace of the world for nearly fifty years, should be righted, in order that peace may once more be made secure in the interest of all.

IX. A readjustment of the frontiers of Italy should be effected along clearly recognizable lines of nationality.

X. The peoples of Austria-Hungary, whose place among the nations we wish to see safeguarded and assured, should be accorded the freest opportunity to autonomous development.

XI. Rumania, Serbia, and Montenegro should be evacuated; occupied territories restored; Serbia accorded free and secure access to the sea; and the relations of the several Balkan states to one another determined by friendly counsel along historically established lines of allegiance and nationality; and international guarantees of the political and economic independence and territorial integrity of the several Balkan states should be entered into.

XII. The turkish portion of the present Ottoman Empire should be assured a secure sovereignty, but the other nationalities which are now under Turkish rule should be assured an undoubted security of life and an absolutely unmolested opportunity of autonomous development, and the Dardanelles should be permanently opened as a free passage to the ships and commerce of all nations under international guarantees.

XIII. An independent Polish state should be erected which should include the territories inhabited by indisputably Polish populations, which should be assured a free and secure access to the sea, and whose political and economic independence and territorial integrity should be guaranteed by international covenant.

XIV. A general association of nations must be formed under specific covenants for the purpose of affording mutual guarantees of political independence and territorial integrity to great and small states alike.

In regard to these essential rectifications of wrong and assertions of right we feel ourselves to be intimate partners of all the governments and peoples associated together against the Imperialists. We cannot be separated in interest or divided in purpose. We stand together until the end.

For such arrangements and covenants we are willing to fight and to continue to fight until they are achieved; but only because we wish the right to prevail and desire a just and stable peace such as can be secured only by removing the chief provocations to war, which this programme does remove. We have no jealousy of German greatness, and there is nothing in this programme that impairs it. We grudge her no achievement or distinction of learning or of pacific enterprise such as have made her record very bright and very enviable. We do not wish to injure her or to block in any way her legitimate influence or power. We do not wish to fight her either with arms or with hostile arrangements of trade if she is willing to associate herself with us and the other peace- loving nations of the world in covenants of justice and law and fair dealing. We wish her only to accept a place of equality among the peoples of the world,—the new world in which we now live,—instead of a place of mastery.

 What They Were Saying

Corporal Barney Tovin, Bronx, New York, 1919:

On the morning of November 11th, [1918] a radio came over the wire at ten o'clock, stating that at eleven all hostility would stop in that hour. Every gun was firing and all infantry went "over the top" and the Yankee gave "Fritz" [the Germans] the grand finale of the war. Promptly at eleven o'clock, all guns ceased firing and we sat in the roads and scattered about like lost sheep, with nothing to do, all dressed up for war, and no place to go. We were lined up and our Company commander read us [General] Pershing's order, which said: "Soldiers of the American Army, this is not peace, but only an armistice. The enemy is not to be trusted. They fooled our Associates in the war before." That night we blew up all our guns and ammunition dumps, throwing hand grenades and rockets into the air. You never saw such a Fourth of July celebration equal to it.

Massachusetts Senator Henry Cabot Lodge, 1919:

I object in the strongest possible way to having the United States agree, directly or indirectly, to be controlled by a league which may at any time, and perfectly lawfully and in accordance with the terms of the covenant, draw us in to deal with internal conflicts in other countries, no matter what those conflicts may be. We should never permit the United States to be involved in any internal conflict in another country, except by the will of her people expressed through the Congress which represents them.

1919 Eighteenth Amendment

The Temperance Movement had its beginnings with women who were tired of their husbands coming home drunk, having spent all of their hard-earned pay on alcohol. By the end of the nineteenth century, a groundswell of support began to build for banning the manufacture and sale of alcohol. States began to implement their own controls over alcohol consumption. By 1915, nine states had implemented Prohibition and seventeen states had near-Prohibition (where more than half of the population was under Prohibition laws of some kind). But proponents knew that if left to the states' authority, nationwide Prohibition would never happen. These "anti-saloon" leaders wanted an amendment to the Constitution. They published literature showing the harmful effects of alcohol—from insanity to poverty to poor education—and got their wish in 1919, when the Eighteenth Amendment was ratified. The amendment affected the jobs of more than seventy-seven thousand people who were employed in the making and distribution of alcoholic beverages. But Prohibition did not stop the consumption of alcohol, it only forced it underground. Backroom saloons and home-brewed liquor (moonshine) were widespread, and gangsters controlled much of the illegal alcohol trade. In 1933, the amendment was repealed by the ratification of the Twenty-First Amendment, and sales of alcoholic beverages were once again legal.

New York City's deputy police commissioner watches federal agents pour illegal alcohol down the sewer, 1921.

Section 1. After one year from the ratification of this article the manufacture, sale, or transportation of intoxicating liquors within, the importation thereof into, or the exportation thereof from the United States and all territory subject to the jurisdiction thereof for beverage purposes is hereby prohibited.

Section 2. The Congress and the several states shall have concurrent power to enforce this article by appropriate legislation.

What They Were Saying

from the Declaration of Principles of the Anti-Saloon League of America, 1913:

The liquor traffic is national in its organization, character and influence. It overflows the boundaries of States and refuses to be regulated or controlled. It is a federal evil; a national menace, too powerful for State authority, requiring national jurisdiction and treatment. It beggars the individual, burdens the State, and impoverishes the Nation. It commercializes vice and capitalizes human weakness. It impairs the public health; breaks the public peace and debauches the public morals. It intimidates and makes cowards of public men. It dominates parties and conventions . . . We therefore declare for its national annihilation by an amendment to the Federal Constitution which shall forever prohibit throughout the territory of the United States the manufacture and sale and the importation, exportation and transportation of intoxicating liquors to be used as a beverage.

1920 Nineteenth Amendment

The efforts of the suffragists finally began to bear fruit during the late nineteenth and early twentieth centuries. By 1917, twelve states allowed women to vote, but the entire American population was not yet in favor of equal suffrage for women. In August 1917 suffragists working at Cameron House, their Washington, D.C., headquarters, were attacked by a mob of government workers and military men. These men threw eggs at the Cameron House and beat and injured the women as they left work for the day. None of the perpetrators were arrested. Between 1917 and 1919, however, more than five hundred women were arrested during various protests around the country, including prominent activists, writers, teachers, and daughters of politicians. Nonetheless, by 1919 the suffragist movement had enough political clout to propel Congress to propose a constitutional amendment to allow women to vote. It was adopted August 26, 1920, in time for millions of women across the country to cast their first ballot in the 1920 presidential election, choosing between Woodrow Wilson and Warren Harding. The ratification was not unanimous; seven states had rejected the amendment.

H. J. Res. 1.

Sixty-sixth Congress of the United States of America;

At the First Session,

Begun and held at the City of Washington on Monday, the nineteenth day of May, one thousand nine hundred and nineteen.

JOINT RESOLUTION

Proposing an amendment to the Constitution extending the right of suffrage to women.

Resolved by the Senate and House of Representatives of the United States of America in Congress assembled (two-thirds of each House concurring therein), That the following article is proposed as an amendment to the Constitution, which shall be valid to all intents and purposes as part of the Constitution when ratified by the legislatures of three-fourths of the several States.

"ARTICLE ————.

"The right of citizens of the United States to vote shall not be denied or abridged by the United States or by any State on account of sex.

"Congress shall have power to enforce this article by appropriate legislation."

F. H. Gillett

Speaker of the House of Representatives.

Thos. R. Marshall

Vice President of the United States and President of the Senate.

The right of citizens of the United States to vote shall not be denied or abridged by the United States or by any state on account of sex.

Congress shall have power to enforce this article by appropriate legislation.

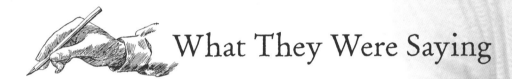 What They Were Saying

The commissioner of education, 1919:

Within the last few years millions of women have been given the franchise and now have all the privileges, responsibilities, and powers of actual citizenship. The adoption of the 19th amendment to the Constitution of the United States will add to these millions millions more. When these women become voters, they will, by their ballots or otherwise, determine wisely or unwisely the policies of municipalities, States, and the Nation. They are conscientious; they realize they need instruction as to the duties and responsibilities of active citizenship and help toward an understanding of the many complex and difficult problems which by their ballot they will help to solve. Through their clubs and various other organizations educational extension workers can do much for them.

from *A History of the United States for Schools*, 1920:

Women now have scholastic advantages formerly limited to men, and have taken their place in many fields of activity once exclusively occupied by men. This has come about, however, not only because of a broader general training, but partly on account of the transfer of many household duties to the mill and factory. As we know, many household supplies which women made by hand in the home a hundred years ago are now made by the use of power machines within factory walls. Women are also doing more than they ever did before in the many forms of public service which make for a finer public spirit and a better civil life. By reason of these and other facts, in 1919 Congress proposed an amendment to the Constitution providing for full suffrage for women throughout the Union.

1935 Social Security Act

The Social Security Act was just one of President Franklin Roosevelt's New Deal programs aimed at providing assistance to Americans during the Great Depression. Roosevelt believed that in order to get America out of the Depression, people needed a helping hand from the government. Some of his programs, such as the Civilian Conservation Corps (CCC), were designed to give people jobs while providing essential services to the country. The Social Security Act was amazing in the scope of its coverage. It helped those out of work or injured and unable to work, those who were retired, and even provided a "death benefit" to go to a surviving spouse.

There were enough proponents of the New Deal that Franklin Roosevelt was elected to office a record four times. His supporters felt that Americans needed something to fall back on in times of need. Of course, there was a catch to this program: Social Security was not free. The system called for employees to pay a percentage of their salary toward the system and also required employers to contribute money.

Not everyone was a fan of the New Deal programs. Some people felt that the Social Security Act and similar programs were symbols of big government, meaning too much government involvement in the everyday lives of citizens.

An act to provide for the general welfare by establishing a system of Federal old-age benefits, and by enabling the several States to make more adequate provision for aged persons, blind persons, dependent and crippled children, maternal and child welfare, public health, and the administration of their unemployment compensation laws; to establish a Social Security Board; to raise revenue; and for other purposes. . . .

Title I Grants to States for Old-Age
Assistance Appropriation

Section 1. For the purpose of enabling each State to furnish financial assistance, as far as practicable under the conditions in such State, to aged needy individuals, there is hereby authorized to be appropriated for the fiscal year ended June 30, 1936, the sum of $49,750,000, and there is hereby authorized to be appropriated for each fiscal year thereafter a sum sufficient to carry out the purposes of this title. The sums made available under this section shall be used for making payments to States which have submitted, and had approved by the Social Security Board established by Title VII (hereinafter referred to as the Board), State plans for old-age assistance. . . .

Title II Federal Old-Age Benefits
Old-Age Reserve Account

Section 201

There is hereby created an account in the Treasury of the United States to be known as the Old-Age Reserve Account hereinafter in this title called the Account. There is hereby authorized to be appropriated to the Account for each fiscal year, beginning with the fiscal year ending June 30, 1937, an amount sufficient as an annual premium to provide for the payments required under this title, such amount to be determined on a reserve basis in accordance with accepted actuarial principles, and based upon such tables of mortality as

the Secretary of the Treasury shall from time to time adopt, and upon an interest rate of 3 per centum per annum compounded annually. The Secretary of the Treasury shall submit annually to the Bureau of the Budget an estimate of the appropriations to be made to the Account. . . .

Old-Age Benefit Payments

Section 202

Every qualified individual . . . shall be entitled to receive, with respect to the period beginning on the date he attains the age of sixty-five, or on January 1, 1942, whichever is the later, and ending on the date of his death, an old-age benefit (payable as nearly as practicable in equal monthly installments) . . .

Payments Upon Death

Section 203

If any individual dies before attaining the age of sixty-five, there shall be paid to his estate an amount equal to 3½ per centum of the total wages determined by the Board to have been paid to him . . .

Title III Grants to States for Unemployment
Compensation Administration

Section 301

For the purpose of assisting the States in the administration of their unemployment compensation laws, there is hereby authorized to be appropriated, for the fiscal year ending June 30, 1936, the sum of $4,000,000, and for each fiscal year thereafter the sum of $49,000,000, to be used as hereinafter provided. . . .

Title IV Grants to States for Aid to Dependent Children

Section 401

For the purpose of enabling each State to furnish financial assistance, as far as practicable under the conditions in such State, to needy dependent children, there is hereby authorized to be appropriated for the fiscal year ending June 30, 1936, the sum of $24,750,000, and there is hereby authorized to be appropriated for each fiscal year thereafter a sum sufficient to carry out the purposes of this title. The sums made available under this section shall be used for making payments to States which have submitted, and had approved by the Board, State plans for aid to dependent children. . . .

Title V Grants to States for Maternal and Child Welfare
Section 501
For the purpose of enabling each State to extend and improve, as far as practicable under the conditions in such State, services for promoting the health of mothers and children, especially in rural areas and in areas suffering from severe economic distress, there is hereby authorized to be appropriated for each fiscal year, beginning with the fiscal year ending June 30, 1936, the sum of $3,800,000. The sums made available under this section shall be used for making payments to States which have submitted, and had approved by the Chief of the Children's Bureau, State plans for such services. . . .

Title VIII Taxes with Respect to Employment: Income Taxes on Employees
Section 801
In addition to other taxes, there shall be levied, collected, and paid upon the income of every individual a tax equal to the following percentages of the wages . . . received by him after December 31, 1936, with respect to employment . . . after such date: (1) With respect to employment during the calendar years 1937, 1938, and 1939, the rate shall be 1 per centum. (2) With respect to employment during the calendar years 1940, 1941, and 1942, the rate shall 1 per centum. (3) With respect to employment during the calendar years 1943, 1944, and 1945, the rate shall be 2 per centum. (4) With respect to employment during the calendar years 1946, 1947, and 1948, the rate shall be 2 per centum. (5) With respect to employment after December 31, 1948, the rate shall be 3 per centum. . . .

Excise Tax on Employers
Section 804
In addition to other taxes, every employer shall pay an excise tax, with respect to having individuals in his employ.

 What They Were Saying

from a letter from Claude W. in New York to a friend in Missouri, 1936:

Business conditions seem improving right along but I do not think we will ever see all the unemployed back at work, unless we reduce the working hours and week days; there has been too many females that have taken up jobs that should go to men, however Roosevelt is doing a good job and if they will only let him carry out his ideas we will all at least have social security and there will be no starving to death, however, I am afraid quite a number of people now on relief will get in the habit of not working and will not work if the opportunity offers.

President Roosevelt's December 8, 1941, Address to Congress 1941

During the 1930s, as Germany built up an army and created an arsenal of weapons, the United States tried hard to maintain its neutrality. After World War II began in 1939, the United States found discreet ways to assist Great Britain in its fight against Germany while still appearing to retain neutrality. A little over two years after the start of World War II, the United States was forced to join the fight when, on the morning of December 7, 1941, Japanese planes conducted a surprise attack on American forces stationed at Pearl Harbor, Hawaii. With neutrality no longer an option, an outraged President Franklin Roosevelt gave a speech before Congress that instantly became one of the best-known and most important presidential speeches in our history. World War II had an even greater scope (with major fronts in Asia, Africa, and Europe) and took a greater toll (in both lives lost and costs) on the country than did World War I.

Roosevelt excelled as a wartime leader. He provided moral support to the millions of Americans who remained on the home front by making the right decisions at the right times. For example, in 1942, he wrote a now-famous "green light" letter to the baseball commissioner, telling the commissioner to let baseball continue during the war. Though not a big fan of baseball himself, Roosevelt knew that baseball was extremely popular, and it was a way for average Americans to get their minds off the troubles of the war for a couple of hours.

TO THE CONGRESS OF THE UNITED STATES:

Yesterday, December 7, 1941 — a date which will live in infamy — the United States of America was suddenly and deliberately attacked by naval and air forces of the Empire of Japan.

The United States was at peace with that nation and, at the solicitation of Japan, was still in conversation with its Government and its Emperor looking toward the maintenance of peace in the Pacific. Indeed, one hour after Japanese air squadrons had commenced bombing in Oahu, the Japanese Ambassador to the United States and his colleague delivered to the Secretary of State a formal reply to a recent American message. While this reply stated that it seemed useless to continue the existing diplomatic negotiations, it contained no threat or hint of war or armed attack.

It will be recorded that the distance of Hawaii from Japan makes it obvious that the attack was deliberately planned many days or even weeks ago. During the intervening time the Japanese Government has deliberately sought to deceive the United States by false statements and expressions of hope for continued peace.

The attack yesterday on the Hawaiian Islands has caused severe damage to American naval and military forces. Very many American lives have been lost. In addition American ships have been reported torpedoed on the high seas between San Francisco and Honolulu.

Yesterday, Dec. 7, 1941—a date which will live in infamy—the United States of America was suddenly and deliberately attacked by naval and air forces of the Empire of Japan.

The United States was at peace with that nation and, at the solicitation of Japan, was still in conversation with the government and its emperor looking toward the maintenance of peace in the Pacific.

Indeed, one hour after Japanese air squadrons had commenced bombing in Oahu, the Japanese ambassador to the United States and his colleague delivered to the Secretary of State a formal reply to a recent American message. While this reply stated that it seemed useless to continue the existing diplomatic negotiations, it contained no threat or hint of war or armed attack.

It will be recorded that the distance of Hawaii from Japan makes it obvious that the attack was deliberately planned many days or even weeks ago. During the intervening time, the Japanese government has deliberately sought to deceive the United States by false statements and expressions of hope for continued peace.

The attack yesterday on the Hawaiian Islands has caused severe damage to American naval and military forces. Very many American lives have been lost. In addition, American ships have been reported torpedoed on the high seas between San Francisco and Honolulu.

Yesterday, the Japanese government also launched an attack against Malaya.

Last night, Japanese forces attacked Hong Kong.

Last night, Japanese forces attacked Guam.

Last night, Japanese forces attacked the Philippine Islands.

Last night, the Japanese attacked Wake Island.

This morning, the Japanese attacked Midway Island.

Japan has, therefore, undertaken a surprise offensive extending throughout the Pacific area. The facts of yesterday speak for themselves. The people of the United States have already formed their opinions and well understand the implications to the very life and safety of our nation.

As commander in chief of the Army and Navy, I have directed that all measures be taken for our defense.

Always will we remember the character of the onslaught against us.

No matter how long it may take us to overcome this premeditated invasion, the American people, in their righteous might, will win through to absolute victory.

I believe I interpret the will of the Congress and of the people when I assert that we will not only defend ourselves to the uttermost, but will make very certain that this form of treachery shall never endanger us again.

Hostilities exist. There is no blinking at the fact that that our people, our territory and our interests are in grave danger.

With confidence in our armed forces—with the unbounding determination of our people—we will gain the inevitable triumph—so help us God.

I ask that the Congress declare that since the unprovoked and dastardly attack by Japan on Sunday, Dec. 7, a state of war has existed between the United States and the Japanese empire.

What They Were Saying

from a speech by President Franklin Roosevelt, February 1942:

This generation of Americans has come to realize, with a present and personal realization, that there is something larger and more important than the life of any individual or of any individual group—something for which a man will sacrifice, and gladly sacrifice, not only his pleasures, not only his goods, not only his associations with those he loves, but his life itself. In time of crisis when the future is in the balance, we come to understand, with full recognition and devotion, what this nation is and what we owe to it. . . .

The task that we Americans now face will test us to the uttermost. Never before have we been called upon for such a prodigious effort. Never before have we had so little time in which to do so much.

"These are the times that try men's souls."

Tom Paine wrote those words on a drumhead, by the light of a campfire. That was when Washington's little army of ragged, rugged men was retreating across New Jersey, having tasted (nothing) naught but defeat.

And General Washington ordered that these great words written by Tom Paine be read to the men of every regiment in the Continental Army, and this was the assurance given to the first American armed forces:

"The summer soldier and the sunshine patriot will, in this crisis, shrink from the service of their country; but he that stands it now, deserves the love and thanks of man and woman. Tyranny, like hell, is not easily conquered, yet we have this consolation with us, that the harder the sacrifice, the more glorious the triumph."

So spoke Americans in the year 1776.

So speak Americans today!

President Roosevelt signs the declaration of war against Japan, December, 1941.

1942 Japanese Relocation Order Issued

⭐⭐

One of the darker moments in our nation's history, the internment of Americans of Japanese descent during World War II, was seen at the time as a necessity. The attack on Pearl Harbor caught the country off guard and struck a nerve. Until 1941 most of our attention was on the Germans' activities in Europe; suddenly all eyes were on Japan. Pearl Harbor was of great concern because the attack took place on our soil. The fear was that the Japanese might try to attack the West Coast. Concern over the presence of many thousands of Japanese Americans in the western states led the government to take rash action and force Americans of Japanese descent away from their homes and into detention. Executive Order 9066 ordered Japanese Americans living on the West Coast to evacuate to relocation centers. Over 120,000 Americans spent the remainder of the war at one of several stark relocation centers, their normal lives on hold. Two cases of Japanese American men convicted of failing to obey military orders went before the Supreme Court in 1943 and 1944. The Court ruled against both men and upheld the constitutionality of the relocation program. In 1988, the government officially apologized to Japanese Americans for the forced relocations and authorized a reparation payment of twenty thousand dollars to those who had been relocated during the war.

EXECUTIVE ORDER

- - - - - -

AUTHORIZING THE SECRETARY OF WAR TO PRESCRIBE
MILITARY AREAS

WHEREAS the successful prosecution of the war requires every possible protection against espionage and against sabotage to national-defense material, national-defense premises, and national-defense utilities as defined in Section 4, Act of April 20, 1918, 40 Stat. 533, as amended by the Act of November 30, 1940, 54 Stat. 1220, and the Act of August 21, 1941, 55 Stat. 655 (U. S. C., Title 50, Sec. 104):

NOW, THEREFORE, by virtue of the authority vested in me as President of the United States, and Commander in Chief of the Army and Navy, I hereby authorize and direct the Secretary of War, and the Military Commanders whom he may from time to time designate, whenever he or any designated Commander deems such action necessary or desirable, to prescribe military areas in such places and of such extent as he or the appropriate Military Commander may determine, from which any or all persons may be excluded, and with respect to which, the right of any person to enter, remain in, or leave shall be subject to whatever restrictions the Secretary of War or the appropriate Military

Whereas the successful prosecution of the war requires every possible protection against espionage and against sabotage to national-defense material, national-defense premises, and national-defense utilities as defined in [list of statutes];

Now, therefore, by virtue of the authority vested in me as President of the United States, and Commander in Chief of the Army and Navy, I hereby authorize and direct the Secretary of War, and the Military Commanders whom he may from time to time designate, whenever he or any designated Commander deems such action necessary or desirable, to prescribe military areas in such places and of such extent as he or the appropriate Military Commander may determine, from which any or all persons may be excluded, and with respect to which, the right of any person to enter, remain in, or leave shall be subject to whatever restrictions the Secretary of War or the appropriate Military Commander may impose in his discretion. The Secretary of War is hereby authorized to provide for residents of any such area who are excluded therefrom, such transportation, food, shelter, and other accommodations as may be necessary, in the judgment of the Secretary of War or the said Military Commander, and

until other arrangements are made, to accomplish the purpose of this order. The designation of military areas in any region or locality shall supersede designations of prohibited and restricted areas by the Attorney General under the Proclamations of December 7 and 8, 1941, and shall supersede the responsibility and authority of the Attorney General under the said Proclamations in respect of such prohibited and restricted areas.

I hereby further authorize and direct the Secretary of War and the said Military Commanders to take such other steps as he or the appropriate Military Commander may deem advisable to enforce compliance with the restrictions applicable to each Military area hereinabove authorized to be designated, including the use of Federal troops and other Federal Agencies, with authority to accept assistance of state and local agencies.

I hereby further authorize and direct all Executive Departments, independent establishments and other Federal Agencies, to assist the Secretary of War or the said Military Commanders in carrying out this Executive Order, including the furnishing of medical aid, hospitalization, food, clothing, transportation, use of land, shelter, and other supplies, equipment, utilities, facilities, and services.

What They Were Saying

from the caption of a photo taken by the Office of War Information, 1942:

Mountain View, California. Members of the Shibuya family are pictured at their home before evacuation. The father and the mother were born in Japan and came to this country in 1904. At that time the father had sixty dollars cash and a basket of clothes. He later built a prosperous business of raising select varieties of chrysanthemums, which he shipped to Eastern markets under his own name. Six children in the family were born in the United States. The four older children attended leading California universities. Evacuees of Japanese ancestry will be housed in the War Relocation Authority centers for the duration.

from *Korematsu v. United States*, 1944:

It should be noted, to begin with, that all legal restrictions which curtail the civil rights of a single racial group are immediately suspect. That is not to say that all such restrictions are unconstitutional. It is to say that courts must subject them to the most rigid scrutiny. Pressing public necessity may sometimes justify the existence of such restrictions; racial antagonism never can. . . . It is said that we are dealing here with the case of imprisonment of a citizen in a concentration camp solely because of his ancestry, without evidence or inquiry concerning his loyalty and good disposition towards the United States. Our task would be simple, our duty clear, were this a case involving the imprisonment of a loyal citizen in a concentration camp because of racial prejudice. Regardless of the true nature of the assembly and relocation centers—and we deem it unjustifiable to call them concentration camps with all the ugly connotations that term implies—we are dealing specifically with nothing but an exclusion order. To cast this case into outlines of racial prejudice, without reference to the real military dangers which were presented, merely confuses the issue. Korematsu was not excluded from the Military Area because of hostility to him or his race. He was excluded because we are at war with the Japanese Empire, because the properly constituted military authorities feared an invasion of our West Coast and felt constrained to take proper security measures, because they decided that the military urgency of the situation demanded that all citizens of Japanese ancestry be segregated from the West Coast temporarily, and finally, because Congress, reposing its confidence in this time of war in our military leaders—as inevitably it must—determined that they should have the power to do just this. There was evidence of disloyalty on the part of some, the military authorities considered that the need for action was great, and time was short. We cannot—by availing ourselves of the calm perspective of hindsight—now say that at that time these actions were unjustified.

Manzanar War Relocation Center in California, one of several camps where Japanese Americans were sent during World War II.

1945 Atomic Bomb Is Dropped

On August 6, 1945, U.S. forces working under the order of President Harry Truman dropped an atomic bomb on the city of Hiroshima, Japan, wreaking tremendous destruction. Another devastating bomb followed a few days later on the city of Nagasaki. More than one hundred thousand Japanese people were killed and many thousands more were severely injured. The U.S. government had been secretly working on the development of an atomic bomb for years, mostly based out of a facility in Los Alamos, New Mexico. It was a massive effort; more than one hundred thousand Americans had been involved in the various stages of the development and creation of the bomb. Because of its serious implications, the decision to drop the atomic bomb was a difficult one for President Harry Truman. Though the war in Europe had ended in May, the war with Japan seemed unlikely to end soon. An American invasion of Japan itself would be extremely difficult to manage, but without it, Japanese surrender was believed to be unlikely. The use of an atomic weapon was thought to be a logical choice. What follows is President Truman's statement about the August 6 event.

Pages from a notebook of calculations for work on the Manhattan Project, the government's secret program to develop the atomic bomb.

Sixteen hours ago an American airplane dropped one bomb on Hiroshima, an important Japanese Army base. That bomb had more power than 20,000 tons of T.N.T. It had more than two thousand times the blast power of the British "Grand Slam" which is the largest bomb ever yet used in the history of warfare.

The Japanese began the war from the air at Pearl Harbor. They have been repaid many fold. And the end is not yet. With this bomb we have now added a new and revolutionary increase in destruction to supplement the growing power of our armed forces. In their present form these bombs are now in production and even more powerful forms are in development.

It is an atomic bomb. It is a harnessing of the basic power of the universe. The force from which the sun draws its power has been loosed against those who brought war to the Far East.

Before 1939, it was the accepted belief of scientists that it was theoretically possible to release atomic energy. But no one knew any practical method of doing it. By 1942, however, we knew that the Germans were working feverishly to find a way to add atomic energy to the other engines of war with which they hoped to enslave the world. But they failed. We may be grateful to Providence that the Germans got the V-1's and V-2's late and in limited quantities and even more grateful that they did not get the atomic bomb at all.

The battle of the laboratories held fateful risks for us as well as the battles of the air, land and sea, and we have now won the battle of the laboratories as we have won the other battles.

Beginning in 1940, before Pearl Harbor, scientific knowledge useful in war was pooled between the United States and Great Britain, and many priceless helps to our victories have come from that arrangement. Under that general policy the research on the atomic bomb was begun. With American and British scientists working together we entered the race of discovery against the Germans.

The United States had available the large number of scientists of distinction in the many needed areas of knowledge. It had the tremendous industrial and financial resources necessary for the project and they could be devoted to it without undue impairment of other vital war work. In the United States the laboratory work and the production plants, on which a substantial start had already been made, would be out of reach of enemy bombing, while at that time Britain was exposed to constant air attack and was still threatened with the possibility of invasion. For these reasons Prime Minister Churchill and President Roosevelt agreed that it was wise to carry on the project here. We now have two great plants and many lesser works devoted to the production of atomic power. Employment during peak construction numbered 125,000 and over 65,000 individuals are even now engaged in operating the plants. Many have worked there for two and a half years. Few know what they have been producing. They see great quantities of material going in and they see nothing coming out of these plants, for the physical size of the explosive charge is exceedingly small. We have spent two billion dollars on the greatest scientific gamble in history—and won.

But the greatest marvel is not the size of the enterprise, its secrecy, nor its cost, but the achievement of scientific brains in putting together infinitely complex pieces of knowledge held by many men in different fields of science into a workable plan. And hardly less marvelous has been the capacity of industry to design, and of labor to operate, the machines and methods to do things never done before so that the brain child of many minds came forth in physical shape and performed as it was supposed to do. Both science and industry worked under the direction of the United States Army, which achieved a unique success in managing so diverse a problem in the advancement of knowledge in an amazingly short time. It is doubtful if such another combination could be got together in the world. What has been done is the greatest achievement of organized science in history. It was done under high pressure and without failure.

We are now prepared to obliterate more rapidly and completely every productive enterprise the Japanese have above ground in any city. We shall destroy their docks, their factories, and their communications. Let there be no mistake; we shall completely destroy Japan's power to make war.

It was to spare the Japanese people from utter destruction that the ultimatum of July 26 was issued at Potsdam. Their leaders promptly rejected that ultimatum. If they do not now accept our terms they may expect a rain of ruin from the air, the like of which has never been seen on this earth. Behind this air attack will follow sea and land forces in such numbers and power as they have not yet seen and with the fighting skill of which they are already well aware.

The Secretary of War, who has kept in personal touch with all phases of the project, will immediately make public a statement giving further details.

His statement will give facts concerning the sites at Oak Ridge near Knoxville, Tennessee, and at Richland near Pasco, Washington, and an installation near Santa Fe, New Mexico. Although the workers at the sites have been making materials to be used in producing the greatest destructive force in history they have not themselves been in danger beyond that of many other occupations, for the utmost care has been taken of their safety.

The fact that we can release atomic energy ushers in a new era in man's understanding of nature's forces. Atomic energy may in the future supplement the power that now comes from coal, oil, and falling water, but at present it cannot be produced on a basis to compete with them commercially. Before that comes there must be a long period of intensive research.

It has never been the habit of the scientists of this country or the policy of this Government to withhold from the world scientific knowledge. Normally, therefore, everything about the work with atomic energy would be made public.

But under present circumstances it is not intended to divulge the technical processes of production or all the military applications, pending further examination of possible methods of protecting us and the rest of the world from the danger of sudden destruction.

I shall recommend that the Congress of the United States consider promptly the establishment of an appropriate commission to control the production and use of atomic power within the United States. I shall give further consideration and make further recommendations to the Congress as to how atomic power can become a powerful and forceful influence towards the maintenance of world peace.

 What They Were Saying

from a letter from Charles O. to Charles O. Jr, a soldier overseas, August 17, 1945:

At last the welcome news has come. We hope for the future that we'll never have to celebrate an event of this kind. In fact, I believe if we have another world war there'll be very few people if any left to do any celebrating. I hope the atomic bomb will be the means of making all peoples of the earth keep the peace.

8

The Modern World

★★

World War II changed the balance of power in the world and began the Cold War era, a time of uneasy relations between the world's two superpowers—the United States and the Soviet Union. With the Soviets in control of Eastern Europe, Americans were worried about the further spread of communism into Asia and much closer to home in Cuba. The atomic power that had been unleashed on Japan and helped end the war was now a daunting threat to the world. Americans twice went to war against Soviet-backed Communist forces, first in Korea and later in Vietnam. The Cold War spurred America to reach new heights in exploration, including sending John Glenn into space in 1962 and sending astronauts to the moon in 1969. The resignation of Republican Richard Nixon due to the Watergate scandal in 1974 helped lead Democrat Jimmy Carter to election in 1976, though he was defeated by Republican Ronald Reagan in 1980. The Reagan era marked an increase in the arms race between Americans and Soviets, but by the time Reagan left office the Soviet Empire was on the verge of collapse. As the twenty-first century dawned, America was first confronted with the contentious 2000 presidential election and then shocked by the horrific 9/11/2001 attacks on the World Trade Center and the Pentagon. New, stricter antiterrorism measures and an American invasion of Iraq took place in the aftermath.

1945 United Nations Is Chartered

When the League of Nations was created after World War I, the United States wanted no part of it despite the pleas of President Wilson. As World War II progressed, President Roosevelt began referring to the Allies as "united nations" and pushed for the creation of a strong international body that could serve as a sentinel to prevent the kind of militarization and aggression that Germany had accomplished as the League of Nations fell apart. This time around, there was less resistance to the idea. Most Americans realized that in the modern world neutrality was no longer an option.

President Roosevelt was looking forward to attending the United Nations Conference to be held in the spring of 1945 in San Francisco, but died before the event. His wish came true, however, as the attendees signed the United Nations Charter on June 26, 1945. When founded, the United Nations was made up of fifty-one countries, including Great Britain, France, China, the Soviet Union, and the United States. Though not a foolproof peacekeeper, the United Nations has defused many crises over the years that may otherwise have led to bloodshed.

Soviet Premier Nikita Khrushchev at the United Nations, 1960.

WE THE PEOPLES OF THE UNITED NATIONS DETERMINED to save succeeding generations from the scourge of war, which twice in our lifetime has brought untold sorrow to mankind, and to reaffirm faith in fundamental human rights, in the dignity and worth of the human person, in the equal rights of men and women and of nations large and small, and to establish conditions under which justice and respect for the obligations arising from treaties and other sources of international law can be maintained, and to promote social progress and better standards of life in larger freedom, AND FOR THESE ENDS to practice tolerance and live together in peace with one another as good neighbours, and to unite our strength to maintain international peace and security, and to ensure, by the acceptance of principles and the institution of methods, that armed force shall not be used, save in the common interest, and to employ international machinery for the promotion of the economic and social advancement of all peoples, HAVE RESOLED TO COMBINE OUR EFFORTS TO ACCOMPLISH THESE AIMS Accordingly, our respective Governments, through representatives assembled in the city of San Francisco, who have exhibited their full powers found to be in good and due form, have agreed to the present Charter of the United Nations and do hereby establish an international organization to be known as the United Nations.

Chapter I Purposes and Principles
Article 1
The Purposes of the United Nations are:

1. To maintain international peace and security, and to that end: to take effective collective measures for the prevention and removal of threats to the peace, and for the suppression of acts of aggression or other breaches of the peace, and to bring about by peaceful means, and in conformity with the principles of justice and international law, adjustment or settlement of international disputes or situations which might lead to a breach of the peace;

2. To develop friendly relations among nations based on respect for the principle of equal rights and self-determination of peoples, and to take other appropriate measures to strengthen universal peace;

3. To achieve international co-operation in solving international problems of an economic, social, cultural, or humanitarian character, and in promoting and encouraging respect for human rights and for fundamental freedoms for all without distinction as to race, sex, language, or religion; and

4. To be a centre for harmonizing the actions of nations in the attainment of these common ends.

Article 2
The Organization and its Members, in pursuit of the Purposes stated in Article 1, shall act in accordance with the following Principles.

1. The Organization is based on the principle of the sovereign equality of all its Members.

2. All Members, in order to ensure to all of them the rights and benefits resulting from membership, shall fulfill in good faith the obligations assumed by them in accordance with the present Charter.

3. All Members shall settle their international disputes by peaceful means in such a manner that international peace and security, and justice, are not endangered.

4. All Members shall refrain in their international relations from the threat or use of force against the territorial integrity or political independence of any state, or in any other manner inconsistent with the Purposes of the United Nations.

5. All Members shall give the United Nations every assistance in any action it takes in accordance with the present Charter, and shall refrain from giving assistance to any state against which the United Nations is taking preventive or enforcement action.

6. The Organization shall ensure that states which are not Members of the United Nations act in accordance with these Principles so far as may be necessary for the maintenance of international peace and security.

7. Nothing contained in the present Charter shall authorize the United Nations to intervene in matters which are essentially within the domestic jurisdiction of any state . . .

 What They Were Saying

President Franklin Roosevelt, 1944:

The Council of United Nations must have the power to act quickly and decisively to keep the peace by force, if necessary. A policeman would not be a very effective policeman if, when he saw a felon break into a house, he had to go to the Town Hall and call a town meeting to issue a warrant before the felon could be arrested. . . . The people of the Nation . . . want their Government to act, and not merely to talk, whenever and wherever there is a threat to world peace.

United States Takes Military Action in Korea 1950

During the 1950s and 1960s, communism was seen as the number one threat to the United States. Our involvement in Korea in the 1950s and then Vietnam in the 1960s and 1970s was based upon the United States' fears of Communist expansion in Asia and around the world. Unlike the isolationist policy of the 1930s, the Cold War policy dictated that the United States act to protect, support, and promote foreign democracies. After the United Nations issued a resolution in 1950 condemning the activities of North Korea, the United States participated in UN–sanctioned military action in Korea to defend South Korea from the Communist North. The Korean conflict (1950–1953) caused the deaths or injuries of more than 130,000 Americans, but ended without any positive result to show for it.

82 (1950). Resolution of 25 June 1950

[S/1501]

The Security Council,

Recalling the finding of the General Assembly in its resolution 293 (IV) of 21 October 1949 that the Government of the Republic of Korea is a lawfully established government having effective control and jurisdiction over that part of Korea where the United Nations Temporary Commission on Korea was able to observe and consult and in which the great majority of the people of Korea reside; that this Government is based on elections which were a valid expression of the free will of the electorate of that part of Korea and which were observed by the Temporary Commission; and that this is the only such Government in Korea,

Mindful of the concern expressed by the General Assembly in its resolutions 195 (III) of 12 December 1948 and 293 (IV) of 21 October 1949 about the consequences which might follow unless Member States refrained from acts derogatory to the results sought to be achieved by the United Nations in bringing about the complete independence and unity of Korea; and the concern expressed that the situation described by the United Nations Commission on Korea in its report* menaces the safety and well-being of the Republic of Korea and of the people of Korea and might lead to open military conflict there,

Noting with grave concern the armed attack on the Republic of Korea by forces from North Korea,

Determines that this action constitutes a breach of the peace; and

I

Calls for the immediate cessation of hostilities;
Calls upon the authorities in North Korea to withdraw forthwith their armed forces to the 38th parallel;

II

Requests the United Nations Commission on Korea:
(a) To communicate its fully considered recommendations on the situation with the least possible delay;
(b) To observe the withdrawal of North Korean forces to the 38th parallel;
(c) To keep the Security Council informed on the execution of this resolution;

III

Calls upon all Member States to render every assistance to the United Nations in the execution of this resolution

*See *Official Records of the Security Council, Fifth Year, No. 15,* 473rd meeting, p. 2, footnote 2 (document S/1496, incorporating S/1496/Corr.1).

4

82 (1950). Résolution du 25 juin 1950

[S/1501]

Le Conseil de sécurité,

Rappelant les conclusions que l'Assemblée générale a formulées dans sa résolution 293 (IV) du 21 octobre 1949, à savoir que le Gouvernement de la République de Corée est un gouvernement légitime qui exerce effectivement son autorité et sa juridiction sur la partie de la Corée où la Commission temporaire des Nations Unies pour la Corée a été en mesure de procéder à des observations et à des consultations et dans laquelle réside la grande majorité de la population de la Corée; que ce gouvernement est né d'élections qui ont été l'expression valable de la libre volonté du corps électoral de cette partie de la Corée et qui ont été observées par la Commission temporaire; et que ledit gouvernement est le seul qui, en Corée, possède cette qualité,

Conscient de ce que l'Assemblée générale, dans ses résolutions 195 (III) du 12 décembre 1948 et 293 (IV) du 21 octobre 1949, s'inquiète des conséquences que pourraient avoir des actes préjudiciables aux résultats que cherchent à obtenir les Nations Unies en vue de l'indépendance et de l'unité complètes de la Corée et invite les Etats Membres à s'abstenir d'actes de cette nature; et conscient de ce que l'Assemblée générale craint que la situation décrite par la Commission dans son rapport* ne menace la sûreté et le bien-être de la République de Corée et du peuple coréen et ne risque de conduire à un véritable conflit armé en Corée,

Prenant acte de l'attaque dirigée contre la République de Corée par des forces armées venues de Corée du Nord, attaque qui le préoccupe gravement,

Constate que cette action constitue une rupture de la paix; et

I

Demande la cessation immédiate des hostilités;
Invite les autorités de la Corée du Nord à retirer immédiatement leurs forces armées sur le 38ᵉ parallèle;

II

Prie la Commission des Nations Unies pour la Corée:
a) De communiquer, après mûr examen et dans le plus bref délai possible, ses recommandations au sujet de la situation;
b) D'observer le retrait des forces de la Corée du Nord sur le 38ᵉ parallèle;
c) De tenir le Conseil de sécurité au courant de l'exécution de la présente résolution;

III

Invite tous les Etats Membres à prêter leur entier concours à l'Organisation des Nations Unies pour

* Voir *Procès-verbaux officiels du Conseil de sécurité, cinquième année, nᵒ 15,* 473ᵉ séance, p. 2, note 2 (document S/1496) et document S/1496/Corr.1 (miméographié) figurant quant au fond dans la déclaration du Président, p. 3 et 4 de la même séance.

The UN resolution on Korea.

Truman's Message to the American People

In Korea the government forces, which were armed to prevent border raids and to preserve internal security, were attacked by invading forces from North Korea. The Security Council of the United Nations called upon the invading troops to cease hostilities and to withdraw to the 38th parallel. This they have not done, but on the contrary have pressed the attack. The Security Council called upon all members of the United Nations to render every assistance to the United Nations in the execution of this resolution. In these circumstances I have ordered United States air and sea forces to give the Korean Government troops cover and support.

The attack upon Korea makes it plain beyond all doubt that Communism has passed beyond the use of subversion to conquer independent nations and will now use armed invasion and war. It has defied the orders of the Security Council of the United Nations issued to preserve international peace and security. In these circumstance the occupation of Formosa by Communist forces would be a direct threat to the security of the Pacific area and to the United States forces performing their lawful and necessary functions in that area. Accordingly I have ordered the Seventh Fleet to prevent any attack on Formosa . . .

I have also directed that United States Forces in the Philippines be strengthened and that military assistance to the Philippine Government be accelerated . . .

I know that all members of the United Nations will consider carefully the consequences of this latest aggression in Korea in defiance of the Charter of the United Nations. A return to the rule of force in international affairs would have far reaching effects. The United States will continue to uphold the rule of law.

 What They Were Saying

from a speech by General Douglas MacArthur to Congress, 1951:

The Communist threat is a global one. Its successful advance in one sector threatens the destruction of every other sector. You cannot appease or otherwise surrender to communism in Asia without simultaneously undermining our efforts to halt its advance in Europe.

from a sergeant's letter home during Korean War, 1952:

We live in long tropical huts with tin roofs and we have a pot stove, oil for fuel…we had had some bad fires here when stoves blew up, so far nobody has been hurt…Our ships load bombs on and go out and bomb, and come back, outside the holes my men and I have to fix so they can go bomb the commies. We are pretty safe and fortunate to be in Mag 33, commonly known as K-3. We are about 125 miles from the battlefront in a place called P'ohang-Dong on the southeast end of Korea on the Sea of Japan. We have an awful lot of work here especially after a bomb run. The North Koreans (communist), they hate us and save all their ammunition to fire everything they get, to try to keep us out.

Twenty-Second Amendment 1951

It was no accident that the Twenty-Second Amendment came not long after President Franklin D. Roosevelt's unprecedented election to four terms of office. Roosevelt was an extremely popular leader through two very difficult times in the country's history; the Great Depression and World War II. If he had served out his full fourth term, Roosevelt, first elected in 1932, would have stepped down as president in early 1949, more than sixteen years later. Though many Americans thought Roosevelt did a good job, they were at the same time wary of a system that allowed for someone to serve indefinitely. Such a system was too reminiscent of the monarchy that Americans had rejected in 1776 and of the dictatorships of Mussolini and Hitler that were still fresh in their minds. Americans were now only willing to let their leaders serve for a total of two terms, or eight years. First proposed by Congress in 1947, the Twenty-Second Amendment took four years to be ratified, but was rejected by only two states (Massachusetts and Oklahoma).

Section 1. No person shall be elected to the office of the President more than twice, and no person who has held the office of President, or acted as President, for more than two years of a term to which some other person was elected President shall be elected to the office of the President more than once. But this Article shall not apply to any person holding the office of President when this Article was proposed by the Congress, and shall not prevent any person who may be holding the office of President, or acting as President, during the term within which this Article becomes operative from holding the office of President or acting as President during the remainder of such term.

1954 *Brown v. Board of Education*

Growing outrage at school segregation came to a head in the early 1950s. First, thirteen parents signed on as plaintiffs in a suit against the Topeka Board of Education. This case, filed in February 1951 under the name of one of the parent plaintiffs, became known as *Brown v. Board of Education*. In Washington, D.C., a group of eleven African American children were refused admission to a whites-only school, setting another lawsuit in motion. The case reached the district court in 1951 as *Bolling v. Sharp*.

A third case arose after 117 African American high school students called a strike at their crumbling blacks-only high school in Richmond, Virginia. Work soon began on a lawsuit that became known as *Davis v. County School Board of Prince Edward County*. In Delaware, African American students and parents decried a ten-mile trip to their school when there was a whites-only school in their neighborhood. An African American mother named Sarah Bulah wanted her daughter to ride on the school bus that passed her house every day. These cases were known as *Bolton v. Gebhart* and *Bulah v. Gebhart*.

These cases were eventually combined into one case, called *Brown v. Board of Education*. On May 14, 1954, the Supreme Court announced its landmark decision; segregated public schools were declared unconstitutional. Children could no longer be kept out of schools because of the color of their skin. Importantly, the Court decided that one could not simply compare tangible aspects such as building size, qualifications of teachers, or the curriculum being taught. The effect of segregation upon the black students had to be considered as well. A key blow had been struck for civil rights, a struggle that would hit full steam during the mid-1960s. Desegregation was a lengthy process and took years to implement. The last of the desegregation cases to go before the Supreme Court, *United States v. Fordice*, was decided in 1992.

Supreme Court of the United States

No. 1 ———— , October Term, 19 54

Oliver Brown, Mrs. Richard Lawton, Mrs. Sadie Emmanuel et al.,

Appellants,

vs.

Board of Education of Topeka, Shawnee County, Kansas, et al.

Appeal from *the United States District Court for the* ————————
District *of Kansas.*

This cause *came on to be heard on the transcript of the record from the United States*
District Court for the ———— District of Kansas, ————————
and *was argued by counsel.*

On consideration whereof, *It is ordered and adjudged by this Court that the judgment*
of *the said* District ———— *Court in this cause be, and the same is*
hereby, reversed with costs; and that this cause be, and the same
is hereby, remanded to the said District Court to take such
proceedings and enter such orders and decrees consistent with
the opinions of this Court as are necessary and proper to admit
to public schools on a racially nondiscriminatory basis with all
deliberate speed the parties to this case.

Per Mr. Chief Justice Warren,
May 31, 1955.

1469

To separate them [African Americans] from others of similar age and qualifications solely because of their race generates a feeling of inferiority as to their status in the community that may affect their hearts and minds in a way unlikely ever to be undone. The effect of this separation on their educational opportunities was well stated by a finding in the Kansas case by a court which nevertheless felt compelled to rule against the Negro plaintiffs:

Segregation of white and colored children in public schools has a detrimental effect upon the colored children. The impact is greater when it has the sanction of the law, for the policy of separating the races is usually interpreted as denoting the inferiority of the negro group. A sense of inferiority affects the motivation of a child to learn. Segregation with the sanction of law, therefore, has a tendency to [retard] the educational and mental development of negro children and to deprive them of some of the benefits they would receive in a racial[ly] integrated school system.

Whatever may have been the extent of psychological knowledge at the time of Plessy v. Ferguson, this finding is amply supported by modern authority. Any language in Plessy v. Ferguson contrary to this finding is rejected.

We conclude that, in the field of public education, the doctrine of "separate but equal" has no place. Separate educational facilities are inherently unequal. Therefore, we hold that the plaintiffs and others similarly situated for whom the actions have been brought are, by reason of the segregation complained of, deprived of the equal protection of the laws guaranteed by the Fourteenth Amendment. This disposition makes unnecessary any discussion whether such segregation also violates the Due Process Clause of the Fourteenth Amendment.

Because these are class actions, because of the wide applicability of this decision, and because of the great variety of local conditions, the formulation of decrees in these cases presents problems of considerable complexity. On reargument, the consideration of appropriate relief was necessarily subordinated to the primary question—the constitutionality of segregation in public education. We have now announced that such segregation is a denial of the equal protection of the laws. In order that we may have the full assistance of the parties in formulating decrees, the cases will be restored to the docket, and the parties are requested to present further argument on Questions 4 and 5 previously propounded by the Court for the reargument this Term The Attorney General of the United States is again invited to participate. The Attorneys General of the states requiring or permitting segregation in public education will also be permitted to appear as amici curiae upon request to do so by September 15, 1954, and submission of briefs by October 1, 1954.

It is so ordered.

 What They Were Saying

President Eisenhower on obstacles to desegregation in Little Rock, Arkansas, 1957:

In that city, under the leadership of demagogic extremists, disorderly mobs have deliberately prevented the carrying out of proper orders from a Federal Court. Local authorities have not eliminated that violent opposition and, under the law, I yesterday issued a Proclamation calling upon the mob to disperse.

This morning the mob again gathered in front of the Central High School of Little Rock, obviously for the purpose of again preventing the carrying out of the Court's order relating to the admission of Negro children to that school.

. . . I have today issued an Executive Order directing the use of troops under Federal authority to aid in the execution of Federal law at Little Rock, Arkansas. This became necessary when my Proclamation of yesterday was not observed, and the obstruction of justice still continues.

It is important that the reasons for my action be understood by all our citizens. As you know, the Supreme Court of the United States has decided that separate public educational facilities for the races are inherently unequal and therefore compulsory school segregation laws are unconstitutional.

Our personal opinions about the decision have no bearing on the matter of enforcement; the responsibility and authority of the Supreme Court to interpret the Constitution are very clear. Local Federal Courts were instructed by the Supreme Court to issue such orders and decrees as might be necessary to achieve admission to public schools without regard to race-and with all deliberate speed.

President Kennedy's
Inauguration
1961

John F. Kennedy was the youngest president ever elected and the first Catholic president. After eight years of Republican Dwight Eisenhower, Americans rejected Eisenhower's vice president, Richard Nixon, and voted for the young senator and World War II hero whose wealthy and powerful father had been an ambassador under President Franklin Roosevelt. Kennedy brought youthful vigor and refreshing ideas to the country. His inaugural speech in 1961, at the height of the Cold War, ranks as one of the most memorable presidential speeches in our history, and his short time as president was eventful. In 1962, a standoff with the Soviet Union over Cuba brought the world close to nuclear war. Alan Shepard become the first American astronaut in space in 1961, and in 1962 John Glenn was the first American to orbit the earth. One of Kennedy's key legacies was his support for a space program, one that eventually led to Americans landing on the moon in 1969. President Kennedy was assassinated in November 1963.

A draft of Kennedy's inaugural speech.

Vice President Johnson, Mr. Speaker, Mr. Chief Justice, President Eisenhower, Vice President Nixon, President Truman, reverend clergy, fellow citizens: We observe today not a victory of party, but a celebration of freedom—symbolizing an end, as well as a beginning—signifying renewal, as well as change. For I have sworn before you and Almighty God the same solemn oath our forebears prescribed nearly a century and three-quarters ago.

The world is very different now. For man holds in his mortal hands the power to abolish all forms of human poverty and all forms of human life. And yet the same revolutionary beliefs for which our forebears fought are still at issue around the globe—the belief that the rights of man come not from the generosity of the state, but from the hand of God.

We dare not forget today that we are the heirs of that first revolution. Let the word go forth from this time and place, to friend and foe alike, that the torch has been passed to a new generation of Americans—born in this century, tempered by war, disciplined by a hard and bitter peace, proud of our ancient heritage, and unwilling to witness or permit the slow undoing of those human rights to which this Nation has always been committed, and to which we are committed today at home and around the world.

Let every nation know, whether it wishes us well or ill, that we shall pay any price, bear any burden, meet any hardship, support any friend, oppose any foe, to assure the survival and the success of liberty.

This much we pledge—and more.

To those old allies whose cultural and spiritual origins we share, we pledge the loyalty of faithful friends. United, there is little we cannot do in a host of cooperative ventures. Divided, there is little we can do—for we dare not meet a powerful challenge at odds and split asunder.

To those new States whom we welcome to the ranks of the free, we pledge our word that one form of colonial control shall not have passed away merely to be replaced by a far more iron tyranny. We shall not always expect to find them supporting our view. But we shall always hope to find them strongly supporting their own freedom—and to remember that, in the past, those who foolishly sought power by riding the back of the tiger ended up inside.

To those peoples in the huts and villages across the globe struggling to break the bonds of mass misery, we pledge our best efforts to help them help themselves, for whatever period is required—not because the Communists may be doing it, not because we seek their votes, but because it is right. If a free society cannot help the many who are poor, it cannot save the few who are rich.

To our sister republics south of our border, we offer a special pledge: to convert our good words into good deeds—in a new alliance for progress—to assist free men and free governments in casting off the chains of poverty. But this peaceful revolution of hope cannot become the prey of hostile powers. Let all our neighbors know that we shall join with them to oppose aggression or subversion anywhere in the Americas. And let every other power know that this Hemisphere intends to remain the master of its own house.

To that world assembly of sovereign states, the United Nations, our last best hope in an age where the instruments of war have far outpaced the instruments of peace, we renew our pledge of support—to prevent it from becoming merely a forum for invective, to strengthen its shield of the new and the weak, and to enlarge the area in which its writ may run.

Finally, to those nations who would make themselves our adversary, we offer not a pledge but a request: that both sides begin anew the quest for peace, before the dark powers of destruction unleashed by science engulf all humanity in planned or accidental self-destruction.

We dare not tempt them with weakness. For only when our arms are sufficient beyond doubt can we be certain beyond doubt that they will never be employed.

But neither can two great and powerful groups of nations take comfort from our present course—both sides overburdened by the cost of modern weapons, both rightly alarmed by the steady spread of the deadly atom, yet both racing to alter that uncertain balance of terror that stays the hand of mankind's final war.

So let us begin anew—remembering on both sides that civility is not a sign of weakness, and sincerity is always subject to proof. Let us never negotiate out of fear. But let us never fear to negotiate.

Let both sides explore what problems unite us instead of belaboring those problems which divide us.

Let both sides, for the first time, formulate serious and precise proposals for the inspection and control of arms, and bring the absolute power to destroy other nations under the absolute control of all nations.

Let both sides seek to invoke the wonders of science instead of its terrors. Together let us explore the stars, conquer the deserts, eradicate disease, tap the ocean depths, and encourage the arts and commerce.

Let both sides unite to heed in all corners of the earth the command of Isaiah—to "undo the heavy burdens . . . and to let the oppressed go free."

And if a beachhead of cooperation may push back the jungle of suspicion, let both sides join in creating a new endeavor, not a new balance of power, but a new world of law, where the strong are just and the weak secure and the peace preserved.

All this will not be finished in the first 100 days. Nor will it be finished in the first 1,000 days, nor in the life of this Administration, nor even perhaps in our lifetime on this planet. But let us begin.

In your hands, my fellow citizens, more than mine, will rest the final success or failure of our course. Since this country was founded, each generation of Americans has been summoned to give testimony to its national loyalty. The graves of young Americans who answered the call to service surround the globe.

Now the trumpet summons us again—not as a call to bear arms, though arms we need; not as a call to battle, though embattled we are—but a call to bear the burden of a long twilight struggle, year in and year out, "rejoicing in hope, patient in tribulation"—a struggle against the common enemies of man: tyranny, poverty, disease, and war itself.

Can we forge against these enemies a grand and global alliance, North and South, East and West, that can assure a more fruitful life for all mankind? Will you join in that historic effort?

In the long history of the world, only a few generations have been granted the role of defending freedom in its hour of maximum danger. I do not shrink from this responsibility—I welcome it. I do not believe that any of us would exchange places with any other people or any other generation. The energy, the faith, the devotion which we bring to this endeavor will light our country and all who serve it—and the glow from that fire can truly light the world.

And so, my fellow Americans: ask not what your country can do for you—ask what you can do for your country.

My fellow citizens of the world: ask not what America will do for you, but what together we can do for the freedom of man.

Finally, whether you are citizens of America or citizens of the world, ask of us here the same high standards of strength and sacrifice which we ask of you. With a good conscience our only sure reward, with history the final judge of our deeds, let us go forth to lead the land we love, asking His blessing and His help, but knowing that here on earth God's work must truly be our own.

What They Were Saying

Soviet Premier Nikita Khrushchev to President Kennedy, 1962:

The Soviet government considers the violation of the freedom of navigation in international waters and air space to constitute an act of aggression propelling humankind into the abyss of a world nuclear-missile war. Therefore, the Soviet government cannot instruct captains of Soviet ships bound for Cuba to observe orders of American naval forces blockading this island. Our instructions to Soviet sailors are to observe strictly the generally accepted standards of navigation in international waters and not retreat one step from them. And, if the American side violates these rights, it must be aware of the responsibility it will bear for this act. To be sure, we will not remain mere observers of pirate actions by American ships in the open sea. We will then be forced on our part to take those measures we deem necessary and sufficient to defend our rights. To this end we have all that is necessary.

from a eulogy by Senator Mike Mansfield, November 24, 1963:

A piece of each of us died at that moment. Yet, in death he gave of himself to us. He gave us of a good heart from which the laughter came. He gave us of a profound wit, from which a great leadership emerged. He gave us of a kindness and a strength fused into the human courage to seek peace without fear.

He gave us of his love that we, too, in turn, might give. He gave that we might give of ourselves, that we might give to one another until there would be no room, no room at all, for the bigotry, the hatred, prejudice and the arrogance which converged in that moment of horror to strike him down.

In leaving us these gifts, John Fitzgerald Kennedy, President of the United States, leaves with us. Will we take them, Mr. President? Will we have, now, the sense and the responsibility and the courage to take them?

I pray to God that we will.

from a letter from First Lady "Lady Bird" Johnson to a New York couple, December 10, 1963:

These have been anguished days for all of us. The prayers, good wishes and confidence of people all over the country support us and help strengthen us to do our best in the task ahead. Please keep us in your thoughts and prayers. We need your help.

President John F. Kennedy's inauguration, January 1961.

★★

Though the Korean War had ended just a decade earlier, conflict in Asia would soon begin again; the situation in Vietnam had been unstable since the end of World War II, with Communist North Vietnam threatening South Vietnam. President Kennedy pledged support to the South Vietnamese in 1961, but involvement was minimal until 1964, when a U.S. destroyer was attacked by three North Vietnamese torpedo boats in the Gulf of Tonkin. This led to Congress's Gulf of Tonkin Resolution calling for increased American engagement. At the time, no one predicted that the conflict would escalate and expand, but by 1966 there were nearly two hundred thousand American troops in South Vietnam and by 1969 there were over five hundred thousand troops there. Protests and demonstrations were commonplace during the Vietnam War. As more time passed without much progress, Americans became less interested in defeating an ambiguous Communist enemy. The United States officially pulled its troops out in 1975 after the fall of Saigon to the Communists. More than fifty thousand Americans died during the conflict.

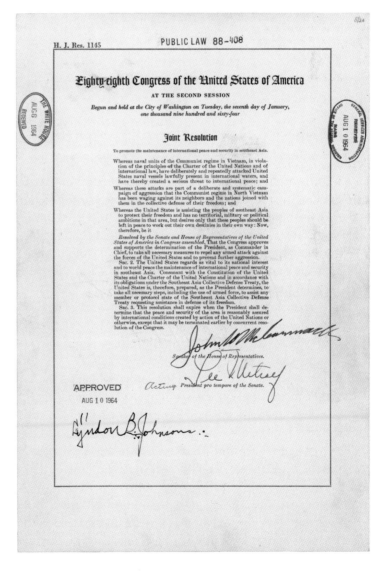

Joint Resolution of Congress, August 7, 1964

Resolved by the Senate and House of Representatives of the United States of America in Congress assembled,

That the Congress approves and supports the determination of the President, as Commander in Chief, to take all necessary measures to repel any armed attack against the forces of the United States and to prevent further aggression.

Section 2

The United States regards as vital to its national interest and to world peace the maintenance of international peace and security in southeast Asia. Consonant with the Constitution of the United States and the Charter of the United Nations and in accordance with its obligations under the Southeast Asia Collective Defense Treaty, the United States is, therefore, prepared, as the President determines, to take all necessary steps, including the use of armed force, to assist any member or protocol state of the Southeast Asia Collective Defense Treaty requesting assistance in defense of its freedom.

Section 3

This resolution shall expire when the President shall determine that the peace and security of the area is reasonably assured by international conditions created by action of the United Nations or otherwise, except that it may be terminated earlier by concurrent resolution of the Congress.

 What They Were Saying

from President Johnson's Message to Congress, August 5, 1964:

Last night I announced to the American people that the North Vietnamese regime had conducted further deliberate attacks against U.S. naval vessels operating in international waters, and I had therefore directed air action against gunboats and supporting facilities used in these hostile operations. This air action has now been carried out with substantial damage to the boats and facilities. Two U.S. aircraft were lost in the action.

After consultation with the leaders of both parties in the Congress, I further announced a decision to ask the Congress for a resolution expressing the unity and determination of the United States in supporting freedom and in protecting peace in southeast Asia.

These latest actions of the North Vietnamese regime has given a new and grave turn to the already serious situation in southeast Asia. Our commitments in that area are well known to the Congress. They were first made in 1954 by President Eisenhower. They were further defined in the Southeast Asia Collective Defense Treaty approved by the Senate in February 1955.

This treaty with its accompanying protocol obligates the United States and other members to act in accordance with their constitutional processes to meet Communist aggression against any of the parties or protocol states.

Our policy in southeast Asia has been consistent and unchanged since 1954. I summarized it on June 2 in four simple propositions:

America keeps her word. Here as elsewhere, we must and shall honor our commitments.

The issue is the future of southeast Asia as a whole. A threat to any nation in that region is a threat to all, and a threat to us.

Our purpose is peace. We have no military, political, or territorial ambitions in the area.

This is not just a jungle war, but a struggle for freedom on every front of human activity. Our military and economic assistance to South Vietnam and Laos in particular has the purpose of helping these countries to repel aggression and strengthen their independence.

The threat to the free nations of southeast Asia has long been clear. The North Vietnamese regime has constantly sought to take over South Vietnam and Laos. This Communist regime has violated the Geneva accords for Vietnam. It has systematically conducted a campaign of subversion, which includes the direction, training, and supply of personnel and arms for the conduct of guerrilla warfare in South Vietnamese territory. In Laos, the North Vietnamese regime has maintained military forces, used Laotian territory for infiltration into South Vietnam, and most recently carried out combat operations—all in direct violation of the Geneva Agreements of 1962.

In recent months, the actions of the North Vietnamese regime have become steadily more threatening . . .

As President of the United States I have concluded that I should now ask the Congress, on its part, to join in affirming the national determination that all such attacks will be met, and that the United States will continue in its basic policy of assisting the free nations of the area to defend their freedom.

from President Richard Nixon, 1969:

I believe that one of the reasons for the deep division about Vietnam is that many Americans have lost confidence in what their Government has told them about our policy. The American people cannot and should not be asked to support a policy which involves the overriding issues of war and peace unless they know the truth about that policy. . . .

My fellow Americans, I am sure you can recognize from what I have said that we really only have two choices open to us if we want to end this war.

—I can order an immediate, precipitate withdrawal of all Americans from Vietnam without regard to the effects of that action.

—Or we can persist in our search for a just peace through a negotiated settlement if possible, or through continued implementation of our plan for Vietnamization if necessary—a plan in which we will withdraw all of our forces from Vietnam on a schedule in accordance with our program, as the South Vietnamese become strong enough to defend their own freedom.

I have chosen this second course.

It is not the easy way.

It is the right way.

It is a plan which will end the war and serve the cause of peace—not just in Vietnam but in the Pacific and in the world.

In speaking of the consequences of a precipitate withdrawal, I mentioned that our allies would lose confidence in America.

Far more dangerous, we would lose confidence in ourselves. Oh, the immediate reaction would be a sense of relief that our men were coming home. But as we saw the consequences of what we had done, inevitable remorse and divisive recrimination would scar our spirit as a people.

We have faced other crisis in our history and have become stronger by rejecting the easy way out and taking the right way in meeting our challenges. Our greatness as a nation has been our capacity to do what had to be done when we knew our course was right.

I recognize that some of my fellow citizens disagree with the plan for peace I have chosen. Honest and patriotic Americans have reached different conclusions as to how peace should be achieved.

In San Francisco a few weeks ago, I saw demonstrators carrying signs reading: "Lose in Vietnam, bring the boys home."

Well, one of the strengths of our free society is that any American has a right to reach that conclusion and to advocate that point of view. But as President of the United States, I would be untrue to my oath of office if I allowed the policy of this Nation to be dictated by the minority who hold that point of view and who try to impose it on the Nation by mounting demonstrations in the street.

For almost 200 years, the policy of this Nation has been made under our Constitution by those leaders in the Congress and the White House elected by all of the people. If a vocal minority, however fervent its cause, prevails over reason and the will of the majority, this Nation has no future as a free society....

Let historians not record that when America was the most powerful nation in the world we passed on the other side of the road and allowed the last hopes for peace and freedom of millions of people to be suffocated by the forces of totalitarianism.

And so tonight—to you, the great silent majority of my fellow Americans—I ask for your support.

from George McGovern's Acceptance of Nomination for President, 1972:

So let us give our—let us give your country the chance to elect a Government that will seek and speak the truth, for this is the time for the truth in the life of this country.

And this is also a time, not for death, but for life. In 1968 many Americans thought they were voting to bring our sons home from Vietnam in peace, and since then 20,000 of our sons have come home in coffins.

I have no secret plan for peace. I have a public plan. And as one whose heart has ached for the past ten years over the agony of Vietnam, I will halt a senseless bombing of Indochina on Inaugural Day.

There will be no more Asian children running ablaze from bombed-out schools. There will be no more talk of bombing the dikes or the cities of the North.

And within 90 days of my inauguration, every American soldier and every American prisoner will be out of the jungle and out of their cells and then home in America where they belong.

And then let us resolve that never again will we send the precious young blood of this country to die trying to prop up a corrupt military dictatorship abroad.

This is also the time to turn away from excessive preoccupation overseas to the rebuilding of our own nation. America must be restored to a proper role in the world. But we can do that only through the recovery of confidence in ourselves.

Civil
Rights Act 1964

One hundred years after slavery was outlawed in the United States, both blatant and subtle racial discrimination was still rampant in many places. Though in theory blacks and other minorities had the same rights as whites, in practice they did not. It became increasingly clear that federal legislation would be necessary to ensure equal rights for all races. As a senator in the late 1950s, Lyndon Johnson had worked to fight for civil rights. Once he became president, he was happy to take up President Kennedy's suggestion that legislation was needed to ban segregation in places such as restaurants and swimming pools. President Johnson was able to work with civil rights leaders such as Dr. Martin Luther King Jr. to create and promote the Civil Rights Act.

The act was met with opposition from those such as Republican Senator Barry Goldwater, the 1964 Republican nominee for president, who claimed it trampled on states' rights; nonetheless it passed in both houses of Congress. The Civil Rights Act sought to level the playing field. Employers could no longer use race as a tool for selecting of prospective employees without punishment.

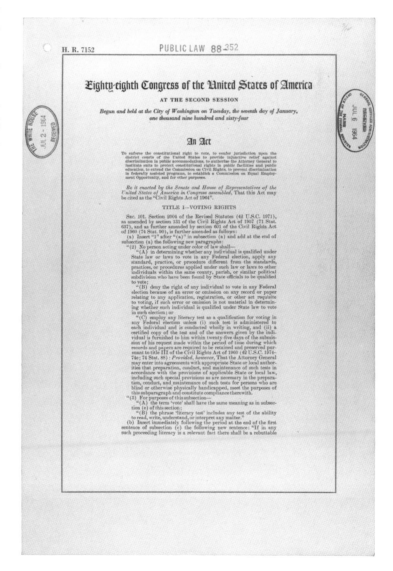

An Act, To enforce the constitutional right to vote, to confer jurisdiction upon the district courts of the United States to provide injunctive relief against discrimination in public accommodations, to authorize the Attorney General to institute suits to protect constitutional rights in public facilities and public education, to extend the Commission on Civil Rights, to prevent discrimination in federally assisted programs, to establish a Commission on Equal Employment Opportunity, and for other purposes.

Be it enacted by the Senate and House of Representatives of the United States of America in Congress assembled, That this Act may be cited as the "Civil Rights Act of 1964." . . .

Title II

(a) All persons shall be entitled to the full and equal enjoyment of the goods, services, facilities, privileges, advantages, and accommodations of any place of public accommodation, as defined in this section, without discrimination or segregation on the ground of race, color, religion, or national origin.

(b) Each of the following establishments which serves the public is a place of public accommodation within the meaning of this title if its operations affect commerce, or if discrimination or segregation by it is supported by State action:

(1) any inn, hotel, motel, or other establishment which provides lodging to transient guests, other than an establishment located within a building which contains not more than five rooms for rent or hire and which is actually occupied by the proprietor of such establishment as his residence.

(2) any restaurant, cafeteria, lunchroom, lunch counter, soda fountain, or other facility principally engaged in selling food for consumption on the premises, including, but not limited to, any such facility located on the premises of any retail establishment, or any gasoline station;

(3) any motion picture house, theater, concert hall, sports arena, stadium or other place of exhibition or entertainment; and

(4) any establishment (A)(i) which is physically located within the premises of any establishment otherwise covered by this subsection, or (ii) within the premises of which is physically located any such covered establishment and (B) which holds itself out as serving patrons of any such covered establishment. . . .

Title VII
Unlawful Employment Practices

(a) It shall be an unlawful employment practice for an employer—

(1) to fail or refuse to hire or to discharge any individual, or otherwise to discriminate against any individual with respect to his compensation, terms, conditions, or privileges of employment, because of such individual's race, color, religion, sex, or national origin; or

(2) to limit, segregate, or classify his employees or applicants for employment in any way which would deprive or tend to deprive any individual of employment opportunities or otherwise adversely affect his status as an employee, because of such individual's race, color, religion, sex, or national origin.

(b) It shall be an unlawful employment practice for an employment agency to fail or refuse to refer for employment, or otherwise to discriminate against, any individual because of his race, color, religion, sex, or national origin, or to classify or refer for employment any individual on the basis of his race, color, religion, sex, or national origin.

 What They Were Saying

President Lyndon Johnson, 1963:

First, no memorial oration or eulogy could more eloquently honor President Kennedy's memory than the earliest possible passage of the civil rights bill for which he fought so long. We have talked long enough in this country about equal rights. We have talked for one hundred years or more. It is time now to write the next chapter, and to write it in the books of law. I urge you again, as I did in 1957 and again in 1960, to enact a civil rights law so that we can move forward to eliminate from this Nation every trace of discrimination and oppression that is based upon race or color. There could be no greater source of strength to this Nation both at home and abroad.

Civil rights march, 1963.

1965 Voting Rights Act

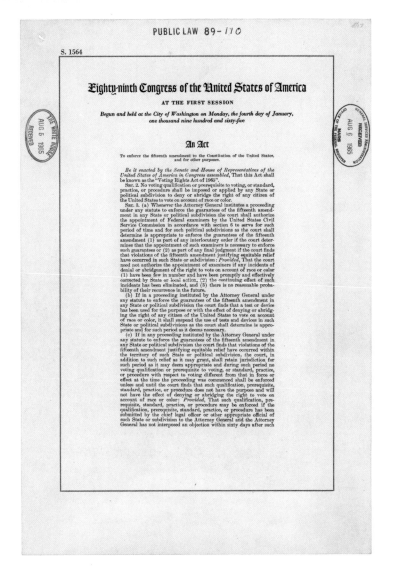

Though by the mid-twentieth century all Americans age twenty-one or over had been granted the right to vote, there were still barriers that prevented many people from doing so. The Voting Rights Act sought to change some of the unfair practices occurring throughout the country by outlawing practices such as the imposition of a poll tax (which would exclude those who could not afford to pay it), the implementation of qualifications or tests for those who wished to vote, or any manner of coercion or threats directed at voters. The act had immediate effects, and millions of new voters were registered as a result.

Be it enacted by the Senate and House of Representatives of the United States of America in Congress assembled, That this Act shall be known as the "Voting Rights Act of 1965." . . .

Section 2

No voting qualification or prerequisite to voting, or standard, practice, or procedure shall be imposed or applied by any State or political subdivision to deny or abridge the right of any citizen of the United States to vote on account of race or color.

Section 3

(a) Whenever the Attorney General institutes a proceeding under any statute to enforce the guarantees of the fifteenth amendment in any State or political subdivision the court shall authorize the appointment of Federal examiners by the United States Civil Service Commission in accordance with section 6 to serve for such period of time and for such political subdivisions as the court shall determine is appropriate to enforce the guarantees of the fifteenth amendment (1) as part of any interlocutory order if the court determines that the appointment of such examiners is necessary to enforce such guarantees or (2) as part of any final judgment if the court finds that violations of the fifteenth amendment justifying equitable relief have occurred in such State or subdivision: Provided, That the court need not authorize the appointment of examiners if any incidents of denial or abridgement of the right to vote on account of race or color (1) have been few in number and have been promptly and effectively corrected by State or local action, (2) the continuing effect of such incidents has been eliminated, and (3) there is no reasonable probability of their recurrence in the future. (b) If in a proceeding instituted by the Attorney General under any statute to enforce the guarantees of the fifteenth amendment in any State or political subdivision the court finds that a test or device has been used for the purpose or with the effect of denying or abridging the right of any citizen of the United States to vote on account of race or color, it shall suspend the use of tests and devices in such State or political subdivisions as the court shall determine is appropriate and for such period as it deems necessary. . . .

Section 4

(a) To assure that the right of citizens of the United States to vote is not denied or abridged on account of race or color, no citizen shall be denied the right to vote in any Federal, State, or local election because of his failure to comply with any test or device in any State with respect to which the determinations have been made under subsection (b) or in any political subdivision with respect to which such determinations have been made as a separate unit, unless the United States District Court for the District of Columbia in an action for a declaratory judgment brought by such State or subdivision against the United States has determined that no such test or device has been used during the five years preceding the filing of the action for the purpose or with the effect of denying or abridging the right to vote on account of race or color. . . . (c) The phrase "test or device" shall mean any requirement that a person as a prerequisite for voting or registration for voting (1) demonstrate the ability to read, write, understand, or interpret any matter, (2) demonstrate any educational achievement or his knowledge of any particular subject, (3) possess good moral character, or (4) prove his qualifications by the voucher of registered voters or members of any other class. . . .

(2) No person who demonstrates that he has successfully completed the sixth primary grade in a public school in, or a private school accredited by, any State or territory, the District of Columbia, or the Commonwealth of Puerto Rico in which the predominant classroom language was other than English, shall be denied the right to vote in any Federal, State, or local election because of his inability to read, write, understand, or interpret any matter in the English language. . . .

Section 10

(a) The Congress finds that the requirement of the payment of a poll tax as a precondition to voting (i) precludes persons of limited means from voting or imposes unreasonable financial hardship upon such persons as a precondition to their exercise of the franchise, (ii) does not bear a reasonable relationship to any legitimate State interest in the conduct of elections, and (iii) in some areas has the purpose or effect of denying persons the right to vote because of race or color. Upon the basis of these findings, Congress declares that the constitutional right of citizens to vote is denied or abridged in some areas by the requirement of the payment of a poll tax as a precondition to voting. . . .

Section 11

(a) No person acting under color of law shall fail or refuse to permit any person to vote who is entitled to vote under any provision of this Act or is otherwise qualified to vote, or willfully fail or refuse to tabulate, count, and report such person's vote. (b) No person, whether acting under color of law or otherwise, shall intimidate, threaten, or coerce, or attempt to intimidate, threaten, or coerce any person for voting or attempting to vote, or intimidate, threaten, or coerce, or attempt to intimidate, threaten, or coerce any person for urging or aiding any person to vote or attempt to vote, or intimidate, threaten, or coerce any person for exercising any powers or duties under section 3(a), 6, 8, 9, 10, or 12(e).

What They Were Saying

Lyndon Johnson to Congress, 1965:

Many of the issues of civil rights are very complex and most difficult. But about this there can and should be no argument. Every American citizen must have the right to vote. . . . No law that we now have on the books . . . can

insure the right to vote when local officials are determined to deny it. . . . There is no Constitutional issue here. The command of the Constitution is plain. There is no moral issue. It is wrong—deadly wrong—to deny any of your fellow Americans the right to vote in this country. There is no issue of States' rights or National rights. There is only the struggle for human rights.

An African American woman votes in the November 1964 election.

Nixon Resigns 1974

President Richard Nixon was newly into his second term of office when he became entangled in a scandal involving a June 1972 break-in at the Washington, D.C., Democratic headquarters in the Watergate Hotel. A special prosecutor was appointed to investigate the scandal and filed suit to have Nixon turn over secret audio tapes that had been revealed. Nixon refused. In March 1974 a district court grand jury indicted seven people as part of the investigation into the Watergate scandal. Though the president himself was not specifically named, the grand jury called him an "unindicted coconspirator." The president's relevant documents and tape recordings were subpoenaed as part of the investigation. In April, Nixon released edited versions of his tapes to the House Judiciary Committee. The district court ordered him to release the original documents in their unaltered state. The president refused to comply and appealed to the court of appeals, citing his right to confidentiality.

The case went to the Supreme Court as *United States v. Nixon* and the decision came down on July 24. The justices ruled that if there was a specific need for evidence in a pending criminal trial, then the president had to yield to any reasonable requests.

By the end of July, the House Judiciary Committee adopted three articles of impeachment against Nixon. The president resigned his office on August 9, 1974, before the impeachment process could progress any further.

President Ford testifies in Congress about his pardon of President Nixon, 1974.

Good evening.

This is the 37th time I have spoken to you from this office, where so many decisions have been made that shaped the history of this Nation. Each time I have done so to discuss with you some matter that I believe affected the national interest.

In all the decisions I have made in my public life, I have always tried to do what was best for the Nation. Throughout the long and difficult period of Watergate, I have felt it was my duty to persevere, to make every possible effort to complete the term of office to which you elected me.

In the past few days, however, it has become evident to me that I no longer have a strong enough political base in the Congress to justify continuing that effort. As long as there was such a base, I felt strongly that it was necessary to see the constitutional process through to its conclusion, that to do otherwise would be unfaithful to the spirit of that deliberately difficult process and a dangerously destabilizing precedent for the future.

But with the disappearance of that base, I now believe that the constitutional purpose has been served, and there is no longer a need for the process to be prolonged.

I would have preferred to carry through to the finish whatever the personal agony it would have involved, and my family unanimously urged me to do so. But the interest of the Nation must always come before any personal considerations.

From the discussions I have had with Congressional and other leaders, I have concluded that because of the Watergate matter I might not have the support of the Congress that I would consider necessary to back the very difficult decisions and carry out the duties of this office in the way the interests of the Nation would require.

I have never been a quitter. To leave office before my term is completed is abhorrent to every instinct in my body. But as President, I must put the interest of America first. America needs a full-time President and a full-time Congress, particularly at this time with problems we face at home and abroad.

To continue to fight through the months ahead for my personal vindication would almost totally absorb the time and attention of both the President and the Congress in a period when our entire focus should be on the great issues of peace abroad and prosperity without inflation at home.

Therefore, I shall resign the Presidency effective at noon tomorrow. Vice President Ford will be sworn in as President at that hour in this office. . . .

I regret deeply any injuries that may have been done in the course of the events that led to this decision. I would say only that if some of my judgments were wrong, and some were wrong, they were made in what I believed at the time to be the best interest of the Nation.

To those who have stood with me during these past difficult months, to my family, my friends, to many others who joined in supporting my cause because they believed it was right, I will be eternally grateful for your support.

And to those who have not felt able to give me your support, let me say I leave with no bitterness toward those who have opposed me, because all of us, in the final analysis, have been concerned with the good of the country, however our judgments might differ.

So, let us all now join together in affirming that common commitment and in helping our new President succeed for the benefit of all Americans.

I shall leave this office with regret at not completing my term, but with gratitude for the privilege of serving as your President for the past 5½ years. These years have been a momentous time in the history of our Nation and the world. They have been a time of achievement in which we can all be proud, achievements that represent the shared efforts of the Administration, the Congress, and the people.

But the challenges ahead are equally great, and they, too, will require the support and the efforts of the Congress and the people working in cooperation with the new Administration. . . .

For more than a quarter of a century in public life I have shared in the turbulent history of this era. I have fought for what I believed in. I have tried to the best of my ability to discharge those duties and meet those responsibilities that were entrusted to me.

Sometimes I have succeeded and sometimes I have failed, but always I have taken heart from what Theodore Roosevelt once said about the man in the arena, "whose face is marred by dust and sweat and blood, who strives valiantly, who errs and comes short again and again because there is not effort without error and shortcoming, but who does actually strive to do the deed, who knows the great enthusiasms, the great devotions, who spends himself in a worthy cause, who at the best knows in the end the triumphs of high achievements and who at the worst, if he fails, at least fails while daring greatly."

I pledge to you tonight that as long as I have a breath of life in my body, I shall continue in that spirit. I shall continue to work for the great causes to which I have been dedicated throughout my years as a Congressman, a Senator, a Vice President, and President, the cause of peace not just for America but among all nations, prosperity, justice, and opportunity for all of our people . . .

To have served in this office is to have felt a very personal sense of kinship with each and every American. In leaving it, I do so with this prayer: May God's grace be with you in all the days ahead.

 # What They Were Saying

Chief Justice Warren Burger, July 1974:

Neither the doctrine of separation of powers, nor the need for confidentiality of high level communications, without more, can sustain an absolute, unqualified Presidential privilege of immunity from judicial process under all circumstances.

from President Gerald Ford's speech pardoning Nixon, September 1974:

I have come to a decision which I felt I should tell you and all of my fellow American citizens, as soon as I was certain in my own mind and in my own conscience that it is the right thing to do. . . .

There are no historic or legal precedents to which I can turn in this matter, none that precisely fit the circumstances of a private citizen who has resigned the Presidency of the United States. But it is common knowledge that serious allegations and accusations hang like a sword over our former President's head, threatening his health as he tries to reshape his life, a great part of which was spent in the service of this country and by the mandate of its people. . . .

The facts, as I see them, are that a former President of the United States, instead of enjoying equal treatment with any other citizen accused of violating the law, would be cruelly and excessively penalized either in preserving the presumption of his innocence or in obtaining a speedy determination of his guilt in order to repay a legal debt to society. . . .

My conscience tells me clearly and certainly that I cannot prolong the bad dreams that continue to reopen a chapter that is closed. My conscience tells me that only I, as President, have the constitutional power to firmly shut and seal this book. My conscience tells me it is my duty, not merely to proclaim domestic tranquility but to use every means that I have to insure it. I do believe that the buck stops here, that I cannot rely upon public opinion polls to tell me what is right. I do believe that right makes might and that if I am wrong, ten angels swearing I was right would make no difference. I do believe, with all my heart and mind and spirit, that I, not as President but as a humble servant of God, will receive justice without mercy if I fail to show mercy. . . .

Now, therefore, I, Gerald R. Ford, President of the United States, pursuant to the pardon power conferred upon me by Article II, Section 2, of the Constitution, have granted and by these presents do grant a full, free, and absolute pardon unto Richard Nixon for all offenses against the United States which he, Richard Nixon, has committed or may have committed or taken part in during the period from July (January) 20, 1969, through August 9, 1974.

1987 Fall of the Berlin Wall

When President Ronald Reagan spoke at the Brandenburg Gate in West Berlin in 1987, he called for an end to the division that had been a result of the Iron Curtain of communism descending on Eastern Europe after Word War II. Though his words themselves were not vested with any particular power or authority, they reflected the changes that had already started to happen with the rise to power of the moderate Soviet leader Mikhail Gorbachev. His words also presaged the near future when the Berlin Wall would in fact come down, and the Soviet Union would collapse, leading to a new round of nation-building among the former components of the vast empire. After forty years of tension and intrigue, the threat of communism would finally diminish. Reagan's genius was to size up Gorbachev and seize the opportunity in West Berlin and in meetings with Gorbachev.

In the 1950s, Khrushchev predicted: "We will bury you." But in the West today, we see a free world that has achieved a level of prosperity and well-being unprecedented in all human history. In the Communist world, we see failure, technological backwardness, declining standards of health, even want of the most basic kind—too little food. Even today, the Soviet Union still cannot feed itself. After these four decades, then, there stands before the entire world one great and inescapable conclusion: Freedom leads to prosperity. Freedom replaces the ancient hatreds among the nations with comity and peace. Freedom is the victor.

And now the Soviets themselves may, in a limited way, be coming to understand the importance of freedom. We hear much from Moscow about a new policy of reform and openness. Some political prisoners have been released. Certain foreign news broadcasts are no longer being jammed. Some economic enterprises have been permitted to operate with greater freedom from state control.

Are these the beginnings of profound changes in the Soviet state? Or are they token gestures, intended to raise false hopes in the West, or to strengthen the Soviet system without changing it? We welcome change and openness; for we believe that freedom and security go together, that the advance of human liberty can only strengthen the cause of world peace. There is one sign the Soviets can make that would be unmistakable, that would advance dramatically the cause of freedom and peace.

General Secretary Gorbachev, if you seek peace, if you seek prosperity for the Soviet Union and Eastern Europe, if you seek liberalization: Come here to this gate! Mr. Gorbachev, open this gate! Mr. Gorbachev, tear down this wall!

I understand the fear of war and the pain of division that afflict this continent—and I pledge to you my country's efforts to help overcome these burdens. To be sure, we in the West must resist Soviet expansion. So we must maintain defenses of unassailable strength. Yet we seek peace; so we must strive to reduce arms on both sides.

Beginning 10 years ago, the Soviets challenged the Western alliance with a grave new threat, hundreds of new and more deadly SS-20 nuclear missiles, capable of striking every capital in Europe. The Western alliance responded by committing itself to a counter-deployment unless the Soviets agreed to negotiate a better solution; namely, the elimination of such weapons on both sides. For many months, the Soviets refused to bargain in earnestness. As the alliance, in turn, prepared to go forward with its counter-deployment, there were difficult days—days of protests like those during my 1982 visit to this city—and the Soviets later walked away from the table.

But through it all, the alliance held firm. And I invite those who protested then—I invite those who protest today—to mark this fact: Because we remained strong, the Soviets came back to the table. And because we remained strong, today we have within reach the possibility, not merely of limiting the growth of arms, but of eliminating, for the first time, an entire class of nuclear weapons from the face of the earth.

As I speak, NATO ministers are meeting in Iceland to review the progress of our proposals for eliminating these weapons. At the talks in Geneva, we have also proposed deep cuts in strategic offensive weapons. And the Western allies have likewise made far-reaching proposals to reduce the danger of conventional war and to place a total ban on chemical weapons.

While we pursue these arms reductions, I pledge to you that we will maintain the capacity to deter Soviet aggression at any level at which it might occur. And in cooperation with many of our allies, the United States is pursuing the Strategic Defense Initiative—research to base deterrence not on the threat of offensive retaliation, but on defenses that truly defend; on systems, in short, that will not target populations, but shield them. By these means we seek to increase the safety of Europe and all the world. But we must remember a crucial fact: East and West do not mistrust each other because we are armed; we are armed because we mistrust each other. And our differences are not about weapons but about liberty. When President Kennedy spoke at the City Hall those 24 years ago, freedom was encircled, Berlin was under siege. And today, despite all the pressures upon this city, Berlin stands secure in its liberty. And freedom itself is transforming the globe…

As I looked out a moment ago from the Reichstag, that embodiment of German unity, I noticed words crudely spray-painted upon the wall, perhaps by a young Berliner: "This wall will fall. Beliefs become reality." Yes, across Europe, this wall will fall. For it cannot withstand faith; it cannot withstand truth. The wall

What They Were Saying

George H. W. Bush accepting the Republican nomination for president, 1988:

And one by one the unfree places fall, not to the force of arms but to the force of an idea: freedom works . . . we have a new relationship with the Soviet Union—the INF treaty, the beginning of the Soviet withdrawal from Afghanistan, the beginning of the end of the Soviet proxy war in Angola, and with it the independence of Namibia. Iran and Iraq move toward peace.

It's a watershed. It is no accident.

It happened when we acted on the ancient knowledge that strength and clarity lead to peace; weakness and ambivalence lead to war. Weakness and ambivalence lead to war. You see, weakness tempts aggressors. Strength stops them. I will not allow this country to be made weak again. Never.

The tremors in the Soviet world continue. The hard earth there has not yet settled. Perhaps what is happening will change our world forever. And perhaps not. A prudent skepticism is in order. And so is hope. But either way, we're in an unprecedented position to change the nature of our relationship. Not by preemptive concession, but by keeping our strength. Not by yielding up defense systems with nothing won in return, but by hard, cool engagement in the tug and pull of diplomacy.

2000 Bush v. Gore

PLACE HOLES OVER POSTS
← →

COLOQUE LOS AGUJEROS SOBRE LOS POSTES

INSERT CARD   **THIS SIDE UP**
INSERTE   *ESTE LADO*
LA TARJETA   *HACIA ARRIBA*

**OFFICIAL BALLOT
GENERAL ELECTION
HILLSBOROUGH COUNTY, FLORIDA
NOVEMBER 7, 2000**

***BALOTA ELECTORAL OFICIAL
ELECCION GENERAL
CONDADO DE HILLSBOROUGH, FLORIDA
7 DE NOVIEMBRE DE 2000***

DO NOT REMOVE – PLACE IN BALLOT BOX
NO SEPARE – DEPOSITE EN LA URNA ELECTORAL

The events following the presidential election of November 2000 were notably bizarre. With the results from forty-nine of the fifty states in, Al Gore was leading George Bush in electoral votes by a count of 266 to 246, with 270 needed for victory. What hung in the balance was a block of twenty-five electoral votes from the state of Florida, where the results were so close that the outcome was not available that night. When America woke up the next morning, there was still no answer. Impossibly, the popular vote was so close in Florida that recounts had to be held. Days passed, and America still had no president-elect. Ballot counting was not straightforward due to confusing ballots and "hanging chads," holes not fully punched in some of the ballots. With the margin of victory hinging on only a few hundred votes, every vote was important. The Bush campaign brought a suit to stop the recount and leave its 537-vote edge over Gore intact. The case made it to the Supreme Court, which found that uniform ballot interpretation standards were not being applied and that a recount could not be conducted before the Florida Legislature's self-imposed date of December 1. Their decision preserved the 537 popular vote margin and gave Florida's electoral votes to George Bush, who became president, despite losing to Al Gore by five hundred thousand popular votes. Following the election, calls were made for reforms of the electoral college system as well as improvements to voting and vote counting systems.

A ballot from Hillsborough County, Florida, November 7, 2000.

Much of the controversy seems to revolve around ballot cards designed to be perforated by a stylus but which, either through error or deliberate omission, have not been perforated with sufficient precision for a machine to count them. In some cases a piece of the card—a chad—is hanging, say by two corners. In other cases there is no separation at all, just an indentation.

The Florida Supreme Court has ordered that the intent of the voter be discerned from such ballots . . . In this instance, however, the question is not whether to believe a witness but how to interpret the marks or holes or scratches on an inanimate object, a piece of cardboard or paper which, it is said, might not have registered as a vote during the machine count. The factfinder confronts a thing, not a person. The search for intent can be confined by specific rules designed to ensure uniform treatment.

The want of those rules here has led to unequal evaluation of ballots in various respects . . . As seems to have been acknowledged at oral argument, the standards for accepting or rejecting contested ballots might vary not only from county to county but indeed within a single county from one recount team to another.

The State Supreme Court . . . mandated that the recount totals from two counties, Miami-Dade and Palm Beach, be included in the certified total. The court also appeared to hold . . . that the recount totals from Broward County, which were not completed until after the original November 14 certification by the Secretary of State, were to be considered part of the new certified vote totals even though the county certification was not contested by Vice President Gore. Yet each of the counties used varying standards to determine what was a legal vote. Broward County used a more forgiving standard than Palm Beach County, and uncovered almost three times as many new votes, a result markedly disproportionate to the difference in population between the counties.

In addition, the recounts in these three counties were not limited to so-called undervotes but extended to all of the ballots. The distinction has real consequences. A manual recount of all ballots identifies not only those ballots which show no vote but also those which contain more than one, the so-called overvotes. Neither category will be counted by the machine. This is not a trivial concern. At oral argument, respondents estimated there are as many as 110,000 overvotes statewide. As a result, the citizen whose ballot was not read by a machine because he failed to vote for a candidate in a way readable by a machine may still have his vote counted in a manual recount; on the other hand, the citizen who marks two candidates in a way discernable by the machine will not have the same opportunity to have his vote count, even if a manual examination of the ballot would reveal the requisite indicia of intent. Furthermore, the citizen who marks two candidates, only one of which is discernable by the machine, will have his vote counted even though it should have been read as an invalid ballot. The State Supreme Court's inclusion of vote counts based on these variant standards exemplifies concerns with the remedial processes that were under way.

That brings the analysis to yet a further equal protection problem. The votes certified by the court included a partial total from one county, Miami-Dade. The Florida Supreme Court's decision thus gives no assurance that the recounts included in a final certification must be complete. Indeed, it is respondent's submission that it would be consistent with the rules of the recount procedures to include whatever partial counts are done by the time of final certification, and we interpret the Florida Supreme Court's decision to permit this. . . .This accommodation no doubt results from the truncated contest period established by the Florida Supreme Court in *Bush I*, at respondents' own urging. The press of time does not diminish the constitutional concern. A desire for speed is not a general excuse for ignoring equal protection guarantees.

In addition to these difficulties the actual process by which the votes were to be counted under the Florida Supreme Court's decision raises further concerns. That order did not specify who would recount the ballots. The county canvassing boards were forced to pull together ad hoc teams comprised of judges from various Circuits who had no previous training in handling and interpreting ballots. Furthermore, while others were permitted to observe, they were prohibited from objecting during the recount.

The recount process, in its features here described, is inconsistent with the minimum procedures necessary to protect the fundamental right of each voter in the special instance of a statewide recount under the authority of a single state judicial officer. Our consideration is limited to the present circumstances, for the problem of equal protection in election processes generally presents many complexities . . .

When a court orders a statewide remedy, there must be at least some assurance that the rudimentary requirements of equal treatment and fundamental fairness are satisfied.

Given the Court's assessment that the recount process underway was probably being conducted in an unconstitutional manner, the Court stayed the order directing the recount so it could hear this case and render an expedited decision . . . The State has not shown that its procedures include the necessary safeguards. The problem, for instance, of the estimated 110,000 overvotes has not been addressed, although Chief Justice Wells called attention to the concern in his dissenting opinion. . . .

Upon due consideration of the difficulties identified to this point, it is obvious that the recount cannot be conducted in compliance with the requirements of equal protection and due process without substantial additional work . . .

The Supreme Court of Florida has said that the legislature intended the State's electors to "participat[e] fully in the federal electoral process," . . . That statute, in turn, requires that any controversy or contest that is designed to lead to a conclusive selection of electors be completed by December 12. That date is upon us, and there is no recount procedure in place under the State Supreme Court's order that comports with minimal constitutional standards. Because it is evident that any recount seeking to meet the December 12 date will be unconstitutional for the reasons we have discussed, we reverse the judgment of the Supreme Court of Florida ordering a recount to proceed.

Seven Justices of the Court agree that there are constitutional problems with the recount ordered by the Florida Supreme Court that demand a remedy . . . The only disagreement is as to the remedy. Because the Florida Supreme Court has said that the Florida Legislature intended to obtain the safe-harbor benefits of 3 U.S.C. §5 Justice Breyer's proposed remedy—remanding to the Florida Supreme Court for its ordering of a constitutionally proper contest until December 18-contemplates action in violation of the Florida election code, and hence could not be part of an "appropriate" order authorized by Fla. Stat. §102.168(8) (2000).

None are more conscious of the vital limits on judicial authority than are the members of this Court, and none stand more in admiration of the Constitution's design to leave the selection of the President to the people, through their legislatures, and to the political sphere. When contending parties invoke the process of the courts, however, it becomes our unsought responsibility to resolve the federal and constitutional issues the judicial system has been forced to confront.

The judgment of the Supreme Court of Florida is reversed, and the case is remanded for further proceedings not inconsistent with this opinion.

What They Were Saying

from Al Gore's concession speech, December 13, 2000:

Over the library of one of our great law schools is inscribed the motto, "Not under man but under God and law." That's the ruling principle of American freedom, the source of our democratic liberties. I've tried to make it my guide throughout this contest, as it has guided America's deliberations of all the complex issues of the past five weeks.

Now the U.S. Supreme Court has spoken. Let there be no doubt, while I strongly disagree with the court's decision, I accept it. I accept the finality of this outcome which will be ratified next Monday in the Electoral College. And tonight, for the sake of our unity as a people and the strength of our democracy, I offer my concession. I also accept my responsibility, which I will discharge unconditionally, to honor the new President-elect and do everything possible to help him bring Americans together in fulfillment of the great vision that our Declaration of Independence defines and that our Constitution affirms and defends.

James A. Baker III, attorney for George W. Bush, in *Our Supreme Court*, 2005:

There are at least two important lessons that can be learned from *Bush v. Gore*, the case which led to the election of George W. Bush as president in 2000. The first is that the rule of law prevailed in the United States. While the case was a controversial one, our legal system determined the outcome. The most important ruling in the case, the one that said the recount process in Florida was unconstitutional on equal protection grounds, was made by seven of the nine Supreme Court Justices, including two appointed by Democrats. The second lesson learned is that our constitutional system in United States worked. We had a smooth transfer of power despite a close election and emotional aftermath. However, there was no rioting in the streets, as there might have been in a country that lacks our stability.

USA PATRIOT Act

It is mainly during times of duress and war that the government has suspended some of our normal civil liberties, going all the way back to the Sedition Act of 1798. It happened again during World War I (with the Espionage Act) and during World War II (with the relocation of Japanese Americans into camps). The terrorist attacks of September 11, 2001, shook the country's sense of security. The USA PATRIOT Act gave the federal government new access to private information and records. The USA PATRIOT Act passed in the senate by a vote of ninety-eight to one. Because the act is very lengthy and many sections consist of modifications to existing laws, an overview of the contents of the act is provided for the reader to understand the ambitious and wide range of activities its scope covered.

The terrorist attacks of September 11, 2001, resulted in the USA PATRIOT Act of 2001 and led to the Iraq War Resolution in 2002.

Sec. 1004. Venue in money laundering cases.

Sec. 1005. First responders assistance act.

Sec. 1006. Inadmissibility of aliens engaged in money laundering.

Sec. 1007. Authorization of funds for DEA police training in south and central Asia.

Sec. 1008. Feasibility study on use of biometric identifier scanning system with access to the FBI integrated automated fingerprint identification system at overseas consular posts and points of entry to the United States.

Sec. 1009. Study of access.

Sec. 1010. Temporary authority to contract with local and State governments for performance of security functions at United States military installations.

Sec. 1011. Crimes against charitable Americans.

Sec. 1012. Limitation on issuance of hazmat licenses.

Sec. 1013. Expressing the sense of the senate concerning the provision of funding for bioterrorism preparedness and response.

Sec. 1014. Grant program for State and local domestic preparedness support.

Sec. 1015. Expansion and reauthorization of the crime identification technology act for antiterrorism grants to States and localities.

Sec. 1016. Critical infrastructures protection.

What They Were Saying

from a speech by President George W. Bush, 2001:

As of today, we're changing the laws governing information-sharing. And as importantly, we're changing the culture of our various agencies that fight terrorism. Countering and investigating terrorist activity is the number one priority for both law enforcement and intelligence agencies.

Surveillance of communications is another essential tool to pursue and stop terrorists. The existing law was written in the era of rotary telephones. This new law that I sign today will allow surveillance of all communications used by terrorists, including e-mails, the Internet, and cell phones.

As of today, we'll be able to better meet the technological challenges posed by this proliferation of communications technology. Investigations are often slowed by limit on the reach of federal search warrants.

Law enforcement agencies have to get a new warrant for each new district they investigate, even when they're after the same suspect. Under this new law, warrants are valid across all districts and across all states. And, finally, the new legislation greatly enhances the penalties that will fall on terrorists or anyone who helps them.

Current statutes deal more severely with drug-traffickers than with terrorists. That changes today. We are enacting new and harsh penalties for possession of biological weapons. We're making it easier to seize the assets of groups and individuals involved in terrorism. The government will have wider latitude in deporting known terrorists and their supporters. The statute of limitations on terrorist acts will be lengthened, as will prison sentences for terrorists.

This bill was carefully drafted and considered. Led by the members of Congress on this stage, and those seated in the audience, it was crafted with skill and care, determination and a spirit of bipartisanship for which the entire nation is grateful. This bill met with an overwhelming—overwhelming agreement in Congress, because it upholds and respects the civil liberties guaranteed by our Constitution.

This legislation is essential not only to pursuing and punishing terrorists, but also preventing more atrocities in the hands of the evil ones. This government will enforce this law with all the urgency of a nation at war. The elected branches of our government, and both political parties, are united in our resolve to fight and stop and punish those who would do harm to the American people.

The decision to send American troops into Afghanistan after September 11 was based on the intelligence that terrorist leader Osama Bin Laden was holed up in the mountains there. The subsequent decision to send American forces into Iraq was more complicated. The resolution that was passed in the Senate in 2002 traced the history of complaints against Iraq back to its 1990 war against Kuwait. A program to develop weapons of mass destruction was also cited, along with the likelihood that Iraq was supporting and harboring the terrorist organization al Qaeda. The resolution passed in the Senate by a vote of seventy-seven to twenty-three. In the years that followed, the debate over our involvement in Iraq intensified as casualties mounted. Unlike the brief and limited 1990 military action, the more recent invasion resulted in the overthrow and capture of Saddam Hussein and in a war against insurgents. The war became one of the central themes of the 2008 presidential race.

Whereas in 1990 in response to Iraq's war of aggression against and illegal occupation of Kuwait, the United States forged a coalition of nations to liberate Kuwait and its people in order to defend the national security of the United States and enforce United Nations Security Council resolutions relating to Iraq;

Whereas after the liberation of Kuwait in 1991, Iraq entered into a United Nations sponsored cease-fire agreement pursuant to which Iraq unequivocally agreed, among other things, to eliminate its nuclear, biological, and chemical weapons programs and the means to deliver and develop them, and to end its support for international terrorism;

Whereas the efforts of international weapons inspectors, United States intelligence agencies, and Iraqi defectors led to the discovery that Iraq had large stockpiles of chemical weapons and a large scale biological weapons program, and that Iraq had an advanced nuclear weapons development program that was much closer to producing a nuclear weapon than intelligence reporting had previously indicated;

Whereas Iraq, in direct and flagrant violation of the cease-fire, attempted to thwart the efforts of weapons inspectors to identify and destroy Iraq's weapons of mass destruction stockpiles and development capa-bilities, which finally resulted in the withdrawal of inspectors from Iraq on October 31, 1998;

Whereas in 1998 Congress concluded that Iraq's continuing weapons of mass destruction programs threatened vital United States interests and international peace and security, declared Iraq to be in "material and unacceptable breach of its international obligations" and urged the President "to take appropriate action, in accordance with the Constitution and relevant laws of the United States, to bring Iraq into compliance with its international obligations" (Public Law 105-235);

Whereas Iraq both poses a continuing threat to the national security of the United States and international peace and security in the Persian Gulf region and remains in material and unacceptable breach of its international obligations by, among other things, continuing to possess and develop a significant chemical and biological weapons capability, actively seeking a nuclear weapons capability, and supporting and harboring terrorist organizations;

Whereas Iraq persists in violating resolutions of the United Nations Security Council by continuing to engage in brutal repression of its civilian population thereby threatening international peace and security in the region, by refusing to release, repatriate, or account for non-Iraqi citizens wrongfully detained by Iraq, including an American serviceman, and by failing to return property wrongfully seized by Iraq from Kuwait;

Whereas the current Iraqi regime has demonstrated its capability and willingness to use weapons of mass destruction against other nations and its own people;

Whereas the current Iraqi regime has demonstrated its continuing hostility toward, and willingness to attack, the United States, including by attempting in 1993 to assassinate former President Bush and by firing on many thousands of occasions on United States and Coalition Armed Forces engaged in enforcing the resolutions of the United Nations Security Council;

Whereas members of al Qaida, an organization bearing responsibility for attacks on the United States, its citizens, and interests, including the attacks that occurred on September 11, 2001, are known to be in Iraq;

Whereas Iraq continues to aid and harbor other international terrorist organizations, including organizations that threaten the lives and safety of American citizens;

Whereas the attacks on the United States of September 11, 2001, underscored the gravity of the threat posed by the acquisition of weapons of mass destruction by international terrorist organizations;

Whereas Iraq's demonstrated capability and willingness to use weapons of mass destruction, the risk that the current Iraqi regime will either employ those weapons to launch a surprise attack against the United States or its Armed Forces or provide them to international terrorists who would do so, and the extreme magnitude of harm that would result to the United States and its citizens from such an attack, combine to justify action by the United States to defend itself;

Whereas United Nations Security Council Resolution 678 authorizes the use of all necessary means to enforce United Nations Security Council Resolution 660 and subsequent relevant resolutions and to compel Iraq to cease certain activities that threaten international peace and security, including the development of weapons of mass destruction and refusal or obstruction of United Nations weapons inspections in violation of United Nations Security Council Resolution 687, repression of its civilian population in violation of United Nations Security Council Resolution 688, and threatening its neighbors or United Nations operations in Iraq in violation of United Nations Security Council Resolution 949;

Whereas Congress in the Authorization for Use of Military Force Against Iraq Resolution (Public Law 102-1) has authorized the President "to use United States Armed Forces pursuant to United Nations Security Council Resolution 678 (1990) in order to achieve implementation of Security Council Resolutions 660, 661, 662, 664, 665, 666, 667, 669, 670, 674, and 677";

Whereas in December 1991, Congress expressed its sense that it "supports the use of all necessary means to achieve the goals of United Nations Security Council Resolution 687 as being consistent with the Authorization of Use of Military Force Against Iraq Resolution (Public Law 102-1)," that Iraq's repression of its civilian population violates United Nations Security Council Resolution 688 and "constitutes a continuing threat to the peace, security, and stability of the Persian Gulf region," and that Congress, "supports the use of all necessary means to achieve the goals of United Nations Security Council Resolution 688";

Whereas the Iraq Liberation Act (Public Law 105-338) expressed the sense of Congress that it should be the policy of the United States to support efforts to remove from power the current Iraqi regime and promote the emergence of a democratic government to replace that regime;

Whereas on September 12, 2002, President Bush committed the United States to "work with the United Nations Security Council to meet our common challenge" posed by Iraq and to "work for the necessary resolutions," while also making clear that "the Security Council resolutions will be enforced, and the just demands of peace and security will be met, or action will be unavoidable";

Whereas the United States is determined to prosecute the war on terrorism and Iraq's ongoing support for international terrorist groups combined with its development of weapons of mass destruction in direct violation of its obligations under the 1991 cease-fire and other United Nations Security Council resolutions make clear that it is in the national security interests of the United States and in furtherance of the war on terrorism that all relevant United Nations Security Council resolutions be enforced, including through the use of force if necessary;

Whereas Congress has taken steps to pursue vigorously the war on terrorism through the provision of authorities and funding requested by the President to take the necessary actions against international terrorists and terrorist organizations, including those nations, organizations or persons who planned, authorized, committed or aided the terrorist attacks that occurred on September 11, 2001 or harbored such persons or organizations;

Whereas the President and Congress are determined to continue to take all appropriate actions against international terrorists and terrorist organizations, including those nations, organizations or persons who planned, authorized, committed or aided the terrorist attacks that occurred on September 11, 2001, or harbored such persons or organizations;

Whereas the President has authority under the Constitution to take action in order to deter and prevent acts of international terrorism against the United States, as Congress recognized in the joint resolution on Authorization for Use of Military Force (Public Law 107-40); and

Whereas it is in the national security of the United States to restore international peace and security to the Persian Gulf region;

Now, therefore, be it resolved by the Senate and House of Representatives of the United States of America in Congress assembled,

Sec. 1. Short Title

This joint resolution may be cited as the "Authorization for the Use of Military Force Against Iraq."

Sec. 2. Support for United States Diplomatic Efforts

The Congress of the United States supports the efforts by the President to—

(a) strictly enforce through the United Nations Security Council all relevant Security Council resolutions applicable to Iraq and encourages him in those efforts; and

(b) obtain prompt and decisive action by the Security Council to ensure that Iraq abandons its strategy of delay, evasion and noncompliance and promptly and strictly complies with all relevant Security Council resolutions.

Sec. 3. Authorization for Use of United States Armed Forces

(a) AUTHORIZATION. The President is authorized to use the Armed Forces of the United States as he determines to be necessary and appropriate in order to

(1) defend the national security of the United States against the continuing threat posed by Iraq; and

(2) enforce all relevant United Nations Security Council Resolutions regarding Iraq.

Selected Bibliography

Abbott, John S. C., and Russell H. Conwell. *Lives of the Presidents of the United States of America, from Washington to the Present Time.* Portland, ME: H. Hallett and Company, 1884.

Adams, James Truslow. *The March of Democracy.* New York: Charles Scribner, 1933.

Allen, Jack. *History: USA.* New York: American Book Company, 1967.

Americans Defending Democracy: Our Soldiers' Own Stories. New York: World's War Stories Inc., 1919.

America's Century, Year by Year from 1900 to 2000. New York: Dorling Kindersley Publishing, Inc., 2000.

Anderson, John J. *A Popular School History of the United States.* New York: Clark & Maynard, Publishers, 1884.

Andrews, E. Benjamin. *History of the United States from the Earliest Discovery of America to the Present Time.* New York: Charles Scribner's Sons, 1914.

Axelrod, Alan, and Charles Phillips. *What Every American Should Know About American History.* Holbrook, MA: Bob Adams, Inc., 1992.

Becker, Carl. *The Eve of the Revolution: A Chronicle of the Breach with England.* New York: United States Publishers Association, 1918.

Bloom, Sol. *The Story of the Constitution.* Washington, DC: United States Constitution Sesquicentennial Commission, 1937.

Carey, M. *The Olive Branch: Or Faults on Both Sides, Federal and Democratic.* Philadelphia: M. Carey and Son, 1817.

Commager, Henry Steele. *Documents of American History.* New York: Appleton-Century-Crofts, 1958.

Croscup, George E. *History Made Visible: United States History with Synchronic Charts.* New York: Cambridge Book Company, 1915.

Ellis, Edward S. *The History of Our Country from the Discovery of America to the Present Time.* New York: Henry W. Knight, 1900.

Gordy, Wilbur F. *A History of the United States for Schools.* New York: Charles Scribner's Sons, 1920.

Herbert, Janis. *The American Revolution for Kids.* Chicago: Chicago Review Press, 2002.

———. *The Civil War for Kids.* Chicago: Chicago Review Press, 1999.

Lawson, Don. *Landmark Supreme Court Cases.* Hillside, New Jersey: Enslow Publishers, Inc., 1987.

Panchyk, Richard. *Our Supreme Court.* Chicago: Chicago Review Press, 2007.

Rubel, David. *Mr. President: The Human Side of America's Chief Executives.* Alexandria, Virginia: Time-Life Books, 1998.

Sanderson, John. *Biography of the Signers to the Declaration of Independence.* Philadelphia: William Brown and Charles Peters, 1828.

Stevens, Joseph E. *1863: The Rebirth of a Nation.* New York: Bantam Books, 2000.

Tryon, Rolla M., and Charles R. Lingley, Frances Morehouse. *The American Nation Yesterday and Today.* Boston: Ginn and Company, 1934.

Turck, Mary C. *The Civil Rights Movement for Kids.* Chicago: Chicago Review Press, 2000.

Wagner, Margaret E. *American Treasures in the Library of Congress.* New York: Harry N. Abrams, 1997.

Whelpley, Samuel. *A Compend of History from the Earliest Times; Comprehending a General View of the State of the World.* Boston: Richardson and Lord, 1828

Web Sites for References

Complete transcripts of many of the documents in this book may be found at www.ourdocuments.gov, a Web site operated by the National Archives.

Other documents and background information may be found at http://memory.loc.gov, the American Memory site of the Library of Congress.

Index